A Nature Company Guide

ECOTRAVEL

A Nature Company Guide

ECOTRAVEL

DWIGHT HOLING, SUSANNE METHVIN,
DAVID RAINS WALLACE

AND

EDWARD L. BOWEN, BEN DAVIDSON, EDWARD R. RICCIUTI,
MICHELE STRUTIN, STEVEN THRENDYLE,
EUGENE J. WALTER JR, SUZANNE WINCKLER

CONSULTANT EDITOR
BEN DAVIDSON

Time-Life Books is a division of Time Life Inc.

The Nature Company Guides are published by Time-Life Books

Conceived and produced by Weldon Owen Pty Limited
59 Victoria Street, McMahons Point, NSW, 2060, Australia
A member of the Weldon Owen Group of Companies
Sydney • San Francisco • London
Copyright © 1995 Weldon Owen Pty Limited
Reprinted 2000

THE NATURE COMPANY
Priscilla Wrubel, Steve Manning, Tracy Fortini

TIME LIFE INC
CHAIRMAN AND CEO: Jim Nelson
PRESIDENT AND COO: Steven L. Janas

TIME-LIFE TRADE PUBLISHING
VICE PRESIDENT AND PUBLISHER: Neil Levin
SENIOR DIRECTOR OF ACQUISITIONS AND
EDITORIAL RESOURCES: Jennifer Pearce
DIRECTOR OF NEW PRODUCT DEVELOPMENT: Carolyn Clark
DIRECTOR OF MARKETING: Inger Forland
DIRECTOR OF TRADE SALES: Dana Hobson
DIRECTOR OF CUSTOM PUBLISHING: John Lalor
DIRECTOR OF DESIGN: Kate L. McConnell
PROJECT MANAGER: Jennifer L. Ward

TIME-LIFE is a trademark of Time Warner Inc. and affiliated companies.

WELDON OWEN PUBLISHING
CEO: John Owen
PRESIDENT: Terry Newell
PUBLISHER: Sheena Coupe
ASSOCIATE PUBLISHER: Lynn Humphries
PROJECT EDITOR: Scott Forbes
COPY EDITOR: Gillian Hewitt
DESIGNER: Clare Forte
JACKET DESIGN: John Bull
PICTURE RESEARCH: Connie Komack, Pictures & Words,
Rockport, Massachusetts; Gillian Manning
ILLUSTRATIONS: Robert Mancini, Ngaire Sales,
Genevieve Wallace, David Wood
MAPS: Stan Lamond; Mark Watson, Pictogram
PRODUCTION MANAGER: Helen Creeke
PRODUCTION ASSISTANT: Kylie Lawson
VICE PRESIDENT INTERNATIONAL SALES: Stuart Laurence

Library of Congress Cataloging-in-Publication Data
The Library of Congress has catalogued the hardcover edition of this book
as follows:

Holing, Dwight
  Nature travel / Dwight Holing, Suzanne Methvin,
David Rains Wallace and Ed Bowen ... [et al.];
  p. cm. - (A Nature Company guide)
    ISBN 0-7835-4753-6 (hardcover—Nature Travel)
    ISBN 0-7370-0097-X (softcover—Ecotravel)
    1. Natural history—North America—Guidebooks. 2. Natural
areas—North America—Guidebooks.
I. Methvin, Susanne. II. Wallace, David Rains, 1945– . III. Title.
IV. Series.
QH102.H64 1995   95–1224
917'.04539—dc20   CIP

Manufactured by Kyodo Printing Co. (S'pore) Pte Ltd
Printed in Singapore
A Weldon Owen Production

How strange and wonderful is our home, our earth,
with its swirling vaporous atmosphere, its flowing and
frozen liquids, its trembling plants, its creeping, crawling,
climbing creatures,...the furry grass, the scaly seas.

EDWARD ABBEY (1927–89),
American writer

CONTENTS

FOREWORD

The most amazing quality of nature is its diversity. You don't have to stray far to find wildflowers that you've never seen before, landscapes of great beauty, wildlife you thought you'd only encounter on television. Without ever leaving the United States and Canada, you can explore deserts, volcanoes, rain forests, alpine meadows, and sweeping grasslands. And that would just be a start.

I've found that, no matter where I travel, spending time with a guide—whether it's a person or several books—opens my eyes to the details. Knowing something about local natural history is a wonderful way to heighten your awareness of the places you visit, to give names to those sights, sounds, and smells and fix them in memory. And learning the details of a place makes it a part of us. That closeness inspires a protectiveness, a desire to preserve the area, to share it with a friend or visit it again ourselves.

That's the idea that inspired The Nature Company to produce this book. We wanted to share with you some of the loveliest, most awe-inspiring places in the world, to guide you to an understanding of the natural features and species that make each place unique, and provide the wilderness basics to make your trip rewarding. We hope that, with each turn of the page, your wanderlust increases, until you find yourself packing your camera and binoculars, lacing up your hiking boots, and heading out to explore. With this book in hand, there's no need to explain to anyone why you had to go; just show it to them and let them discover why for themselves.

Happy travels,

PRISCILLA WRUBEL
Founder, The Nature Company

INTRODUCTION

On a warm summer day a few years ago, I took
a boat trip through the James River National
Wildlife Refuge in southeastern Virginia. Shady
woodlands lined the banks of the river as it traced a gentle
course through the rolling hills toward Chesapeake Bay.
As I floated downstream, dozens of bald eagles soared
above me. Few experiences since have touched me as
deeply as watching those magnificent birds in graceful flight.

Many North Americans have shared similar experiences.
Our parks, reserves, and wildlife refuges offer easy access
to the wonders of the natural world, and a peaceful escape
from the city. These still-wild places and the creatures that
inhabit them are also an important part of our heritage.
From the lush forests of the Northeast to the spectacular
canyons of the Southwest, North America's landscapes
and wildlife are among her greatest assets. By safeguarding
places such as the Florida Everglades, the Alaskan wilds,
and Oklahoma's Tallgrass Prairie, we are not only
protecting unique terrain and saving such creatures as the
timber wolf and the American bison from extinction, but
are also preserving a singular North American experience.

Today, organizations such as The Nature Conservancy are
working with businesses, government, and private citizens
to continue to protect these assets. The Nature Company is
also doing its part by encouraging appreciation of nature in
its many forms. *Nature Travel* is one tool with which to
encounter and understand the natural world. Whether you
are an armchair traveler or outdoor adventurer, this book
invites you to experience our wild places. May it enhance
your enjoyment of the natural beauty of this land.

JOHN SAWHILL
President and Chief Executive Officer, The Nature Conservancy

And so, in every conceivable shape that can appeal to the eye of the poet, artist or geologist, Nature has piled up her changeless masonry on creation.

Picturesque America, WILLIAM CULLEN BRYANT (1794–1878), American poet and newspaper editor

CHAPTER ONE
THE NATURE
of AMERICA

A CONTINENT *of* MARVELS

As our cities have expanded and wilderness areas have shrunk, the wild places of the continent have become increasingly precious.

A WILDERNESS EXPERIENCE
Canoeing in Quetico Provincial Park in Ontario (above). A bald eagle diving for fish (above left).

People make their way into the wild in search of experiences that are rare in our world of convenience and artificiality. Little can equal the joy of finding a mountain meadow bright with wildflowers after a day of strenuous climbing, the excitement of watching a bear catch salmon in a river, or the fascination of canoeing through a swamp where the baldcypresses and alligators have remained unchanged since the time of the dinosaurs.

AREAS TO EXPLORE

The national park has been called the United States' unique contribution to world culture. The first one, Yellowstone, was created in 1872. Now there are 53 United States national parks, 102 national monuments and memorials, and a growing number of national seashores, lakeshores, and riverways. In addition, the United States has over 450 national wildlife refuges and countless national and state wilderness areas, forests, preserves, parkways, and trails. Canada, too, offers the nature traveler a remarkable range of national and provincial parks and wilderness areas. Throughout North America, the number of designated nature areas is continuing to grow.

In the West, vast regions are now national parks and wilderness areas, and remnants of eastern woodlands and midwestern prairies have also been preserved in a natural state. Some places that are now accessible, such as Hawaiian rain forest and Alaskan and Canadian tundra, were beyond the reach of even the most adventurous early explorers.

Increasingly, conservationists are directing their attention to maintaining and reclaiming wilderness areas around existing parks and preserves so that large enough areas can be maintained or restored to support viable populations of animals such as bears and wolves. Wilderness areas are playing an ever more important role in restoring what has been all but lost. In New England, for

PARKS AND REFUGES *play a crucial role in protecting endangered species. Bison (left) have been reintroduced to areas such as Wichita Mountains National Wildlife Refuge. Saguaro National Monument in Arizona protects some of the Southwest's most significant forests of saguaro cacti (right).*

In God's wilderness is the hope of the world—the great fresh, unblighted, unredeemed wilderness.

JOHN MUIR (1838–1914)
Scottish-born American
naturalist and writer

SCENES FROM THE WILD *Hawaii's mist-shrouded tropical forests (above); a grizzly bear catching a salmon in Denali National Park in Alaska (right); and a crystal clear morning in California's Sierra Nevada (far right).*

instance, moose and other large wild animals are returning to recovering forests; native red wolves have recently been restored to the swamps and mountains of the Southeast; in the Midwest, reintroduced bison herds graze among the wildflowers of prairie preserves.

DIFFERING APPROACHES

Many people are content to make short trips into the edges of wilderness, and usually find plenty to see. Others choose to walk or boat for days, weeks, or even months through wild country. This is often arduous and can even be dangerous, but may lead to once-in-a-lifetime experiences such as seeing a pine marten chase a squirrel through the treetops, or watching a nesting eagle bring food to its young. Such experiences remind us that nature is still flourishing, no matter how remote from it our lives have become, and that we too are part of it.

Offering a refuge from civilization's stresses, nature travel's popularity has led to crowding becoming a problem in some areas. Yet wilderness will only continue to exist if people value it, and to do so they must experience it. What is vital is that people avoid harming these unspoiled places, and actively support wilderness protection against the demands of commercial growth. Traveling in this way has recently come to be known as ecotourism or ecotraveling. If we create conditions that safeguard the world's glorious wild country, we will be working towards protecting living things everywhere.

YELLOWSTONE *(left), the first national park, home today to mammals such as the moose (below).*

THE LAY *of the* LAND

Whatever a nature traveler's interests, they'll be nourished by

the wealth of environments found

in the United States and Canada.

Examples of virtually every type of habitat and ecological community on Earth can be found on the North American continent or on the islands of Hawaii.

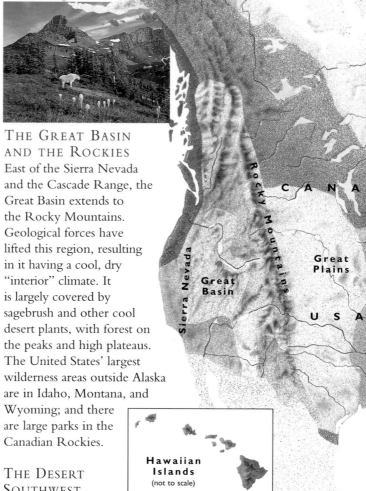

HAWAII AND THE FAR WEST

Hawaii's unique native flora and fauna have evolved from organisms that arrived on these isolated volcanic islands over millennia. There are also many unique species in the Far West, as the region is cut off from eastern ecosystems by stretches of desert.

The mountains contribute to natural diversity by distributing rainfall unevenly, resulting in lush temperate rain forests with huge, old trees lying adjacent to semi-arid grasslands. Much wilderness remains close to heavily urbanized coast and valleys.

Chaparral, which covers major portions of California, is characterized by thickets of fire-adapted shrubs.

The Pacific Ocean teems with wildlife, notably marine mammals, nourished by nutrient-rich upswellings from the ocean depths.

THE GREAT BASIN AND THE ROCKIES

East of the Sierra Nevada and the Cascade Range, the Great Basin extends to the Rocky Mountains. Geological forces have lifted this region, resulting in it having a cool, dry "interior" climate. It is largely covered by sagebrush and other cool desert plants, with forest on the peaks and high plateaus. The United States' largest wilderness areas outside Alaska are in Idaho, Montana, and Wyoming; and there are large parks in the Canadian Rockies.

THE DESERT SOUTHWEST

The Rockies continue south into Mexico, but the climate of the Southwest is milder than that of the Great Basin. Although lower elevations are dry, occasional summer rains from the Gulf of Mexico foster some of the world's richest desert vegetations. Wildflowers are striking in rainy years. Much desert has been protected in parks and wilderness areas.

The Southwest is by no means all desert: mountain and streamside forests provide habitat for a wide range of species.

Hawaiian Islands
(not to scale)

PLAINS AND PRAIRIES

From Texas to Saskatchewan, the Great Plains and Midwest Prairies stretch east from the Rockies. Most wild land in the region is on the drier western edge. Ranching occupies most of the shortgrass plains where bison once roamed, and the tallgrass prairies have become a productive farming region. Gone is the dramatic transition from forest to prairie that struck early travelers. Soybeans and corn have replaced the forests of the eastern Mississippi Basin.

THE SOUTHEAST

Forests are more prevalent in the Appalachians and along the east coast. Southeastern forests are species rich because they escaped the effects of glaciation. Trees such as magnolias grow on the uplands, while southern swamps are famous for bald-cypresses. Despite the large human population, much wilderness is protected in the mountains and in swampy regions. The warm waters of the Atlantic coast and the Gulf of Mexico support coral reefs, mangroves, and other tropical habitats, and some tropical forest species grow in southern Florida and Texas.

THE NORTHEAST

Northeastern and mid-Atlantic forests are more diverse than those of Europe, because many species that survived glaciation in the south spread north again as the ice receded. With their many deciduous species, these broad-leaf forests display spectacular fall colors. The continent's most urban region, the Northeast still retains much wilderness in the northern Appalachians and in the north woods that run from the Great Lakes to New Brunswick.

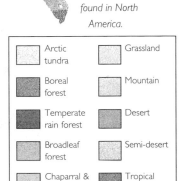

HABITATS *The map shows the principal types of environment found in North America.*

Arctic tundra	Grassland
Boreal forest	Mountain
Temperate rain forest	Desert
Broadleaf forest	Semi-desert
Chaparral & woodland	Tropical forest

THE FAR NORTH

In northern Quebec, the north woods grade into boreal forest (the taiga)—a vast, boggy region of stunted conifers and birches that stretches to central Alaska and the Arctic, sparsely populated by Native Americans and scattered mining and logging communities.

The last large, wild bison herd inhabits the boreal forest of Alberta's Wood Buffalo National Park, also the endangered whooping crane's nesting ground. This country provides winter shelter for the continent's last free-ranging migratory herds of caribou.

THE ARCTIC

Each summer the caribou travel to their calving grounds in the arctic tundra which extends across the continent's northern rim. Alpine tundra also covers mountain peaks south to New England and Mexico. Tundra vegetation, such as lichens, mosses, wild-flowers, and dwarf willows, grows on permafrost—permanently frozen soil, the surface of which thaws in summer. Yet the Arctic supports some of the world's largest mammals, such as musk oxen and brown bears. Summer breeding populations of migratory waterfowl are enormous. Marine mammals such as polar bears, walruses, and beluga whales live in the icy Arctic Ocean.

FLORA AND FAUNA *(clockwise from far left) Diver and trumpetfish in Hawaii; a mountain goat in Montana; the roseate spoonbill, found in the Everglades; Alaskan taiga in winter; a polar bear in Manitoba; New Hampshire forest in fall; a bison herd in South Dakota; a prickly pear cactus in flower.*

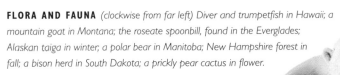

THE SHAPING
of a CONTINENT

The landscapes around us have been created by geological and climatic forces over millions of years.

U ntil the 1960s, when the theory of plate tectonics became widely accepted, geologists thought that the continents and oceans had not changed position since the time the Earth's crust cooled.

According to plate tectonics, the planetary crust is formed from a number of more or less rigid plates of rock which are constantly moving very slowly over the partly melted rock of the lower mantle, miles beneath the surface, driven by forces in the Earth's core. Where plates meet, the edge of one plate is forced downward under the other in a region called a subduction zone—an area of intense earthquake and volcanic activity. ("Hot spot" volcanoes, such as those in the Hawaiian Islands, are associated with weak points in the Earth's crust.) When plates pull apart, molten rock from the mantle erupts and forms new crust.

MOUNT ST HELENS, *in Washington State, erupting in May 1980 (left). Dinosaur tracks in Utah (right), which indicate that this rock must be at least 65 million years old.*

PLATE INTERACTIONS
North America rides on the North American Plate, which is being created in the mid-Atlantic and is moving west at the rate of one or two inches a year. As it moves, this plate pushes against the plate lying beneath the Pacific Ocean. As oceanic plates are denser than continental plates, for most of the past 100 million years or so the Pacific Plate has been subducted into the mantle beneath the North American Plate, causing a build-up of sediments on the continental crust margin.

The enormous stresses of plate interactions in the western regions of North America have fractured and upthrust the continental crust, which is why this area is so much more mountainous than the East.

Traveling westward from the east coast of North America is like traveling forward in geological time. Most eastern rocks have lain relatively undisturbed for hundreds of millions of years. Oceans and swamps deposited eastern Mississippi Basin sediments long before dinosaurs evolved and the Appalachians are the remnants of much larger mountains that were formed when North America was still united with Europe. The surface rocks of the Great Plains are younger, dating from the time of the dinosaurs and later, but the mountains of the Far West reached their jagged heights only in the past few million years.

Earthquakes and volcanic eruptions are a reminder of this continuing process of mountain building.

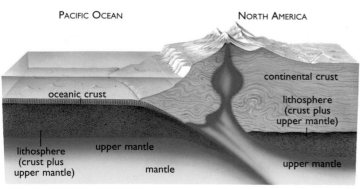

PACIFIC OCEAN   NORTH AMERICA

oceanic crust

continental crust

lithosphere (crust plus upper mantle)

lithosphere (crust plus upper mantle)

upper mantle

mantle

upper mantle

CONTINENTAL COLLISION *Where an oceanic plate meets a continental plate, the denser oceanic plate subducts. Magma may then be forced to the surface to form a volcano.*

THE GRAND CANYON *(left), carved by the Colorado River over a period of nearly 6 million years. Road cuts (below) often expose rock strata, showing how layers of rock have built up over the centuries.*

WIND AND WATER *carve rocks into an unimaginable range of shapes (left).*

GLACIATION

Ice is another force that has shaped the continent. About two million years ago, for reasons that are still unclear, global temperatures dropped significantly. Over centuries, snow that earlier had melted from mountains and arctic regions every summer began to accumulate. In time, this snow turned into glaciers—masses of compacted ice that flowed under their own weight.

A single glacier over a mile thick eventually covered the northeastern corner of North America south to Ohio, while smaller glaciers covered western mountains. (Glaciation did not affect northern regions such as lowland Alaska and north-western Canada because they were drier and snow did not accumulate.) The glaciers acted as giant conveyor belts, hauling rocks and soil plucked from high altitudes or latitudes and depositing them sometimes hundreds of miles away.

Many North American lakes, from the Great Lakes to the tarns that lie on the northerly sides of high western peaks, were formed during the ice age. Glacial ice carved their beds and they were then filled with meltwater. Even desert lakes are relics of the ice age's humid climate, when grassland and trees covered today's arid Southwest.

In the West, mountain glaciers carved dramatic U-shaped valleys such as Yosemite Valley, polishing granite cliffs that prompted early traveler John Muir to call California's Sierra Nevada "the Range of Light". Manhattan Island is a terminal moraine—a heap of debris left by a retreating glacier, while the fertile plains of the Midwest are glacial till—sand and soil deposited by the ice sheet. Much of eastern Canada has only a thin layer of soil because glaciation dragged the rest southward.

EROSION

Gravity, water, and wind have worked on the rocks and soils, carving them into an endless variety of landscapes. In the East, continental glaciation and water erosion have created rounded hills and broad valleys, although there are dramatic gorges in the Appalachians.

In the drier West, especially the deserts, wind and occasional cloudbursts have created bad-lands such as the Missouri River bluffs, which early traveler George Catlin likened to "some ancient and bound-less city in ruins". Elsewhere, tectonic forces have lifted the land, through which streams have carved gorges. The finest example is the Grand Canyon, where the Colorado River has cut a gorge a mile deep, exposing sediments from the dawn of multicellular life.

RIVER OF ICE *Bear Glacier in Kenai Fjords National Park, Alaska. U-shaped valleys, small lakes called cirques, and hanging valleys result from glaciation in mountainous regions.*

WILDERNESS TRAVELERS

So wonderful were the tales of the explorers who

penetrated the interior of the New World that

people didn't always believe them.

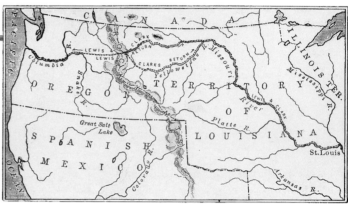

The wonders of the New World were first seen by Europeans in the East. John Bartram, a farmer and self-taught botanist, roamed the forests of the eastern seaboard in the late 1700s, seeking new plants for the gardens of wealthy British patrons. A practical, hard-headed frontiersman, he regarded the wilderness mainly as an obstacle to his plant collecting. His son William, however, who was an artist, responded differently. Where John described one of Florida's limestone springs as smelling "like bilge" and boiling up "like a pot", William saw "an enchanting and amazing crystal fountain...the blue ether of another world".

Samuel Taylor Coleridge based his poem "Kubla Khan" on descriptions of Florida springs given in William Bartram's *Travels*—a book that became widely influential. The Bartrams' travels provided encouragement for several young naturalists, including bird painters Alexander Wilson and John James Audubon, both of whom roamed the eastern states in the early 1800s.

THE LEWIS AND CLARK EXPEDITION

In 1803, President Thomas Jefferson sent Meriwether Lewis and William Clark across the continent on an expedition to find out about land recently acquired by the United States from the

CAROLINA PARAKEET *(left), depicted here by John James Audubon, is now extinct. A nineteenth-century engraving of Lewis and Clark's route (above).*

French. Traveling from St Louis to the Pacific coast and back in the course of three years, they found a wonder-filled world. The Mississippi Basin appeared to stretch westward for ever, first spread with forests where migrating passenger pigeons obscured the sky for days, then with prairies where wildflowers grew higher than the horsemen's heads.

Beyond the Mississippi lay a sea of grass where bison darkened the ground for miles.

Lewis described the Rockies as "one of the most beautiful picturesque countries that I ever beheld, through the wide expanse of which innumerable herds of living animals are seen". The expedition provided the first records of hundreds of plants and animals, including bighorn sheep, pronghorns, and grizzly bears.

AMAZING SIGHTS

In the West, mountain men such as Jim Bridger and Jedediah Smith reported stranger sights: valleys where streams boiled and the earth bubbled and steamed; deserts so dry that lakes and rivers were salt; trees as wide as houses. Bridger told of glass mountains that hunters tried to shoot deer through, but much of what he described really did exist and was later found to be widespread.

Artists and scientists soon followed in the footsteps of explorers and trappers. Botanist Thomas Nuttall ascended the Missouri into the Great Plains in 1811, explored Arkansas and Oklahoma in 1818, and followed the Oregon Trail to the Pacific in 1834, naming hundreds of new plant and animal species as he went. Nuttall was so

BUFFALO CHASE *George Catlin painted this image of the Plains Indians hunting bison in 1832 (left).*

careless of frontier dangers that he used his rifle barrel to dig up plant specimens. "All his enthusiasm was awakened at beholding a new world", wrote his friend, Washington Irving. "He went groping and stumbling along among a wilderness of sweets, forgetful of everything but his immediate pursuit." George Catlin's paintings of Indians and Plains landscapes provided easterners with their first authentic view of the West. So strange did his works appear that many people regarded them as fraudulent when he first exhibited in the 1830s. However, once painters such as Albert Bierstadt and Thomas Moran returned from western journeys to paint huge canvases of mountains and plains, and photographers such as William Henry Jackson displayed their work (see p. 24), Americans came to regard the West as a realm of great beauty as well as an obstacle to be tamed.

JOHN MUIR

In 1869, a traveler who would do more than any other to change America's values about wilderness walked into the Yosemite Valley. John Muir, a Scottish-born farmer and inventor, grew up in Wisconsin and was a passionate lover of the natural world. In 1867, he had walked from Indiana to Florida to experience the Appalachian forests. He then decided to explore the wild hills and valleys of California. Deeply moved by the Sierra Nevada, Muir spent the next decade walking the range, sometimes living on little more than tea and stale bread.

His enthusiasm for the wonders around him was unbounded and his brilliantly descriptive books and articles on his explorations are still widely read. Far from being a detached observer, he always insisted on nature's intrinsic spiritual value and on our duty to protect it. "It took more than three thousand years to make some of the trees in these western woods," he wrote. "God has cared for these trees, saved them from drought, disease, avalanches, and a thousand straining, leveling tempests and floods; but He cannot save them from fools...."

John Muir (right), with John Burroughs.

THE HUMAN IMPACT

*The influx of European settlers brought a wave
of change to North America that transformed
vast tracts of the continent.*

Following close on the heels of the explorers came European trappers, traders, and settlers, who viewed the continent as a source of unlimited riches. Moving by degrees from east to west, they exploited whatever they came across. Everywhere wilderness was destroyed in the name of progress.

NATIVE AMERICANS

Native Americans saw their lands as a realm of spiritual powers from which humans could derive many benefits. Eastern and southwestern cultures had been farming corn, beans, and other crops for thousands of years before the Europeans arrived and all the native cultures had sophisticated technologies for managing and harvesting wild ecosystems. But in both their farming and their harvesting from the wild, an ecological

OSCEOLA NICK-A-NO-CHEE, *an Indian boy (left), painted by George Catlin in 1840. A typical village of the people of the Secotan tribe in North Carolina (right), painted in watercolors by John White at the end of the sixteenth century.*

balance had been maintained, and the lands on which they lived remained fertile and unpolluted.

William Bartram, who traveled in Georgia and Florida during the 1770s, described the lives of the Creek and Cherokee with admiration, observing that wild animals such as deer, cranes, and even wolves co-existed with the Creeks' livestock and cornfields.

Sixty years later, the painter and writer George Catlin traveled widely among the nomadic tribes of the Great Plains and was filled with awe at the sight of the great expanses of grass and the Indians' way of life. But he was able to see that the life of the Plains tribes was doomed in the face of European settlement.

To the Plains Indians, the bison was an all-important object of veneration, providing them with food, and hides for clothing and shelter. With the coming of the Europeans, however, the balance between humans and nature altered. Once they had horses and guns, the Indians could kill more game than they needed, and trade the excess with the whites. Easterners shot bison for sport; the military encouraged the destruction of game so that the Indians would go hungry and could be brought to heel; cattle ranching began and countless miles of fences were erected by the ranchers.

BISON BONES, *mainly skulls, at the Michigan Carbon Works in Detroit in about 1895. The bones were ground into bonemeal.*

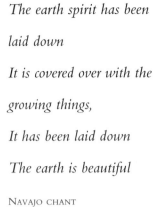

The earth spirit has been

laid down

It is covered over with the

growing things,

It has been laid down

The earth is beautiful

In 1883, a group of white and Indian hunters killed the last remaining bison herd in Montana, leaving a small herd in Yellowstone as the last free-living bison in the entire United States. Without the staple of bison, the Plains tribes were destitute.

THE LAST OF THE BUFFALO, *painted by Albert Bierstadt in 1889 (above). The extinct passenger pigeon (right). A mining camp in Colorado, in about 1880 (below right).*

A NEW LANDSCAPE

During the nineteenth century, settlers tamed the eastern half of the continent with unprecedented speed, cutting forests, plowing prairies, and draining swamps. The United States government exiled native nations such as the Cherokees and Creeks west of the Mississippi. Wildlife declined everywhere, and several species became extinct, most notably the passenger pigeon, which dwindled from an estimated 9 billion birds in 1800 to a single captive individual in 1914.

In the Far West, the influx of Europeans and other migrants had a devastating effect on the indigenous people and on the environment. The California gold rush in the mid-1800s resulted in the arrival of miners in their thousands, shanty towns springing up, hills being laid bare, and streams becoming muddy trenches.

Many disappointed miners became farmers, turning the vast seas of grass into agricultural land and felling huge swathes of timber for housing and the railroads.

Herds of elk, pronghorns, and bighorn sheep that had once been abundant everywhere disappeared within decades, ranchers replacing them with sheep and cattle. The ranchers saw wildlife as competition to be eliminated. "The wolves that howled at evening about the travellers camp-fire have succumbed to arsenic and hushed their savage music," wrote Francis Parkman, historian of the Oregon Trail, "the mountain lion shrinks from the face of man, and even grim 'Old Ephraim', the grizzly bear, seeks the seclusion of his dens and caverns."

LOGGED REDWOODS *in a Californian forest in the 1890s.*

A NEW AWARENESS

A growing awareness of the inherent worth of wilderness
led to increasing efforts being made
to safeguard what little remained.

As early as 1832, George Catlin had envisaged government preservation of wilderness, writing of "a nation's park, containing man and beast, in all the wild freshness of their nature's beauty". By the end of the century this was no longer possible on the Plains, but wilderness preservation elswhere was more successful.

The Yosemite Valley was the first region to be saved for its beauty. In 1864 the US government granted the valley and the Mariposa Grove of Giant Sequoias to the state of California, on condition that "the premises shall be held for public use, resort, and recreation…for all time".

Soon after, the Yellowstone Plateau became a *cause célèbre* among conservationists. The work of artist Thomas Moran and photographer William Henry Jackson, who explored the area with a government survey team in 1871, was so impressive that Congress created Yellowstone National Park the following year. As no money was appropriated to manage the park, however, squatters and hunters arrived, as well as

GRAND CANYON OF THE YELLOWSTONE, *painted by Thomas Moran in 1872.*

tourists. Poaching soon reduced the last US bison herd to 22 animals. Logging, grazing, and other commercial enterprises were also allowed in the park.

Rocky Mountains Park (later Banff National Park) in Canada was formed in 1885 to preserve a hot spring and the surrounding peaks. But the government's scheme for the West (the National Policy) also allowed fur trading, mining, and logging.

Clearly, it would take new values and institutions to save wilderness.

THE SIERRA CLUB

By the turn of the century, many Americans had come to feel that wild places had intrinsic value.

STAMPS *promoting national parks (top) and a poster advertising tours to Yellowstone (above).*

GARDEN OF THE GODS, COLORADO *(right), photographed by William Henry Jackson.*

GREAT EGRETS, *threatened with extinction, were saved by the efforts of private conservation societies.*

The rapid loss of untouched country led to the formation of organizations such as the Sierra Club, founded in 1892 by a group that included John Muir (see p. 21). Through lobbying and press articles, he had played a major part in having the area around the original Yosemite Valley park declared a national park, and in 1906 the Sierra Club succeeded in having both areas combined in a federal park.

Wilderness conservation benefited from the 1901–8 Roosevelt presidency, and the early 1900s saw several parks created, including Rocky Mountain, Rainier, Olympic, Hawaii Volcanoes, and Glacier. In 1916, a Park Service was created to manage them.

FOREVER WILD

Wilderness protection, however, remained an uphill fight, for only in national parks were lands fully protected. Other conservation bodies, such as the Forest Service, the Bureau of Land Management, and the Fish and Wildlife Service, allowed business activities of one sort or another. Even park administrations sometimes favored tourism, building roads into wild areas.

In 1935, Bob Marshall and Aldo Leopold started the Wilderness Society, devoted to saving wild areas. While working for the Forest Service in the 1920s, Leopold had pioneered the concept of federal wilderness areas, where roads and machines were banned. However, administrators could terminate these areas. In 1964, the Wilderness Act was finally passed, enabling Congress to designate federal lands as "forever wild". The Act created 9.1 million acres of wilderness, and conservationists have added more. Currently about 1 percent of US land is in the wilderness system—about the same amount as is paved.

In Canada, between 1968 and '74, ten new parks were set aside, doubling the size of the park system. In 1991, the Canadian parliament resolved that at least 12 percent of the country would remain free from development. A year later, federal and provincial governments passed legislation to preserve natural regions and unique ecosystems.

OTHER INITIATIVES

Federal wilderness in the US is not evenly distributed, much being in the West or Alaska. In addition, many threatened animals and plants survive only on private land.

A growing awareness of the need for more conservation areas led the states to begin creating natural park systems, mostly during the 1920s and '50s. Private groups also began acquiring wild land, as when Audubon societies bought rookeries at the turn of the century to help save egrets and herons under threat from the millinery trade.

In the 1940s, The Nature Conservancy was set up to protect vulnerable ecosystems. It cares for millions of acres and is acquiring other land for transfer to government.

Despite these moves, wilderness destruction is still taking place at a rate far exceeding the rate at which land is being set aside for protection. The US has lost half its wetlands, about 90 percent of its old forests, and almost all its tallgrass prairie.

THEODORE ROOSEVELT
and John Muir, photographed in Yosemite (far right). Bob Marshall (right).

WILDERNESS CONSERVATION TODAY

Conservationists are now working on new initiatives to provide land for wildlife, including wilderness management of lands surrounding national parks.

SILENT SPRING (left) by lifelong conservationist Rachel Carson (right), was one of the first books to draw public attention to environmental issues.

Although the explosion of environmental concern which began in 1961 with the publication of Rachel Carson's *Silent Spring* brought increased attention to bear on wilderness protection, progress has been slow in acquiring wilderness land since then, and there have been many setbacks. For example, a highly significant proposal for a Tallgrass Prairie National Park in the Midwest was derailed in the 1980s by ranching interests and Native American concern about losing mineral rights. However, there have been notable successes. The Alaska National Interest Lands Act of 1980 added large areas to the wilderness system, as did various state bills. The passing of the California Desert Protection Act in 1994 was noteworthy, creating two new national parks—Death Valley and Joshua Tree—and carving out millions of acres of federally protected wilderness.

HABITAT DESTRUCTION, *highlighted by these postage stamps (above right), poses a major threat to many species. For example, logging of old-growth forest in the Northwest has endangered the spotted owl (below).*

THE ENDANGERED SPECIES ACT

The Endangered Species Act, passed in 1966, prohibits activities that threaten endangered species on federal lands and has saved some species from likely extinction, notably the American alligator and the bald eagle. The Act also provides for the protection of endangered animals' habitats. This precipitated the biggest conservation struggle of the 1980s, when harvesting of old-growth national forests in the Pacific Northwest threatened the spotted owl's habitat. When conservation groups sued the government, an injunction was issued against further logging of old growth in most Northwest forests until the government showed it could provide for the owl's survival. Many other plants and animals depend on uncut forest, so the decision was a major victory, if a temporary one, since the timber industry continues to press for logging of old-growth areas.

In nature there are neither rewards nor punishments— there are consequences.

R.G. INGERSOLL (1833–99), American attorney

ENVIRONMENTALISTS *protesting against logging in the Pacific Northwest (left). United States postage stamps promoting wildlife conservation (below).*

WILDLIFE CORRIDORS

The spotted owl controversy has focused attention on the inadequacy of protecting wilderness only through parks and wilderness areas. The Pacific Northwest has a significant number of parks and designated areas of wilderness, yet, despite this, some of the region's native animal species have disappeared. Mount Rainier National Park in Washington, for instance, lost 13 of its mammal species between 1920 and 1976.

Parks are often too small to provide sufficient habitat for native animals that travel long distances to breed and feed. Because of this, conservationists are working to protect habitat surrounding parks and wilderness areas. In the place of clear-cutting adjacent forest, as has occurred around Olympic National Park, for example, they advocate leaving wildlife corridors of mature forest and other habitat along which animals can migrate. At Yellowstone, conservationists are trying to provide for wildlife not just in the park, but also on surrounding public and private lands. This is the only way that at least one species, the grizzly bear, will survive here, since this bear population, now reduced to a few hundred, is isolated from other grizzly populations to the north.

REINTRODUCING WOLVES

Common throughout the continent when Europeans arrived, by 1970 wolves had been wiped out almost everywhere south of Canada. Wolf attacks on livestock were the main motivation for this. In the East, the Massachusetts Bay Colony paid bounties on wolves as early as 1630, and most states later followed suit. By the mid-nineteenth century, wolves had been shot, trapped, and poisoned out of the East and Midwest. They survived longer in the West, but by the 1930s almost all were gone. Significant numbers survive only in Canada, Alaska, and northern Minnesota.

With growing environmental awareness, the public has realized that the wolf plays a crucial ecological role as a predator. After the Endangered Species Act was passed in 1966, several wolf restoration programs were set up. The red wolf, of southeastern forests and swamps, was the first to be affected. Remaining wild red wolves were caught for a captive breeding program. Individuals are now being reintroduced to Alligator River National Wildlife Refuge and Great Smoky Mountains National Park and have already begun breeding.

Since the 1970s, wild gray wolves have been entering the United States from Canada, and there are now small packs in Montana and Idaho.

THE RED WOLF named for its reddish fur, is a little larger than the coyote.

The US Fish and Wildlife Service is currently trapping Canadian wolves and releasing them in Yellowstone, to help control the park's game herds. Some local ranchers oppose this, although conservationists have offered to pay for livestock losses. Some environmentalists question the value of artificially reintroducing wolves to Yellowstone when the wolves would return by themselves, if allowed. Wolf restoration is also being considered in areas such as Colorado and New England.

THE ECOTRAVELER

The more we avoid harming the wilderness areas we visit,

the better are the chances of their being preserved

for future generations.

In 1950, there were 30 million visitors to US national parks; in 1993, there were 270 million. Clearly, every step that each visitor takes in a park is significant, for a vast number of steps are being taken in our wild places. And what about the way we use campgrounds, the way we use water, the way we interact with wildlife?

Ecotourism, or ecotravel, is an approach to nature travel that focuses on avoiding harm to wild places and contributing to their conservation wherever possible. Over the years, many lovers of nature have behaved in this way, but today this approach is vital if future generations are to experience the wonders of nature in the way that we can.

TOURIST RUSH HOUR *at Pigeon Forge, Tennessee, near the entrance to Great Smoky Mountains National Park (above). An early cartoon (right) depicting a possible outcome if Yellowstone were leased to speculators.*

MINIMIZING HUMAN IMPACT

Being an ecotraveler means leaving wild places exactly as you find them. Litter is an obvious problem, and one that is easily resolved if visitors conscientiously carry out all their own litter and any other refuse that they come across.

Ecotravelers also avoid uprooting plants, picking flowers, or even collecting seeds. They leave eggs in their

LOW-IMPACT CAMPING *involves camping only at designated sites, using a portable stove rather than a campfire, washing well away from water sources, and packing out all waste materials.*

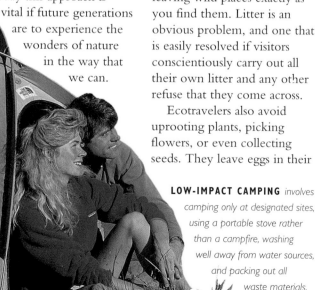

nests, and rocks where they lie. Seashells and driftwood, which are used by wildlife for all sorts of purposes, can disappear altogether from a place as a result of the souvenir collecting of thousands of visitors.

Apparently harmless activities such as washing in a lake or collecting fuel for a campfire can result in water pollution and soil being worn bare in heavily visited places. It is always best to stay on trails, for fragile flora can be harmed by people tramping over it. Shortcutting switchbacks on trails to save a little time can cause major soil

erosion, for rain tends to carve the shortcuts into gullies.

Contributing to the conservation of wild places ranges from picking up somebody else's litter at a campsite, to volunteering for one of the wilderness stewardship projects sponsored by environmental groups. These projects involve participants in vital tasks such as planting trees, and restoring trails and streams. Ecotourism also offers people opportunities to become involved in wildlife research programs (see p. 82).

VISITOR NUMBERS

Regrettably, maintaining the quality of nature areas increasingly entails limiting the number of people entering them. To be allowed into many wilderness areas you now need a permit. This helps to keep visitor numbers at a manageable level.

In some cases, it has become necessary to close hiking trails or entire areas to allow them to recover from overuse. This presents a paradox, since the principle of "use it or lose it" applies to wilderness. If people are unable to enjoy an area, they may well be unwilling to advocate protecting it against logging or other commercial uses, or to have their taxes spent on its conservation.

The principles of ecotravel are vital in this context, because if people adhere to them, large numbers of us will be able to enjoy wilderness without degrading it. The unity of the Earth's ecosystems must be respected and we must recognize that the human species is but a part of the whole.

The love of wilderness is more than a hunger for what is always beyond our reach; it is also an expression of loyalty to the earth, the only home we shall ever know, the only paradise we ever need—if we only had the eyes to see.

EDWARD ABBEY (1927–89),
American writer

GUIDELINES FOR ECOTRAVELERS

• Plan your trip carefully and use the proper equipment, so that costly and intrusive rescues can be avoided.

• Stay on trails when possible and avoid taking shortcuts across switchbacks. Shortcuts contribute to erosion.

• Unless wilderness camping is permitted, camp only in designated campsites.

• Pack out all litter, including toilet paper, and bury wastes well away from water sources. If others before you have left litter, try to carry it out with you.

• Use soap and detergent sparingly, if at all, and never allow them (or anything else) to enter streams or lakes.

• Avoid making animals uneasy by your presence. If you come too close to them, they have to expend energy in keeping their distance and defending their territory. If you scare birds from their nests, their eggs or young will be vulnerable to predators. When taking photos, the best approach is to use a telephoto lens.

• Avoid the temptation to take souvenirs home with you, such as flowers, seedpods, shells, and rocks. In other words, take nothing except photos and memories.

• Respect the solitude of other nature travelers, and be considerate of local people.

Thousands of tired, nerve-shaken, over-civilized people are beginning to find out that going to the mountains is going home; that wildness is a necessity; and that mountain parks and reservations are useful not only as fountains of timber and irrigating rivers, but as fountains of life.

Our National Parks, JOHN MUIR (1838–1914),
Scottish-born American naturalist and writer

CHAPTER TWO

PREPARING
for NATURE

MAKING PLANS

Whether you're setting off on a day hike in your local park
or a six-month trip around North America, you
will need to do some careful planning.

STARTING POINTS
Maps and leaflets (left), available from park offices, will help you plan your trip. The Kearsarge Pass entrance to Kings Canyon National Park (right).

The first step, for a potential nature traveler, is to decide where you're going. Would you like your trip to be a challenging wilderness experience or a relaxing vacation? What aspects of nature interest you particularly? The field guide section of this book, Pathways to Nature (p. 76), will be helpful, as it covers a wide variety of destinations and environments, from windswept arctic tundra to lush tropical swamps.

TAPPING RESOURCES
Once you have decided roughly where you would like to go and what you would like to do, you can refer to Pathways to Nature for the addresses of those places that best fit your require-ments. You will also find

the Resources Directory useful (p. 272), as it lists a wide range of nature travel publications, organizations, and tour operators. Special interest guidebooks, such as birding guides for specific regions, help in planning a trip. They provide detailed maps and information about trails, campgrounds, and lodging; and tell you what species can be seen each season and where to find them.

Special interest magazines also provide this sort of information, and list tour companies that run organized trips. Detailed maps are necessary both in the planning stages and on the road. In many cases, park services will provide maps and tell you about significant events to plan your trip around, such as migrations of animals or birds. It's also worth-while talking to tour operators and people who know the area, as they can give you firsthand information and alert you to potential problems.

YOUR ITINERARY
The next step is to start making basic arrangements for your trip. A day-by-day outline of your

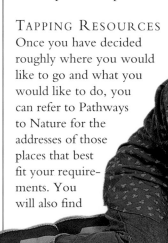

THE RIGHT ROUTE *Plan for as full an experience as possible by allowing time for stops at other nature areas on the way to your final destination.*

THE NEVER-ENDING TRAIL *North America offers the nature traveler an inexhaustible supply of magnificent destinations. Sometimes the most difficult task is deciding where to go next.*

itinerary will help you decide where to stay and how much you can do in the time available. With the map laid out in front of you, plot out the route and figure out how many miles you can cover on travel days. Don't try to cram too much in and allow plenty of time for walking— by far the best way to experience nature. Some of the most exhilarating nature experiences occur on rest days, such as when an unexpected animal appears in camp.

BUDGETING
You will also find it useful to make a budget. Nature travel can be relatively inexpensive if you camp, but be sure to include estimates for food, transport, lodging, entrance and camping fees, special services (a one-day dive trip in the Florida Keys, for instance), souvenirs, and emergency funds. Make reservations well in advance (up to one year for some lodges), particularly if you are traveling at peak season.

For a more tranquil experience, travel in the off-season or to less visited areas, such as Coronado National Forest in southeast Arizona instead of the Grand Canyon. A trip to one small area is often more rewarding and far more relaxing than rushing around trying to see as many places as possible, particularly when it comes to experiencing nature.

ORGANIZED NATURE TOURS

A great way to learn about nature travel is to join the local chapter of a national nature organization. Groups such as the Sierra Club sponsor regular hiking and backpacking trips while other organizations such as the Audubon Society run hiking and birding trips, as well as nature classes and nature camps for children and adults. Joining one of these societies will put you in touch with people from a range of backgrounds who all share an interest in nature.

A number of non-profit groups organize nature travel activities for travelers with disabilities. These range from bird-song classes for the visually impaired to sea kayaking tours for the disabled.

One advantage of any organized tour is that you can leave the arrangements in the hands of professionals, while you relax and concentrate on the wildlife. See p. 277 for a list of nature organizations.

NATURE STUDY EQUIPMENT

*You don't need much in the way of equipment
to observe nature, but there are a few items
that will add to your enjoyment.*

A good pair of binoculars is an excellent investment. They open up a whole new world of birds and animals, and, if you turn them upside down, they can be used as magnifying lenses for taking a close look at plants and insects.

There are a number of things to consider when choosing a pair of binoculars, including magnification, brightness, focus, weight, durability, and price.

All binoculars have a set of numbers on them, such as 7 x 35. The 7 x refers to the magnification, meaning that the image will look seven times larger than it appears to the naked eye. The second number is the diameter of the objective (front) lenses in millimeters. The larger these are, the more light will enter

the binoculars and the brighter the image will be, but also the heavier the binoculars will be. Magnification of between 7 and 10, and objective lenses of between 30 and 40 are recommended for nature study.

On the whole, compact binoculars are not well suited to all-round nature observation because of their narrow field of view and lack of brightness at dawn and dusk.

Selecting a pair of binoculars should be a hands-on experience. Look through several kinds to compare their weight and fit in your hands; to see if the eyepieces are comfortable; and to check the focus. The closer they can focus, the better. Some binoculars have a rubber

ESSENTIAL EQUIPMENT for any nature travel trip includes binoculars (above left), relevant field guides (left), and a notepad and pencil or pen.

coating, making them more durable.

Generally, you get what you pay for. An inexpensive pair of binoculars may go out of alignment if dropped or fog up in humid weather. It's wise to buy the best pair you can afford, making sure that they come with a good warranty.

ROOF PRISMS

light path

focus wheel · exit pupil

prisms

objective lens

BINOCULARS come in two basic styles: porro and roof prism. The compact design of roof prisms makes them lighter, but they are usually more expensive. Porro prisms are normally cheaper but are also heavier.

PORRO PRISMS

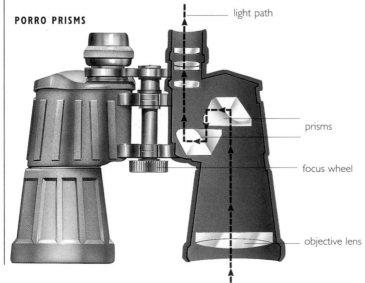

light path

prisms

focus wheel

objective lens

USING AND CARING FOR BINOCULARS

Learning to use binoculars takes practice. Start out aiming at something almost stationary, such as a bird at a birdfeeder. Note its surroundings and then try to locate it and focus on it as quickly as you can. With practice, you'll be able to anticipate where a moving bird will be by the time you get the binoculars up to your eyes. Store your binoculars and scope in protective carrying cases and use cotton cloth to clean the lenses and eyepieces in the field. If properly cared for, high quality optical equipment will last a lifetime.

EVER READY *When out in the field, wear your binoculars around your neck on a wide strap. This will allow you to focus immediately on whatever appears in your field of view.*

The hours when the mind is absorbed by beauty are the only hours when we really live.

The Life of the Fields,
RICHARD JEFFERIES (1848–87), English naturalist and novelist

COMPLETING YOUR NATURE KIT

Binoculars are certainly the main tools for nature observation, but you might also include some of the following in your nature kit: camera and lenses (see p. 58), tape recorder, magnifying lens, spotlight, notebook and pen, field guides, and ziplock plastic bags. You may even decide to make or buy a portable blind for field observation and photography.

Today's field equipment is geared toward nature observation, rather than toward collecting plant and wildlife specimens, as once was the case. If you bring back only memories and pictures from your walks, then wildflowers, butterflies, and shells are left to continue as part of the chain of life, and to be enjoyed by others.

SPOTTING SCOPES

Experienced naturalists sometimes invest in a spotting scope and a tripod to complement their binoculars. Spotting scopes offer magnifications from 20x to 60x and are useful for studying wildlife at a distance, such as large mammals or waterbirds.

Scopes with lenses in the 20x to 30x magnification range are the most useful. Zoom scopes give a wider magnification range but the optics are usually not as sharp and the image may be dimmer at high magnification. Be sure to look through scopes with offset

A MAGNIFYING GLASS
(above) will allow you to look at insects and plants more closely.

eyepieces as well as those with ones that are aligned with the barrel: the former are easier on the neck and back whereas the latter are easier to aim.

A range of light-weight but sturdy tripods are available to use with spotting scopes and cameras. Try setting up various kinds and look for one with a head that is easy to use. Those with tubular legs and screw locks can be steadier but ones with square legs and flip locks are easier to set up.

SPOTTING SCOPES *(right) are ideal for observing shorebirds (far right). A tripod will keep the image steady.*

OUTDOOR CLOTHING

*Functional clothing and comfortable footwear
will ensure that you are able to make
the most of your time outdoors.*

A potentially enjoyable trip can be a miserable experience if you aren't wearing the right clothes. If you are going to visit more than one habitat, it's a good idea to make a list of what clothing you will need for each environment.

ACCESSORIES *Synthetic fleece gloves (right) worn under waterproof overmitts will provide effective insulation in cold conditions. High-quality UV sunglasses (left and opposite) offer essential protection in bright weather.*

Inner layer: thin synthetic under-shirt and pants

Middle layer: lightweight fleece

Outer layer: waterproof jacket and pants

Footwear: sturdy hiking boots and comfortable socks

As you gain experience in the field, you can build your wardrobe around certain basic items and then refine it for differing conditions.

Specialty clothing for nature trips is functional. For example, naturalist's vests are available with pockets designed to carry your field equipment: binoculars, field guide, notepad and pen, sunscreen lotion, and insect repellent. Neutral colors, such as tan, olive, or camouflage designs will help you blend into your surroundings and get closer to wildlife. However, during the hunting season brighter colors will alert hunters to your presence. (If you hear hunters drawing near you should move away or shout to warn that you are there. If you try to hide you are more likely to be shot at.)

LAYERING

In cold weather, you need to wear three layers to keep warm and dry. The thin inner layer, such as long underwear, should be made from a combination of fibers that will wick moisture away from your body. Synthetics such as polypropylene, or a combination of polyester and nylon, are highly effective. Synthetic fleece pullovers and pants are ideal for the middle layer. Lightweight and very warm, they dry quickly if you get wet.

The outer layer, or shell, protects you from rain, snow, and wind. Most outer wear is

COLD WEATHER GEAR *Modern materials provide clothes that are durable, lightweight, and waterproof. If you follow the basic principles of layering (left), you will remain warm and comfortable even in adverse weather conditions (above).*

FUNCTIONAL CLOTHING *Naturalist's vests (left) have large pockets for carrying field equipment. Muted colors (below) will help you blend with your surroundings and get closer to wildlife.*

Look for tropical-weight, light-colored cotton or cotton blend fabrics, as these breathe, dry faster, and are more durable than synthetics. Sunglasses with UV protection and a wide-brimmed hat are essential to protect you from the sun, but make sure your hat brim doesn't get in the way of your binoculars. Lightweight waterproof parkas and ponchos that can be rolled up and stored in a pocket are ideal for protection in spring showers and summer storms. And a bandanna comes in handy as a headband or handkerchief.

now made of Gore-Tex, or a similar material, which is water repellent and windproof but also lets air in and out.

The layering system can be applied to hats, gloves, and footwear too. For example, you might wear Thermax and Lycra glove liners under fleece gloves and Gore-Tex overmitts.

One drawback to Gore-Tex fabrics is that they tend to rustle when you move. Some naturalists therefore prefer to wear cotton or wool jackets coated with a synthetic sealant, because they are quiet.

All waterproof materials have to be kept clean or they will lose their effectiveness.

HOT WEATHER WEAR

In hot weather, wearing few clothes does not necessarily mean you will be cool. Loose-fitting, long-sleeved shirts and long pants will keep you cooler than shorts and a T-shirt, and will protect you from the sun and bugs.

COMFORTABLE FEET

It's vital to have appropriate footwear, and of course the type of outing you are taking will dictate the kind you'll need.

Low-top, lightweight hiking shoes made of durable materials, such as leather and Cordura nylon, are suitable for most trail hiking. If you will be hiking over rough terrain and carrying heavy loads, you should consider leather hiking boots with high tops, firm arch support and a thick, durable outsole. For hiking in the snow, boots with leather uppers and rubber bottoms, plus removable liners, will keep your feet dry and warm.

Sports sandals can be worn for short hikes and river crossings, and are available with a range of soles for different uses.

Mid-calf to knee-high rubber boots are good for hiking in wet climates, such as tropical rain forests and Alaskan tundra. Look for ones that don't slip up and down and wear two pairs of socks for long hikes.

Make sure boots or shoes fit well before you buy them. Break them in on short hikes before taking off on a long trip. To maintain their effectiveness in wet weather, both leather and Gore-Tex boots should be treated regularly with waterproofing spray or cream.

Socks should also be chosen carefully. Look for cushioned soles and materials that will wick away moisture.

On long hikes, change your socks daily and apply moleskin (available at camping stores) to areas where your shoe is rubbing to avoid getting blisters.

FOOTWEAR *Sports sandals (left) are suitable for watersports and short hikes. For long backcountry trips over rough terrain, sturdy leather boots with tough soles (above) are a must.*

THE DAY HIKE

By far the best way to experience the outdoors is to walk.

In the peace, you can absorb your surroundings

and really feel a part of nature.

When planning a day hike, you will need to think about where you want to go, what you hope to see (and therefore when to go), your clothing, and what to take with you.

DECIDING WHERE TO GO

Detailed maps of the area in question will help you plan your route. If you are visiting a new area, consult the map for general information, such as

TREAD LIGHTLY *Lightweight hiking boots (right) combine breathable uppers with rugged soles and firm ankle support.*

the length of the trail and whether it's a loop. If you are hiking cross-country, it's advisable to refer to a topographical map (see p. 45). Allowing enough time in the area is the key to seeing wildlife. You will see much more if you walk slowly and softly and pause frequently to look and listen. Plan to have

a picnic at a viewpoint, such as on the shore of a lake where animals may come to drink.

Take into account the physical fitness of your group, the weather, and the terrain. By using common sense and allowing a generous amount of time to complete the hike, you can usually avoid getting into dangerous situations and becoming exhausted.

Physical training may be necessary before undertaking some of the classic trails, such as hiking to the bottom of the Grand Canyon from the rim. Safety rules for hiking include traveling with a companion and letting someone know exactly where you are going and when you expect to return.

Ah to be alive

on a mid-September morn

fording a stream

barefoot, pants rolled up,

holding boots, pack on,

sunshine, ice in the shallows,

northern rockies.

For All,
GARY SNYDER (b. 1930),
American poet

PREPARING FOR THE TRAIL

In choosing a day pack, be sure to select one that is made of a lightweight but durable fabric, such as Cordura; it should distribute the weight evenly with two padded shoulder straps, be reinforced at the bottom, have compartments for easy access, and be roomy enough to carry your gear.

When packing for a day trip, consider including the following:
• hat, jacket, additional layer of clothing, bandanna
• binoculars, notepad and pencil, field guide
• energy food, water bottle
• pocket knife, flashlight, whistle, signal mirror
• compass, map
• sunscreen lotion, insect repellent, first aid kit
• camera and film.

THE DAY KIT
Some of the items you should pack for a day hike.

PLAN YOUR ROUTE
carefully and register before venturing into wilderness (below). The Pinnacle Peak Trail in Mount Rainier National Park (right).

TRAVELING LIGHT *For short hikes, a lumbar pack with compartments for water bottles (right) can replace your day pack.*

WHAT DO YOU HOPE TO SEE?

Check with rangers, locals, and books to find out where and when you are likely to see the species that you are looking for. Birds and mammals are at their most active in the early morning and in the evening, so these are usually the best times to see them.

If you're making an early start, lay out your gear ahead of time so that you get into the field early and arrive at the target area at an ideal viewing time. If it's hot, hike early and late in the day, rest at midday, and carry plenty of water.

CLOTHING

Consider what kind of weather conditions you might run into and prepare for the worst. The basics for most habitats include a long-sleeved shirt or top, long pants, comfortable walking shoes, hat, sunglasses, and an outer-wear shell, such as a poncho or wind-breaker (see page 36).

TAKE YOUR TIME *Make sure you allow time to stop, rest, and take in the scenery.*

WHAT TO TAKE WITH YOU

Purchase a day pack that will be durable and comfortable to carry for long periods. Pack it with the items listed in the box opposite. Make sure you include plenty of water (between 2 quarts and a gallon [2.5 and 5 l] per person), and some snacks for picnic stops along the way and for emergency situations. Lightweight food bars that are high in energy are convenient. If you keep some of these and your water bottle constantly at the ready, then you'll be able to hit the trail at a moment's notice.

And what should you leave at home? Radios, pets, brightly colored clothing, loud talking, and, if you are traveling in bear country, strong-smelling foods, hair-spray, and perfume.

ON THE TRAIL

In most parks, maps are available at the entrance and there are mileage posts at the trailheads. If there are no maps, look for a kiosk displaying a map of the area and make notes on the trail you have chosen to follow.

Always stay on the trail and follow markers, both for your own safety and to preserve the habitat. If you are in a wilderness area, be sure to sign the trail register in case you lose your way and need help.

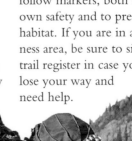

CAMPING OUT

Once you have equipped yourself with a range of basic camping equipment, you will be ready for any number of rewarding trips around the continent.

When considering camping, you must decide how comfortable you wish to be and how far you intend to go from civilization. Backpackers carry everything on their backs and camp in the wilderness. Car campers use the vehicle for transport and storage, and set up camp in campgrounds for cooking and sleeping. Other travelers go camping in recreational vehicles (RVs), which are mobile homes.

The equipment and supplies you need for backpacking and car camping are basically the same, except that backpacking gear is lighter and smaller (see p. 44). The basics include a sleeping bag and pad, tent or shelter, light source, food and water, storage containers, and cooking equipment.

SLEEPING BAGS

Sleeping bags come in a wide variety of materials, weights, and prices. First you need to consider the range of temperatures you expect to camp in. For cold weather, snow camping, and mountaineering, a down bag with a Gore-Tex water-repellent shell will provide the most protection. Goose down is

the warmest, lightest, and most compressible fill, but it loses its loft when wet and is very expensive. For all-round use, synthetic-filled bags are available in a variety of comfort ratings, retain their loft when wet, and are less expensive than down. Additional cold-weather features to look for include draft tubes along the zippers, plus collars and hoods. The weight of the bag (particularly if you are backpacking) and its shape are also important considerations. Tapered bags are warmest, whereas rectangular bags are more roomy, allowing for air circulation in warm climates.

THE INSULATION LAYER

No matter how warm your sleeping bag is, you will be

SLEEP GEAR
For maximum warmth, choose a tapered sleeping bag with draft tubes and a hood.

cold if you don't have a layer of insulation between it and the ground. A ground cloth and insulation pad are recommended. A polyethylene ground cloth can be used for shade or rain protection during the day and then be folded over, as well as under, your sleeping bag to protect you from dew if you're sleeping under the stars. Where pads are concerned, material and construction are more important than thickness. You can choose from waffled polyurethane foam mats to

SLEEPING UNDER THE STARS *(above) is possible with a warm sleeping bag and a tarp. Kits are widely available that convert your insulation pad into a comfortable chair (left).*

DOME TENTS *(left) are easy to set up and, as they don't necessarily have to be pegged, can be erected on rocky ground.*

HEADLAMPS *(above) are excellent for camping, as they provide light while leaving your hands free for other tasks.*

compact, self-inflating mattresses of waterproof nylon that can be made into camp chairs with the purchase of a frame.

TENTS

Tents come in all sorts of sizes, styles, fabrics, and prices. Price is usually related to specialty materials and construction for durability, lightness of weight, and weather protection.

When choosing a tent, consider its versatility, size, weight, ease of erection, and its suitability for the environments you will be using it in. For rainy climates, you'll need a tent with a rain fly. For hot climates, large airy tents with big netted windows are most comfortable. Family tents are roomy but heavy; backpacking tents are light-weight and compact; mountaineering tents are sturdy backpacking tents that will withstand high winds and snow load.

The most common tent shapes are domes, A-frames, and hoops. Most are easy to assemble, consisting of only a few parts and shock-corded poles. Practice setting up your tent before the inaugural trip and air it on your return: if you store it wet it will become mildewed. If you commonly camp in wet weather, apply sealant regularly to fly and tent seams to prevent leaks.

SELECTING A CAMPSITE

When you reach a campground, have a good look at all the available sites to see how secluded they are, whether they have a flat area for sleeping, how close they are to the bathrooms, and what the views are like.

(Part of the fun of camping is waking up to the sight of a mountain peak or your own private wilderness garden.) If you are in rainy country, select a site on high ground so that it doesn't turn into a bog. If it's cold, choose one that's sheltered. As cold air tends to settle in valleys and canyons at night, select a site in a raised position.

BACKPACKING TENTS *(left) are ideal for long treks in wilderness areas. They are light, take up little space in your backpack, and will provide a sturdy shelter even in extreme weather conditions (above).*

STORING FOOD

Scavenging mammals, such as bears, raccoons, and mice, often search campsites for food, particularly at night. Make sure you leave nothing out to attract them. Some camps provide bear-proof storage lockers. If none

A SMARTER THAN AVERAGE BEAR *making a quick getaway.*

is available, store all food in your car or hang it out of reach of animals (see p. 45), well away from where you are sleeping. Bears are attracted to all sorts of smells, so keep yourself and your campsite clean. Careful planning before a trip can eliminate much packaging and therefore reduce waste levels. Whatever garbage there is should be stored in airtight containers. Never take food or toothpaste into your tent at night, and never use perfume or hairspray.

OUT OF REACH *This safety cache is designed to keep food beyond reach of bears, mice, and other scavengers.*

FOOD AND COOKING EQUIPMENT

With so many exciting things to do outdoors, everybody is happiest in camp, including the cook, with meals that are quick to prepare and need little cleaning up afterwards.

Before you set out on your trip, plan menus for each day and then make a list of the ingredients and equipment you will need. Your basic menu should include dry items such as cereals and crackers, and quick-cooking grains that can form the basis of one-pot meals. (Don't forget carbo-hydrate "fuel" foods, like pastas, for hikes.) As cooler space is limited, buy small amounts of perishable items and replenish stocks along the way. Buy a block of ice as it will last longer than cubes.

Kitchen equipment should include an insulated cooler (if you are car camping) matches, eating utensils, plates, cups, cutting knife, cutting board, skillet, cook pot with lid,

biodegradable dishwashing liquid, scrubber, dish towels, ziplock bags, and perhaps a spatula and a long-handled fork. If space is limited, look for nesting cookware.

CAMP STOVES

Cooking on an open fire remains a potent symbol of camping, but camp fires pollute the air and result in people stripping areas near campgrounds of timber and twigs. Responsible campers use camp stoves instead.

If you are cooking with wood, never take it from natural areas, cook only on designated fire rings and grills, and be sure your fire is out before leaving.

Single-burner camp stoves are ideal for backpacking, whereas stoves with two or three burners are more suitable for car camping. Most stoves operate on prefilled cartridges (usually butane), or on refillable tanks that use white gas— an inexpensive, clean-burning fuel available from general stores. Both have good track records; it's a matter of personal preference which you choose.

BACKPACKING STOVES *(below) come with refillable tanks that must be sealed tightly to prevent leakage.*

DUTCH OVENS *(above left) allow you to cook large quantities efficiently. Cartridge stoves (above) are simple to operate, but cartridges may not be available on the road.*

DRINKING WATER *Even water from the most pristine-looking mountain stream should be treated before you drink it (below). Compact water filters (right) make this a relatively simple task.*

water), treat it with chemicals (such as iodine tablets), or use a filtering system. Water purifying tablets are quick and easy to use but leave an aftertaste. Portable water filters are amazingly compact, and come in a variety of styles.

CAMPING ACCESSORIES
You will definitely need a flashlight or headlamp for finding your way in the dark and spotlighting animals. Lanterns, either butane cartridge or white gas, are handy for nighttime cooking and reading.

If you are setting up camp in one spot for a week or two, you may want to bring such items as a solar shower, hammock, inflatable raft, tarp and poles for shade, portable table, camp chairs, and books and games. Duffel bags are handy for carrying clothing and gear and easy to pack into the car.

Try the stove out at home first, before taking it camping, and make sure you recycle the empty fuel containers. Be extremely careful with fire in camp and make sure everyone knows how to use the stove properly.

WATER
Always take water in a multi-gallon container for the car and base camp, and include water bottles for day hikes. Between 2 quarts and a gallon (2.5 and 5 l) or more per person per day is the recommended amount for hikers and backpackers. Potable water is available at most campgrounds but not at primitive campsites or on the trail. *Giardia lamblia*, a bacteria that comes from mammal excrement, is now prevalent in water throughout North America, so no matter how inviting a stream or lake looks, don't drink the water without treating it. There are three ways to do this: boil it (for 10 minutes for completely sterile

PORTABLE TRANSPORT *An inflatable kayak like this one, which fits into a medium-sized duffel bag when deflated, will allow you to reach areas of the backcountry that are otherwise inaccessible.*

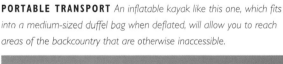

CREATURE COMFORTS *Accessories such as a solar shower can turn a backcountry campsite into a home away from home.*

BACKPACKING

For nature travelers who venture on extended trips into the magnificent wilderness areas of the continent, the rewards are high.

Backpacking requires physical fitness, self-reliance, and careful planning. You have to carry in your backpack all you are likely to need in order to survive out in the wild.

CHOOSING A BACKPACK

Backpacks with internal frames are most suitable for cross-country and active travel; ones with external frames are best for hiking in hot weather and carrying large loads.

Once you've decided which frame you need, it's best to try several loaded packs on and then walk around the store. Most of the weight should rest on the padded hip belt, not on your shoulders. Consider how the pack is divided for ease of access, look for one made of durable water-repellent fabric such as Cordura, and choose an unobtrusive color.

EQUIPMENT

Make a list of the clothing and camping gear you will require (see pp. 34–43). In addition, you'll need an

orienteering compass; topo-graphical maps; toiletries; toilet paper; a pocket knife; candles; a first aid kit (including moleskin to prevent blisters); nylon cord (50 feet [15 m]) to tie your tarp to trees and to hang food out of the reach of bears; and stuff bags in which to carry food, clothing, and garbage.

Food and fuel are heavy and should therefore be divided among the members of the group. Dehydrated and freeze-dried foods need to be divided into daily portions, labeled, and repackaged in ziplock bags.

Most backpackers carry between one-fifth and one-third of their body weight and hike with at least one companion for safety's sake and to share the weight of the gear.

PERMITS AND REGULATIONS

You'll need wilderness permits for camping in federal and state wilderness areas and fire permits for using stoves and building fires. You can obtain these from park authorities and visitor centers.

Permits are issued to control the number of campers and to provide information about regulations. Read the rules

INTERNAL FRAME PACKS *keep the load close to your own center of gravity. They are best suited to off-trail activities such as cross-country hiking and skiing.*

EXTERNAL FRAME PACKS *are ideal for carrying large loads. They are preferable in hot weather, as the frame allows air to circulate between your body and the pack.*

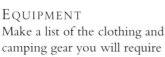

ON A BACKPACKING TRIP *you carry everything you need for your survival. Small and versatile, a pocket knife (top left) is part of any backpacker's kit.*

carefully, both for your own safety and to ensure that the wilderness is left pristine. Before setting off, register at the trailhead.

BACKCOUNTRY CAMPING
Camp in an area where you will have minimal impact on the land and cook only on a stove. Open fires scar the land and use wilderness resources. If you have to make an open fire, make it only in a previously made fire ring.

Respect fragile environments, such as alpine meadows, either keeping on trails or hiking abreast to lessen your impact. Wash all dishes and make latrine stops at least 300 feet (90 m) from water to avoid pollution. Take all garbage, including used toilet paper, out with you, cover wastes with soil or leaves, and use biodegradable soap.

Store all food, garbage, and smelly items such as toothpaste in stuff bags outside your pack and the sleeping area. In places

BACKCOUNTRY CAMPING *can provide unique experiences in the wild (above). In bear country, hang your food from a branch 20 feet (6 m) off the ground (right). Choose a spindly branch that cannot support a bear's weight.*

where there are few trees, prop pans against the bags to set off the alarm if an animal tries to get at the food during the night. In bear country with sufficiently tall trees, hang your food as shown above.

OFF-TRAIL HIKING *demands initiative and a high level of self-reliance.*

CROSS-COUNTRY TRAVEL

If you are planning to head cross-country into wilderness, a topographical map and an orienteering compass will be essential. Topographical maps have contour lines showing elevations and carry names of major landscape features. In the United States, the most widely used topographical maps are published by the United States Geological Survey (USGS). Index maps showing the maps available for each state can be obtained free of charge from USGS offices.

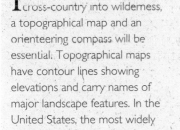

A TOPOGRAPHICAL MAP AND COMPASS
are essential tools for finding your way around in backcountry.

In Canada, topographical maps can be obtained from the Surveys and Mapping section of the Canadian Map Office. (See p. 277 for addresses.)

In an orienteering compass, the needle turns within a circular housing filled with liquid, which in turn rotates on a clear plastic base. The 360 degree directional dial is generally marked off in increments, and the end of the north-pointing needle is usually red. Sometimes the base plate has measurements marked on it, for calculating distances on maps.

It's as well to practice using a map and compass on local hikes first. Place the compass on the map, lining up north on both, then orient yourself in relation to the major landscape features. Most topo maps show a small angle of

declination to the east or west of true north for magnetic north, since compasses point to magnetic north. To be as accurate as possible, place the compass on the map, north lined up with north, and rotate the dial the number of degrees east or west of north indicated by the angle of declination. You will then be oriented to true north.

Plot out your route before you set off. Navigating is not difficult if you check your map and compass against landmarks from time to time. In forested areas, take bearings often and adjust your course accordingly.

SAFETY OUTDOORS

Make sure that you recognize when a situation is dangerous, and that you know what to do in the case of an accident or illness.

As long as you use your common sense and are careful, there are few dangers involved in nature travel. In addition, rangers are usually not far away, unless you are traveling in some of the vast wilderness areas of the West or Alaska.

Make sure that at least one member of your party is familiar with basic first aid and that you always have a first aid kit in your backpack. First aid courses are run by the Red Cross and are held at many community centers.

Most injuries you'll have to deal with will be minor, such as scrapes and cuts, but safety outdoors requires being on the lookout at all times. Accidents usually result from carelessness or foolhardiness.

Most accidental deaths outdoors are either drownings or the result of a fall. Life preservers should always be worn when boating and young children must be closely supervised when near water.

FIRST AID KIT

You can buy a first aid kit or assemble your own. These are the basics: sterilized gauze pads, antiseptic cleaning tissues, adhesive tape, scissors, stretch bandage, butterfly closures, antiseptic ointment, Band-Aids, needle, and aspirin. (Salt tablets are sometimes provided to replace minerals lost through perspiration, but

they should only be used if taken with large amounts of water.) To this you should add items appropriate to your needs, such as personal medications.

It's also a good idea to have a survival kit in case you become stranded. You can buy one or put together your own

EMERGENCY ASSISTANCE *is seldom far away, but always tell friends where you're going and when you plan to return.*

to include waterproof matches, candle, signal mirror, whistle, plastic tube tarp or instant pocket tent, bouillon, sugar, tea, and salt.

sterile dressings

stretch bandage

adhesive tape

TROUBLE ON THE TRAIL

Even when taking great care, accidents do occasionally happen. Three basic first aid rules should be followed in the case of serious injuries and life-threatening situations.

First, stay calm and do what you can to save the patient's life, such as giving artificial respiration or stopping the blood flow. Second, treat for shock by making the patient as comfortable as possible and supplying food and liquids as required. Third, seek help or take the patient to civilization.

It's a good idea to hike in backcountry with at least one companion, so that someone can go for help. A group of three is ideal.

Illnesses can also develop on the trail, such as heat exhaustion, hypothermia, or altitude sickness. These

conditions can affect one's ability to think clearly and can be deadly if not dealt with immediately (see p. 51).

If you think you are lost or you've become separated from your group, don't panic. First, stop and rest, and have something to eat. Get out your map and try to remember the last landmark. You will probably be able to work your way back to the trail by thinking calmly and using

BEING PREPARED

means making sure that you are properly equippped, down to small items for emergencies.

your map and compass. If you really are lost, stay put, make a shelter with the tarp from your survival kit, and signal from time to time. You can use the whistle or mirror from the kit to signal or make a smoky fire with green wood and leaves.

ALTITUDE SICKNESS

Many people experience mild altitude sickness in the form of a headache, shortness of breath, or nausea when they ascend quickly to high altitudes. If such symptoms develop, take it easy for a few days and get plenty of sleep so that your body can become accustomed to a lesser amount of oxygen. Allow a recovery day for each 1,000 feet (300 m) climbed above 10,000 feet (3,000 m).

Two serious forms of altitude sickness can some-times develop: high-altitude pulmonary edema and cerebral edema. In the former, fluid accumulates in the lungs and in the latter it accumulates on the brain. If you cough up blood, or if headaches persist or intensify, descend immediately. As impaired judgement is a basic symptom, always travel in high country with a companion.

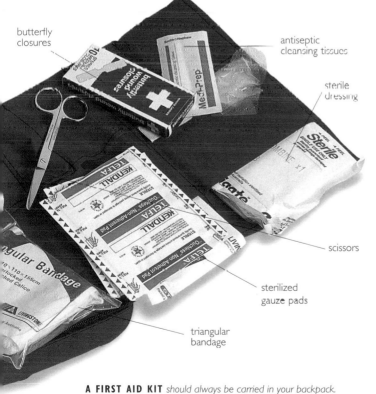

A FIRST AID KIT *should always be carried in your backpack. Most basic kits contain the above items. Band-Aids, antiseptic ointment, a needle, aspirin, safety pins, and a pair of tweezers should be added. You might also like to include moleskin for blisters, lip balm with sunscreen, and corticosteroid cream for rashes and itching caused by insect bites or contact with poisonous plants.*

butterfly closures — antiseptic cleansing tissues — sterile dressing — scissors — sterilized gauze pads — triangular bandage

Natural Hazards

*Few encounters with animals and plants are
life-threatening, but it's wise to know how to recognize
the dangers and what to do if there's an emergency.*

Mammals in the wild are unpredictable, but they are usually afraid of humans and will retreat when people approach. Most accidents with wild animals occur because people have not treated them with respect. Never try to pet or feed animals, or to photograph friends or family near them.

In grizzly country, it's a good idea to tie bells to your pack or talk loudly as you walk, so that bears can move off before you become threateningly close. If you come face to face with a bear, stop and assess the situation. If there are cubs nearby or if the bear is a grizzly, move with extreme caution. Never get between a mother and her cubs for she may charge to protect her young.

In the extremely unlikely event of a bear flattening its ears, facing you squarely, and starting to huff, retreat at once—up a tree if possible (they see tree climbing as a mollifying retreat)—or lie face down and play dead.

Watching Out for Snakes

You will be lucky to even see a snake on your trip and it's very unlikely that one will move toward you, for they seldom attack unless provoked. Most venomous ones occur in the swamps of the Southeast and the deserts and rocky areas of the Southwest. They are sluggish except in temperatures of over 72 degrees Fahrenheit (22° C), but can be aggressive in hot weather.

When in snake country, be careful where you step and where you put your hands when climbing. Long pants, long-sleeved shirts, socks, and hiking shoes will offer some protection. If you meet a snake, stop and let it move on its way, or back away slowly.

Current wisdom on snake-bite treatment is for the patient to stay calm, keep exertion to a minimum, elevate the affected area to minimize swelling, and to seek medical attention without delay. If you are in a remote area without medical help, the immediate use of a venom-extraction syringe and the intake of antibiotics can be effective, in addition to staying still and keeping the affected area elevated.

Troublesome Insects

Most insects are more bothersome than dangerous. An effective insect repellent will keep most away. Apply it to your skin and your clothing. Citronella-based repellents are the safest on exposed skin.

Where there is an acute bug problem, wear protective clothing, such as "bug shirts" which have mosquito netting sewn into the hood and body, or secure mosquito netting over your hat.

Wasps and bees are sometimes hard to avoid. If you are allergic to bee stings, always carry oral medication or an anaphylactic shock kit.

Poisonous Plants

It's important to be able to recognize poisonous plants, particularly if you are traveling with children. Poison oak, poison ivy, and poison sumac are the best known toxic plants. Brushing against any of them can cause anything from mild dermatitis to huge blisters. Even when they are bare in winter they can transmit sap to your skin and clothes. Wash clothes and yourself in hot water as soon as possible. Various lotions, creams, and soaps are available that help stop the itching. In serious cases, consult a doctor.

KEEP YOUR DISTANCE
Found in the swamps and waterways of the Southeast, alligators (left) can be aggressive. You should therefore never approach one, even if it appears docile. A poison ivy leaf (above).

POISON OAK *is a shrub that grows in woods along the Pacific Coast. Its oily looking compound leaves, that have three rounded leaflets, make it easy to identify. In early fall the leaves turn a bright red.*

POISON IVY *grows throughout eastern forests. Usually a vine, but sometimes an erect shrub, it has toothed, compound leaves with three leaflets. It has whitish flowers and white berries, and the leaves turn red in fall.*

POISON SUMAC *grows up to 20 feet (6 m) in swampy pine forests in the East. The tree has pinnate leaves with seven to thirteen untoothed leaflets which turn a brilliant color in fall.*

COTTONMOUTHS *are found in south-eastern swamps. A triangular head and white mouth lining (hence the name) are distinguishing features. When agitated, a cottonmouth opens its mouth and vibrates its tail.*

RATTLESNAKES *are common in the southwest: there are 17 species in Arizona. They are identified by their triangular heads and their rattle—a series of loosely connected horny segments at the end of the tail.*

CORAL SNAKES *are identified by their red, yellow, and black bands. Several species mimic these markings, such as the Sonora mountain kingsnake, but on all of them the red and yellow bands are separated by black.*

DEER TICKS *and black-legged ticks transmit Lyme disease. Check your body thoroughly for ticks after a walk in woody or grassy areas and detach any you find with care. If a bull's eye rash develops, seek medical attention.*

SCORPIONS *are nocturnal arachnids, common in the South and West. They kill their prey (spiders and large insects) by striking with their tail, which ends in a stinger. Few attack humans, but they should be avoided.*

FEMALE BLACK WIDOWS *have a red hourglass mark on the underside of the abdomen and their venom is poisonous to people. They are found mainly under wood piles. Seek medical help if you are bitten.*

THE BLACK BEAR, *the most common bear in North America, varies from brown to black. Smaller than a grizzly, it can be distinguished by a straight profile to the face and the lack of a shoulder hump on the back.*

THE GRIZZLY (BROWN) BEAR *(above and right) has a dished profile to the face, a distinctive hump on the shoulders, and is considerably larger than a black bear. It is restricted to wilderness area in the northern Rockies and Alaska.*

WATCHING *the* WEATHER

*On all outings, keep your sixth sense tuned in to
the weather, learn to recognize warning signs,
and be prepared for the unexpected.*

THUNDERHEADS *indicate an
approaching storm in Yosemite
National Park (right). A hat,
sunglasses, and water bottle
(left) are essentials for any hike.*

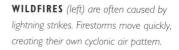

WILDFIRES *(left) are often caused by
lightning strikes. Firestorms move quickly,
creating their own cyclonic air pattern.*

To enjoy nature travel, you have to be ready for all types of weather. If you are well prepared and have the right equipment, there is no reason why a little inclement weather should spoil your trip. In fact, you will be in a position to savor what other people may consider adverse conditions: a rain shower revitalizing a meadow of wildflowers and releasing a heady bouquet of scents; a snowfall transforming a winter landscape.

PREPARATION

Before setting out on a trip, find out what sort of weather to expect. The Weather Channel on television will give you a good picture of the weather throughout the continent, season by season, and provides localized information on a daily basis.

When on your trip, if you are in lodgings or a car, tune in to the local or national weather reports from time to time. The National Weather Service and Environment Canada monitor storms and immediately release information to the media if dangerous conditions, such as a hurricane, a whiteout blizzard, an earthquake, a firestorm, or a tornado, are imminent.

STORMS

Make sure you wear clothing to suit the prevailing conditions (see p. 36) and keep a close eye on the weather. Learn to read the signs of an approaching storm. Watch for towering gray cumulonimbus clouds building on the horizon, gusting winds, or low visibility. Head back if time allows, or take cover at once and wait it out.

If there is lightning and you are wearing rubber-soled shoes, crouch as low as possible with only your shoes touching the ground. Alternatively, lie flat on the ground or take cover in a ditch or head-high bushes. Avoid any metal objects and the

BE PREPARED *for
all types of weather
in the mountains and pay close
attention to warning signs.*

AVALANCHE
DANGER!
SNOW TRAVEL IN AREA BEYOND THIS SIGN
PROHIBITED

LIGHTNING *To assess the distance between yourself and a storm, allow 1 mile (1.6 km) for every 5 second gap between a lightning flash and the subsequent clap of thunder. As the storm approaches, move away from exposed areas.*

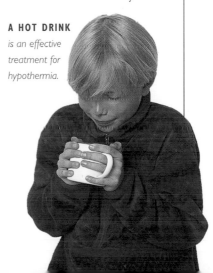

highest objects in the area, such as a single tree.

In the Southwest, storms can cause flash floods. You should therefore avoid narrow canyons when there is a likelihood of a downpour and camp away from dry stream beds.

Some of the most unusual photographs and sightings of rare birds occur in storms, but always use your common sense.

IN THE SUN

Sunshine may create the most pleasant traveling conditions, but it is important to minimize your exposure to the sun and protect yourself against its more harmful effects. Dress appropriately; take plenty of water; apply liberal amounts of sunscreen with 15 to 30 UV protection; and wear UV sunglasses.

PROTECT YOURSELF *when out in the sun by applying sunscreen to exposed skin.*

ADJUSTING TO EXTREMES

Hyperthermia and hypothermia are conditions that develop when the body becomes too hot or too cold respectively. Both develop gradually and cause irrationality, so that the sufferer is unaware of what corrective action to take. You should therefore always travel with a companion and keep a close watch on how your body is reacting to extreme temperatures.

If you are hiking in a hot climate, take time to become acclimatized, exercise intermittently, and drink plenty of water. The first signs of heat exhaustion are a fast, irregular heartbeat, and profuse sweating. If these symptoms develop, stop at once. Find a shaded area where you can rest, cool off with wet cloths or in a nearby body of water, drink plenty of water, and then return to base.

Hypothermia can occur whenever people allow themselves to get wet and cold, and exhaustion and inadequate clothing are often contributing factors. This condition results in uncontrollable shivering and stiff muscles. If these symptoms develop, take shelter at once,

get as warm and dry as you can, eat something, drink hot liquids, and rest.

When hiking in freezing temperatures over a prolonged period, check the feeling in your fingers and toes from time to time. If necessary, loosen shoelaces to increase circulation and place your hands in your armpits to warm your fingers. If extremities do become frostbitten—danger signs include pain and inflammation of the skin followed by loss of sensation and color—head for help immediately. Wherever possible, seek medical advice before trying to thaw out the affected area. Permanent damage can occur if this is done incorrectly.

A HOT DRINK *is an effective treatment for hypothermia.*

BACKCOUNTRY TRAVEL

SEA LEVEL

Nature travelers can have a wonderful time combining their favorite sporting activities with visiting backcountry areas.

There are many enjoyable ways of making your way into the more remote corners of parks and nature reserves, but make sure you consider the impact you'll have on the environment and on other people.

High impact modes of travel—either those that use horses and mules, or are motor-driven, such as motorcycles, snowmobiles, jet skis, and motorboats—should only be used on designated trails and waterways. Bikes, snowshoes, cross-country skis, canoes, rafts, kayaks, and rowboats are low impact, in that they are quiet and don't use fuel. Of course, users must also behave responsibly, such as biking only on paths, for their activities to be low impact.

A MOUNTAIN BIKE
is a low-impact means of transport, but always ride on bike-approved trails.

Most pack animals are harmful, as they eat the plants, soil the wilderness with their wastes, and tear up the trails and meadows. Motor vehicles have the highest impact of all. They use up fuels, pollute the air, tear up the land, and destroy the peace. Riding off-trail and driving off-road are prohibited in all natural areas.

BIKING

Biking provides quick backcountry access and is fun. Most bikes are made of aluminum and steel alloys, but the best

ACTIVITIES OFF-TRACK
include rock-climbing and llama trekking. Llamas make ideal pack animals as they are docile and their hooves do not damage the vegetation.

(and also the most expensive) are made of titanium. When selecting a model, consider carefully the kind of country you will be biking in. Mountain bikes are versatile and sturdy. They have numerous gears that make climbing hills easier, and they allow you to sit upright and enjoy the scenery. You will need to buy a bike helmet and a tool kit that includes at least a spare tube, a mini-pump, a patch kit, and tire levers.

Check in advance to find out where mountain biking is allowed, if at all. Always stay on the trail, as tire treads damage habitats quickly and give wild areas a "used" look.

ACROSS THE SNOW

Snowshoeing and cross-country skiing enable people to visit wilderness areas in winter.

With a little practice, anyone who can walk can snowshoe. Use ski poles at first, for support. Look for snowshoes that are made of

THE BEST WAY INTO THE WILDERNESS
*when there is snow on the ground is to use
snowshoes (below) or cross-country skis (right).*

DOG-SLEDDING *in
Brooks Range in Gates of
the Arctic National Park.*

lightweight materials (such as aluminum and neoprene), and that are fitted with crampons to prevent you from sliding backward. Warm winter boots and ankle-to-knee gaiters will keep your feet dry and warm.

Cross-country skiing is quicker and therefore more exhilarating than snowshoeing. The best skis are ones that do not need waxing and that have clip-on bindings and scales to provide "climbing" traction. You will need poles that reach from the ground to your arm-pits and cross-country boots with firm support.

In some regions, such as Minnesota and Alaska, you can travel by dog sled, which can be a magical experience.

BOATING

Canoeing, kayaking, rafting, rowing, and organized boat trips offer access to wildlife along waterways.

Try out several types of craft before purchasing one, to see what suits you best. Kayaks are designed for one or two people and are suitable for whitewater rivers and open sea. Canoes are designed for two people and for calm waters,

such as marshes and quiet lakes. Inflatable canoes and folding kayaks (made of canvas with wooden struts) are versatile for stowing in a car or airplane. More durable kayaks are made of plastic or fiberglass; sturdier canoes are made of aluminum, fiberglass, wood, or canvas and wood. Kayaks and canoes of this sort can be carried on top of a vehicle. Consider weight if your trip involves portage. Double-bladed kayak paddles that have adjustable blades and can be taken apart are the handiest. Canoe paddles should be single-bladed and reach to your armpits when held by your side.

ADVENTURE TRAVEL

Adventure tours provide excellent ways to take part in sporting activities in the great outdoors and have all the arrangements made by experts.

Soft adventure trips include biking tours on the side roads of New England. More adventurous travel will take you to remote areas, such as whitewater rafting through the Grand Canyon or helihiking in the Rockies. For the hardcore adventurer, there are mountain climbing tours of some of the country's famous peaks, such as Mount Rainier.

Choose a company that has been in

business for some time, specializes in certain destinations or activities, has knowledgeable staff and guides, and follows ecotourist principles (see p. 28). Be sure to ask for references from people who have toured with the company, and compare the responses, itineraries, and prices of several organizations before making a decision.

IN A KAYAK *you can take on
white water or the open sea.*

NATURE ACTIVITIES

*One way to add to your enjoyment of nature and
to inspire you to travel widely is to
develop an outdoor hobby.*

There is certainly no shortage of plants and wildlife in North America, as a quick glance through Chapter 4, Pathways to Nature, will illustrate. Whatever the time of year, there's always something that will interest a naturalist. Whether your specialty is birds, plants, or animals, our wild places offer a diversity of wildlife that promises to keep you enthralled for a lifetime.

BOTANY

Plants are divided into the major categories of trees, shrubs, grasses, wildflowers, nonflowering plants (ferns, lichens, mosses, and seaweeds) and fungi. There are about 750 species of tree, 15,000 species

DESERT FLOWERS *Owl's clover and Mexican poppy, blooming in the Sonoran Desert.*

of wildflower, and innumerable species of grass and nonflowering plant.

A field guide and a good magnifying glass are all you need for identifying plants. Look closely at the leaves, fruit, bark, overall shape, and where the plant is growing.

The wildflower season varies depending upon an area's latitude and altitude, starting as early as February along the Californian coast and extending into July in alpine meadows. Fall is when tree

A BIRD BLIND *in California (left). Birding (below) is among the most popular of all nature activities.*

foliage is at its most dramatic. Always stay on trails and do not collect plants. Take photographs instead.

BIRDING

If you visit a range of habitats at different seasons, you'll be able to see a good many of the 850 bird species that occur in North America. A good pair of binoculars and a field guide are all you need. Schedule your birding for the best time to view the types of bird you're looking for: landbirds in the morning and late afternoon; ducks and geese all day; shorebirds on an ebb tide; and owls and nightjars at night.

A bird's size and shape, particularly the shape of the bill, will help you determine its family. Other details, such as color patterns, habitat, behavior, range, and song will indicate its species. Range maps in your field guide show which birds are resident and which are migratory.

BASKING WALRUSES *in their hundreds being photographed at Bristol Bay in southwest Alaska (left). An organized whale-watching trip (below) is the best way to see whales and dolphins up close.*

Stay at a distance from nests and don't harass birds with tape recordings of their songs.

MAMMALS

As many as 290 species of land mammal and 40 species of marine mammal have been recorded in North America. To go mammal spotting, you'll need a good pair of binoculars, a field guide—preferably with pictures of tracks and scats as well as the animals—and a spotlight for night outings.

Land mammals are found across the continent, with many of the large ones in western mountains and on northern plains. Marine mammals are found along both coasts and in the waters of the Hawaiian islands. Land mammals are generally active early in the morning, in the evening, and at night. On day hikes, you'll probably see tracks and scat more often than the animals themselves.

Driving at night and spotlighting is the best way to see nocturnal mammals, and you really need at least two people—one to drive and one to spotlight.

Some marine mammals, such as sea otters, are resident but most are migratory. You may see marine mammals from the shore, but organized boat trips along the coast are the best way to view whales and dolphins up close.

Make sure that your behavior in no way intrudes on the animals. Use a blind if photographing at a den; always stay at a respectful distance; and take care not to harm marine wildlife or habitat with motorboat propellers.

REPTILES AND AMPHIBIANS

There are close to 300 species of reptile (crocodilians, turtles, lizards, and snakes) and almost 200 species of amphibian (salamanders, toads, and frogs) in North America. Florida is home to alligators, crocodiles, and many turtle species; the Southwest has numerous lizards

and snakes; the Appalachians and western coastal ranges are salamander country; and frogs are abundant in eastern forests.

You'll need a pair of binoculars, a field guide, and a spotlight for night excursions. Most reptiles and amphibians are active at dawn and dusk. Snakes and lizards can best be seen by driving slowly on backroads on warm nights. Frogs and salamanders are most evident on the first rainy nights of spring. During the day, look in ponds for frogs and turtles; and check for salamanders, lizards, and snakes under logs and rocks (turning them away from you and replacing them as they were).

First learn to distinguish reptiles and amphibians by family characteristics and then look for field marks, such as stripes or rings on the body or face. In the case of a poisonous snake, stand several body lengths away and look at it through binoculars.

Never harass reptiles or amphibians; never capture them to take home as pets; and do all you can to help local conservation organizations protect their habitats.

TRACKS of a white-tailed jack rabbit (left). Collared lizard (above), native to the Midwest and the Southwest.

BEACH WALKING AND TIDEPOOLING: MOLLUSKS

Walking along the edge of the sea offers opportunities galore to observe mollusks: crabs, sea stars, anemones, and other strange creatures.

You'll need a tide table to determine when to visit and a field guide on seashore life. It's also advisable to wear a pair of water-walking shoes, such as sports sandals, and have a good sense of balance. Start at the farthest pool from the shore and move inshore with the tide. Do not collect specimens or shells.

SNORKELING AND DIVING: SEALIFE

Snorkeling and diving are delightful pursuits in the tropical waters around the Florida Keys and in the Hawaiian islands, and are enjoyed by the more hardy in California's cool waters.

TIDEPOOLING *is a fascinating activity when the tide is out (below). Sea stars (right) are among the many marine creatures you'll come across.*

For snorkeling, you need a mask, snorkel, fins, underwater flashlight (for nighttime snorkeling) and a local fish guide (plastic-coated, for underwater use). You may also want to invest in a prescription mask, if needed, and a wetsuit. The best time for snorkeling is

UNDERWATER WORLD *A diver surrounded by butterfly fish (below) in the waters of Hawaii, where you'll also find the endangered green sea turtle (left).*

in broad daylight, when sunlight penetrates the water.

Scuba diving is undoubtedly the best way to experience the underwater world, but you must become certified through attending classes and exercise proper safety precautions.

To learn how to identify fish, first familiarize yourself with the shapes of different families, then look for field marks and patterns of color to determine the species.

You can play your part in protecting our reefs and tropical waters by not having a saltwater aquarium, not buying jewelry made of coral, not standing on or taking living coral, not anchoring your boat in coral, and by not dumping garbage into open water.

INSECTS AND ARACHNIDS

Insects are by far the largest group of animals in the world and there are over 100,000 species of insect in North America alone. This fascinating group includes highly complex

LIFE ON THE PRAIRIE *A katydid on a purple coneflower.*

FIELD GUIDES

Field guides are tools that enable people in the field to identify wildlife, plants, and geological features. The first mass-market field guides were written and illustrated by Roger Tory Peterson, beginning in 1934 with *A Field Guide to the Birds*. A birder, painter, and writer, this remarkable man revolutionized the way that we observe nature by introducing the concept of field marks— physical features that allow one to quickly and decisively distinguish particular species. Since that time, all sorts of field guides have been published by a range of naturalists. You can now find ones that will help you identify everything from trees and wildflowers to fossils.

[Nature] is the one place where miracles not only happen, but happen all the time.

THOMAS WOLFE (1900–38), American novelist

PETRIFIED WOOD, (shown in cross-section) in which the cells of an ancient piece of timber have been replaced by mineral deposits.

social animals (bees and ants); creatures that undergo amazing metamorphoses (butterflies, moths, and beetles); delicate fliers (damsel and dragonflies); luminescent fireflies; and venomous stingers (wasps and bees). Arachnids include spiders and scorpions. Field guides are available for certain groups, such as butterflies and beetles.

Insects perform the vital task of pollinating plants, and the number of pesky ones is relatively small. Open-air, wire-encased bug jars allow children to catch insects, observe them for a while, and then set them free.

ROCKS AND FOSSILS

To learn about the various geological processes that formed the landscape around you, obtain a field guide to rocks and minerals and a guide to the geological history of your area.

TAKE A GOOD LOOK *at the rocks you find (right), but don't take them away. Tiger swallowtail butterfly (above).*

Geologists identify rocks by the way they were formed. For example, igneous rocks are volcanic in origin; sedimentary rocks were laid down in layers in lakes and seas; and metamorphic rocks are igneous and sedimentary rocks that have been transformed by heat and pressure.

Parks and preserves in North America and the islands of Hawaii offer some of the most magnificent geological examples on Earth, in addition to excellent preserved examples

of life that lived millions of years ago, in the form of fossils.

Never hack away at the ground with a pick or take rocks and fossils away with you: leave what you have seen for others to enjoy.

NATURE ACTIVITIES FOR THE DISABLED

Increasingly, at parks across the continent, information is being provided in braille, large print, and in tape-recorded form; and special trails and boardwalks are being constructed so that travelers with disabilities can participate fully in nature activities.

For example, the Anhinga Trail in Everglades National Park is not only wheelchair accessible but offers audio tapes and textured cue pads for the visually impaired. And in Yosemite National Park you can join a nature walk conducted in sign language.

Write or call the park you intend to visit for further information on similar activities.

RECORDING YOUR TRIP

Whether it be in the form of photographs or a journal, keeping a record of your trip adds another dimension to your experience and heightens your perception.

A ZOOM LENS *on your camera provides great versatility.*

For many people, nature photography is the perfect way to enjoy being in the wild. To be successful, you need to be familiar with how your camera works and have a keen eye for composition and light.

CAMERA EQUIPMENT

Basic field equipment should include at least one quality 35 mm camera, a zoom lens or several fixed lenses, film, carrying case, lens cloth, notepad, pen, and ziplock bags to keep everything dry. The camera and lenses will be your most expensive investment: be sure to consider quality, clarity, versatility, weight, magnification, and guarantee, as well as price.

For maximum flexibility, you should be able to focus and select your shutter speeds manually. Ideally, you should have a 55 mm as your basic lens, a macro for plants and insects, a 200 to 500 mm telephoto for wildlife, a wide-angle for landscapes, and a zoom for versatility. Always take more film

than you think you will need and consider the weather and lighting you will be using it in. You'll need 64 and 100 ASA films for full sun, 200 ASA for sunny to partially cloudy weather, and 400 and 1000 ASA for dusk and dark areas, such as forests. You may also want a tripod, filters,

polarizers, a flash attachment, and a portable blind. Specialty cameras include panoramic cameras for getting the "whole" view, amphibious cameras for underwater or whitewater shots, and video cameras for capturing wildlife sounds and behavior.

Allow ample time for photographing and relaxing in your favorite spots, so that you don't have to leave just

PHOTOGRAPHIC OPPORTUNITIES *While you should never harass animals to obtain a photo, some are only too keen to be in the picture (left). A photographer setting up to take a shot of Yosemite Valley in earlier times (above).*

*are available
that will help you
identify the sounds
of nature.*

when the lighting is at its best.
Streamline your equipment
to an amount you can carry
comfortably. Respect wildlife
and make sure you don't
jeopardize the breeding success
of birds by approaching their
nests too closely. You need
patience, quick reflexes, and
fast film to catch the perfect
view of a bird or mammal
before it moves.

The best times of day for
nature photography are usually
early in the morning and late
afternoon. This is when the
lighting lends a warm glow
to the landscape and when
wildlife is most active.

SOUND EQUIPMENT

A small, hand-held digital
recorder can be used in
the field to record
dawn choruses
and memorable
sounds, such
as "singing"
coyotes in
the desert.

If you are really serious
about making high quality
recordings, you'll need a
parabolic reflector with a high
quality directional microphone
and a digital recorder. This
equipment is not as heavy and
bulky as it once was, but it can
still be cumbersome. Once

ANSEL ADAMS

One of the most famous
photographers of the
twentieth century, Ansel Adams
(1902-84) was closely associated
with the Sierra Club and
spent much of his adult life in
Yosemite National Park.

He took thousands of
photographs of Yosemite and
other parks throughout the
United States and wrote
numerous articles, essays, and
books, bringing the wonders of
the wilderness to the attention
of the American public.

Adams worked tirelessly for
the environmental movement
and campaigned widely for
the creation of new parks.
His photographs speak

eloquently of the need to
preserve our wilderness.

In 1980 he received the
Presidential Medal of Freedom
from President Carter for his
visionary work.

you start recording in the
field, you'll quickly become
sensitive to interfering sounds,
such as wind, running water,
cars, and airplanes.

The use of tape recorders
has become common among
avid birders to try to lure
difficult-to-see-species, such
as owls, into the open. This
technique should be used
sparingly, as males will desert
their territories if they are
subjected to it repeatedly.

KEEPING A
WRITTEN RECORD

Recording in a journal
the places you visit and
what you do and see
is a rewarding way
of remembering
your trip and the
material can be used later for
developing your experiences
into articles and stories.

Scientists and
amateur naturalists
take notes each day
they are in the
field, which record
the date, the
weather, time spent
in the field, species
seen and heard,

behavior observed,
and the number of
each species. Notes
of this sort should
be written up as
soon as you return
home. Over the
years, if you record
information from the field
in this way, it will increase
your knowledge of species
distribution and behavior
and may provide rewarding
research data.

The knowledge and field
skills of dedicated amateurs are
being called upon increasingly
for scientific studies, such as
surveys of breeding birds, or
the assessment of remaining
critical habitats for species that
are endangered or threatened.

TAKING FIELD NOTES *helps you
develop your powers of observation.*

NATURE TRAVEL *with* KIDS

If you introduce children to the outdoors in a rewarding way and nurture their curiosity about the world around them, they'll be nature lovers from the start.

If you're taking children with you on a trip, especially if you're going camping, planning is vital. It's a good idea for them to practice camping in the backyard. They'll have a great time and will then be accustomed to the tent and their sleeping bags before you set off. And if you take them hiking near home, they'll become used to wearing their backpacks and you can work out what length of walk they can handle comfortably.

Once you've made your short list, involve the children

in deciding where you're going. Make sure you choose places with plenty of habitats to explore and where they can run around, climb trees, investigating tide pools, or explore a lakeshore.

HAVING A GOOD TIME

The best approach is to make a backcountry visit so enjoyable that it will be a home away from home. Don't forget your child's favorite stuffed animal, if they have one, and also a few bedtime story books.

On the trail, kids can carry their own nature gear in their backpack—items such as binoculars, bug jar, magnifying glass, field guide, paper, and colored pencils. It's important for children to have a pair of

ORGANIZED NATURE ACTIVITIES

Organized nature activities are available for a wide range of ages, including preschoolers. Many local parks and recreation departments offer summer day camps and some run week-long nature camps.

Natural history museums and aquariums offer kids' classes and day trips to go tidepooling, looking for reptiles, and birding. If your'e planning a trip to a

national park, check with the visitor center to see if youth programs are available.

Some nature organizations sponsor nature camps for kids. The Youth Ecology Camp in Maine, for example, is sponsored by the Audubon Society, and Camp Chiricahua, held every summer in Arizona for budding birders, is run by Victor Emanuel Nature Tours.

Some nature tour companies run tours especially for families, such as llama pack trips, river rafting trips, and biking tours. These allow the whole family to enjoy an outdoor experience together and leave all the planning and guiding to experts.

HAVING THEIR OWN BACKPACK
means that children can carry their own nature gear, snacks, and drinks, plus maybe a few extra items of clothing.

TAKING THE KIDS WITH YOU

Parents show a great sense of ingenuity when taking their children with them into wild country. Be sure to choose equipment that is comfortable and safe and is sturdily built.

binoculars early on, as it's hard to share binoculars. Be sure to get a pair that little fingers can focus. Always bring snacks, drinks, and extra clothes along as kids need frequent refueling along the way and may well get wet or muddy. Don't make a big deal about them getting dirty. Mud washes off but exciting experiences outdoors will stay with your child for a lifetime.

When planning a hike, select an area where there are various trails to choose from, preferably loops of differing lengths, and choose one without steep hills so that little legs do not become worn out too quickly. Give your child a chance to lead the hike and set the pace—distance covered is nowhere near as important as having fun. Avoid trails that go near clifftops or alongside fast-flowing rivers, and take plenty of breaks.

DISCOVERIES

During breaks, or in camp, focus the child's attention on something specific. If you see a salamander, for instance, you can lie on your bellies and watch it climb over rocks and eventually dive into the stream; this can lead to discussions and discoveries about the lives of salamanders. There is always a drama unfolding, if you look and listen carefully.

By following the interests of your child, the time spent together will be a joyful learning experience for both

of you. If he or she is interested in reptiles, for instance, take a field guide on reptiles and amphibians with you. With some guidance, children quickly learn how to use field guides and are soon spouting scientific names.

Our wildlife and ecosystems are facing crises of monumental proportions that we will soon be handing over to our children. By teaching them to love and respect nature and by showing them how to take care of our wild places, we'll be raising a generation inspired to work for its preservation.

If a child is to keep alive his inborn sense of wonder...he needs the companionship of at least one adult who can share it, rediscovering with him the joy, excitement and mystery of the world we live in.

The Sense of Wonder,
RACHEL CARSON
(1907–64),
American
naturalist
and
writer

WITH A LITTLE GUIDANCE,

children soon learn how to use a field guide and binoculars.

Those who contemplate the beauty of the earth find
reserves of strength that will endure as long as life lasts.

The Sense of Wonder, RACHEL CARSON (1907–64),
American naturalist and writer

CHAPTER THREE
TRAVELING
THROUGH NATURE

TRAVELING *in* FORESTS

Few things can do more to restore the jaded senses than the sight of forest greenery or a walk in the velvety silence of the woods.

FLY AGARIC MUSHROOMS *(far left) grow in temperate forests throughout North America and are very poisonous. The only treefrog species in the Pacific states, the Pacific treefrog (left) has toe pads that enable it to cling to vertical surfaces, such as tree trunks. When their wings are folded, monarch butterflies (below) resemble dead leaves.*

Nearly 150 distinct types of forest containing some 1,390 different species of tree are found in North America. Picture these forests as a lush, green mantle draped over the continent. The western shoulder is covered thickly with conifers—pine, cedar, fir, spruce, and hemlock. The tallest, biggest, and oldest species (redwoods, giant sequoias, and bristlecone pines, respectively) grow in California. Conifers mixed with such hardwoods as maples, birches, and beeches

MOUNTAIN LIONS *can occasionally be seen in northern upland forests, in semi-arid mountainous terrain, and in tropical forests.*

spread across North America's upper back. This patchwork-like pattern continues down the eastern shoulder, with loblolly, slash, and longleaf pines joining thickets of sweetgums, tupelos, and oaks in the south. At the southern tip of the mantle dangles a tropical fringe of mangroves, mahoganies, and baldcypresses.

Beneath the shady limbs of these imposing members of the forest community grow thousands of kinds of shrub, vine, herb, fern, moss, and mushroom. And feeding upon the forest plants are legions of small mammals, birds, and insects, which, in turn, provide food for other creatures.

ANIMAL SIGNS
Each of these creatures signals its presence in a particular way, so take a field guide, binoculars, and a magnifying glass. Bears, bobcats, and mountain lions claw trees to mark their territories. Gray squirrels, horned owls, and wood ducks nest in tree

cavities, while badgers dig their dens in the soil below. Porcupines eat conifer, beech, and sugar maple bark, leaving chunks of outer bark on the ground, and a Jeffrey pine with its trunk peppered with acorns will be a woodpecker's larder.

The most conspicuous signals are the songs of the birds, especially in spring when males are calling for mates and fending off rivals. Even the nonsingers find ways to signal their presence: the male ruffed grouse rapidly beats his wings, producing a drumming sound.

The beauty of silence

And the broken boughs

And the homes of small

animals…

But So As By Fire,
GEORGE OPPEN (1908–84),
American publisher and
political activist

BOREAL OWLS *live in the coniferous forest of the Far North.*

OLD-GROWTH FORESTS

Old-growth forests contain trees that are at least 175 years old. These last vestiges of ancient forest are dominated by cone-bearing trees—Douglas fir, Sitka spruce, and redwood—which are heavier and genetically older than the broadleafs that grow among them, such as tanoak, Oregon white oak, and madrone.

Significant old-growth areas include the red-wood and sequoia

forests of the Sierra Nevada and the narrow strip of temperate rain forest that stretches from Northern California to the Alaskan panhandle.

Because of their great bio-diversity, ancient forests support a wide array of wild-life, much of which is now endangered because over-cutting has re-duced the size of these once-great forests by 90 percent.

WHEN TO GO

The first signs of warmer weather in deciduous wood-lands are the wildflowers taking advantage of sunlight streaming through bare branches, and robins greeting worms that have tunneled up through the unfrozen ground. Then the green awning of leaves begins to unfurl, starting with the lowest shrubs and culminating with the leafing of the tall canopy.

Summer's heat triggers a mad hatch of insects, which brings trout in the rivers and lakes to the surface to feed. If you look in the mud along the banks you may find box turtles escaping the heat. Dawn and dusk bring deer to the meadows to feed.

Activity in the forest increases in fall as the trees and animals prepare for winter. This is the easiest time of the year to spot wildlife. Small mammals throw caution to the wind as they scurry about collecting nuts and seeds. The scenery is magnificent, the changing climate triggering a blaze of color as the leaves turn from green to yellow, to rust, to red. Look for color on the forest floor as well: August through October are mushroom months from Washington to Maine.

Most wildlife quietly disappears from view in winter. Migrants such as Cape May warblers and monarch butterflies will all have flown south and hibernating bears and chip-munks will be snug in their dens and burrows. If you exchange your hiking boots for cross-country skis or a pair of snowshoes, you'll be able to penetrate deep into the woods to relish their silent, snowy beauty.

TOP FOREST AREAS

RED FOXES, *shy and nocturnal, are found in wooded areas and brushland.*

TRAVELING *in the* MOUNTAINS

Mountain country offers nature travelers endless opportunities for exploration and refreshment in breathtaking scenery.

THE HIGH LIFE *Bighorn sheep (left) have adapted to living at high altitudes. A blue haze rising from the Blue Ridge Mountains (right).*

From the 500 million-year-old Appalachians in the East, rounded by wind and rain, to the fire-breathing summits of Kilauea and Mount St Helens in the West, North American mountains offer vast areas of wilderness to explore. To hike a mountain trail is to follow in the footsteps of legendary men such as Daniel Boone, Lewis and Clark, Jim Bridger, Jeremiah Johnson, and John Muir. Each range has a story to tell of prehistoric cultures, gold nuggets glistening in a creek, wolves howling at the moon, or aspens dancing in the wind.

Mountains are characterized by diversity. The Great Smokies and the Blue Ridge Mountains get their names from the haze that is given off by the vegetation that blankets their slopes. Mountain goats and bighorn sheep cling sure-footedly to the steep sides of the Rockies. Giant grizzlies rule the Alaskan Range. At 430 miles (690 km), the Sierra Nevada comprises the longest wall of granite on the planet. And the Earth's highest surface wind speed, 231 miles (372 km) per hour, was recorded atop New Hampshire's White Mountain.

SPECIAL EQUIPMENT

Mountain travel should be approached with caution and requires careful planning. Altitude sickness can kill. Weather is often tempestuous. Trails on a map differ from those underfoot. Take your time acclimatizing to high altitudes: allow one day for each 1,000 foot (300 m) climb above 10,000 feet (3,048 m). Plan for every contingency, and always call ahead to check local conditions. Remember, even in July snowstorms occur in the Rockies.

ELK *live in mountain habitats but may feed in valleys.*

SCALING THE HEIGHTS *A group of hikers on the northwest ridge of Mount Clark in Yosemite National Park (left). The plumage of the white-tailed ptarmigan (below left) turns white in winter to camouflage the bird against the snow. Gray wolves (below) hunt elk, bighorn sheep, and deer at high elevations.*

Register with area rangers or local authorities before setting out on any wilderness excursion of more than a day, and remember to take a compass and topographical map as they will come in handy if you find unsigned forks on a trail. Tie a bell on your pack or carry a whistle when hiking in mountain lion and bear country. A water filtration system is essential even in the most pristine of settings. In clear skies at high altitudes, ultraviolet radiation is intense, so protect your skin by wearing a hat and applying a strong sunscreen. When taking photos, use a UV or polarizing filter on your lens.

WHEN TO GO

Summer is the most popular time of year for visiting the mountains as the trails are usually free of snow and the rivers right for running. The high meadows look like giant bouquets, brimming with such colorful wild-flowers as lupine, Indian paintbrush, and mountain bluebells. The high country attracts numerous birds, including tanagers, mountain chickadees, warblers, and rosy finches. Deer, elk, and other large mammals also move to higher ground in search of food when the days are warm.

Fall brings cooler weather and fewer bugs, and because there are not so many people out on the trail it's a good time to visit such popular destinations as Yellowstone and Yosemite. At lower elevations, animal life bustles at a feverish pace as resident species prepare for winter.

TOP MOUNTAIN AREAS

Denali National Park and Preserve, Alaska (p. 88)

Gates of the Arctic National Park and Preserve, Alaska (p. 92)

Yosemite National Park, California (p. 108)

Mount Rainier National Park, Washington (p. 118)

Rocky Mountain National Park, Colorado (p. 124)

Glacier National Park, Montana (p. 132)

White Mountain National Forest, New Hampshire (p. 234)

Banff National Park, Alberta (p. 254)

Winter snows change mountain travel and outdoor recreation conditions dramatically. Many areas become inaccessible but in an increasing number of places you will find that trails are being marked and groomed for cross-country skiing. Skiers should be aware of the dangers of hypothermia and avoid slopes that are susceptible to avalanches.

Snow can last until June, making high-country hiking any earlier in the year a chancy business. Nothing is more tiring than having to slog through slush or force your way through crusty, thigh-high snowdrifts.

GRIZZLY BEARS *are found in upland areas of western Canada and Alaska and in the Rocky Mountains.*

WILDFLOWERS *fill alpine meadows late spring through summer in most mountain areas of North America.*

67

TRAVELING *in* GRASSLANDS

The great oceans of grass that spread from Alberta to Texas are at once desolate and beautiful, tumultuous and serene.

Waves of shortgrass, midgrass, and tallgrass prairie cover North America's midsection. These expanses may not inspire the excitement that a rugged coastline or a craggy mountain does, but their drama and diversity soon become apparent to anyone prepared to pay them close attention.

Although much has fallen to the plow, remnants of three types of grassland can still be found. Tallgrass is comprised of grasses over 4 feet (120 cm) tall that grow in Iowa, Illinois, Minnesota, and along the eastern edges of Kansas, Nebraska, South and North Dakota, and parts of Canada. Midgrass—between 2 and 4 feet (60 and 120 cm) tall—covers parts of north-central Texas, Oklahoma, Nebraska, Kansas, and most of the Dakotas. The shortgrass prairie—grasses under 2 feet (60 cm) tall—is bounded by the Rockies on the west. The largest expanses are found in parts of eastern Colorado, Wyoming, and New Mexico. Native short-grass species

GRASSLAND *flowers include the golden coreopsis (above). Pronghorns (below), were almost wiped out by hunters in the nineteenth century but are now making a comeback.*

THE TALLGRASS PRAIRIE PRESERVE in *Oklahoma (above) protects one of America's largest remaining areas of native tallgrass prairie. The ring-necked pheasant, an introduced species, is now common in grasslands and farmlands throughout North America.*

include buffalo, blue grama, June, and green needle grasses.

Millions of years ago, in these regions, saber-toothed cats, mammoths, ancient badgers, prongbucks, giant camels, rhinoceroses, and llamas fed among grassy meadows, cattail marshes, and groves of cottonwoods, hack-berry trees, and elms. As the Earth warmed, this savanna gave way to prairie and great herds of bison, pronghorn, and elk took over.

Hunters destroyed most of these herds in the 1800s, but

the big ungulates are making a comeback. About 800,000 pronghorns inhabit the prairie today and you can see large herds along Interstate 80 in Wyoming. More than 70,000 bison are now roaming, and they can be found at a number of preserves, including Yellowstone National Park in Wyoming, and Wichita Mountains National Wildlife Refuge and the Tallgrass Prairie Preserve in Oklahoma. Elk are common in Yellowstone and in Lake Scott State Park in Kansas.

TOP GRASSLAND AREAS

Grasslands teem with birdlife. In upland areas, keep an eye out for circling red-tailed, Swainson's, and ferruginous hawks looking for prairie dogs, pocket mice, and kangaroo rats. Ring-necked pheasants and northern bobwhites scurry through the fields, while mountain plovers, long-billed curlews, greater yellowlegs, and sandpipers congregate along the shores of seasonal ponds and pools.

FOSSILS

The Great Plains contain some of the world's biggest boneyards. Over 100 million years ago, much of the region was covered by a giant inland sea. Carnivorous fish 15 feet (4.5 m) long swam in its warm, shallow waters, while 4 ton dinosaurs resembling overgrown

BIRDS OF PREY, *such as the prairie falcon (left), hunt over open fields. Prairie dogs (below) take refuge from predators in their burrows.*

armadillos waded in its shallows, and Tyrannosaurus rexes roamed the marshy plains. Among the best places to see dinosaur fossils are Morrison, Colorado; Como Bluffs, Wyoming; and Hell Creek, Montana. Always leave fossils where they are for others to enjoy.

Badlands National Park in South Dakota is known as the world's largest animal grave-yard. Its soft sediments contain the remains of more than a hundred species of mammal, including extinct horses, saber-toothed cats, monkeys, and alligators. There are informational displays and guided tours, and local natural history museums and univer-sities will let you know how to join scientists on a dig.

WHEN TO GO

Grasslands are beautiful throughout the year, with wildflowers reaching their peak in spring and animal life most apparent in spring and fall. Remember, however, that the Great Plains have some of the most violent and unpredictable weather anywhere. Winters can be bitterly cold, with dry winds sweeping across the prairie at speeds of over 100 miles (160 km) per hour. Summers, on the other hand, can be blazingly hot, with tornadoes occurring frequently.

OUT IN THE OPEN *At one time, 50 to 60 million bison (above) roamed the prairies. In the badlands of North Dakota (above), prairie merges with mountains.*

There is not a sprig of grass that shoots uninteresting to me.

THOMAS JEFFERSON
(1743–1826),
United States President

WILDFLOWERS

Native grasses are far from being the prairie's only plants. Willow, cottonwood, box elder, ash, and elm trees grow alongside creeks and rivers, while desert shrubs like salt-bush, sagebrush, and mountain mahogany populate drier areas.

It is the wildflowers, though, that provide the greatest show. Once the snow melts, wave after wave of blooms color the prairies like a giant Impressionist painting. First to come from nature's palette are the buttercups that appear in early spring, just as the snow is starting to recede. Dandelions follow, and by May all their flowers have opened. Next come pussytoes and morning glories, followed by asters, blazingstars, and lupine. Coneflowers are among the last to bloom, while sunflowers last all the way through September.

TRAVELING *in the* DESERT

Far from being barren wastelands, American deserts offer the naturalist a startlingly diverse range of scenery and some intriguing wildlife.

CACTI *provide food and shelter for a variety of animals. White-winged doves nest on saguaros (left). Birds and bats feed on the flower of the agave (right).*

Deserts are deceptive. A region that appears stark, lifeless, and monochromatic at first glance becomes, on closer inspection, a place of great beauty that's home to a fascinating array of plants and wildlife. Strange reptiles such as fringe-toed lizards, sidewinders, and Gila monsters skitter, slither, and lumber across the sandy floor. Roadrunners sprint between clumps of buckhorn chollas and creosote bushes, while verdins, phainopeplas, and cactus wrens flit among flowering honey mesquites.

Four great deserts covering hundreds of square miles—the Mojave, Sonoran, Great Basin, and Chihuahuan—sprawl across parts of California, Nevada, Utah, Arizona, Texas, and New Mexico. Each has been colored and sculpted by a combination of plate tectonics, volcanic activity, wind, and rain. Spectacular landscapes abound. Take Death Valley National Park in California's Mojave Desert, where snow–dusted peaks up to 11,000 feet (3,350 m) high tower above a dazzling white salt pan 280 feet (85 m) below sea level. In between lie sand dunes and highly eroded cliffs as variegated as a rainbow.

SPECIAL EQUIPMENT

Travel in the desert requires planning. For all its beauty, the desert can be harsh and unrelenting. Distances are deceptive and dimensions can become distorted. Tantalizing pools of water seem to hover on the horizon, forever out of reach. Temperatures can range from 120 degrees Fahrenheit (48° C) during the day to freezing at night. Water is as valuable as gold. Cactus spines prick. Rattlesnakes bite. Being properly equipped makes all the difference and a canteen is essential.

Many desert areas are rich in minerals. Wind, rain, and geological forces have brought deposits to the surface, exposing such beauties as agate, quartz, and turquoise for visitors to see. Desert night skies glitter, too. With no city lights and few clouds to obscure them, the planets and stars appear close enough to touch. A constellation guide and a telescope or binoculars will add to an evening spent around the campfire.

To see wildlife you will need to rise early and go to bed late, as most creatures are active before the sun rises and after it sets, but if you find

DESERT COLORS *The muted colors of the sagebrush lizard and the varied tones of the Artists Palette in Death Valley (above). Brittlebrush (below) bursts into bloom in late winter and early spring.*

working to preserve and protect what's left. Canada and the United States have launched a joint program—the North American Waterfowl Management Plan—to protect waterfowl habitat, and both The Nature Conservancy and Ducks Unlimited continue to buy wetland areas for preservation and restoration.

SPECIAL EQUIPMENT

Wetlands are wet, and to visit many areas you'll need a canoe or a boat. Poling or paddling is best, but if you must use a motor, consider an electric outboard of the kind used for trolling. Powered by car batteries, they're slow and quiet, so they leave little wake to disturb floating nests and won't drown out the sounds of the swamp.

Rubber hip boots or chest waders also come

MUSKRATS *(below) build multi-chambered dwellings out of mud and plants. Generally nocturnal, they feed on sedges, water lilies (left), and cattails.*

in handy. Sturdy soles guard your feet against sharp stalks sticking up from the mud. Use a walking stick for balance when wading and for testing the depth of muddy water. You might consider putting your binoculars and camera in ziplock plastic bags for protection, or bringing along waterproof versions.

WHEN TO GO

In spring, wetlands are brimming with runoff from snowmelt and winter rains. Wildflowers appear in waves. In the prairie potholes of the Midwest and the vernal pools of the West, varying species encircle the pools in rings of color, as water levels first

rise and then slowly fall. Birdlife grows increasingly active as migrants join residents to breed and rear their young. The relative scarcity of predators in these watery regions ensures a reasonable success rate for their broods.

With summer comes an explosion in the insect population. Mosquitoes breed and hatch close to the shore—areas frequented by human visitors—giving the false impression that wetlands are pest-ridden through and through.

In fall, activity is constant, with migrating waterfowl progressing southward from wetland to wetland as if they were watery stepping stones. In winter, northern marshes freeze, allowing visitors to "walk on water". While there are fewer birds to watch, this can be the best season to spot mink, weasels, and muskrats.

CANADA GEESE *(above) can often be found on ponds and rivers in urban parks. Cattails (below).*

TOP WETLAND AREAS

Kauai Refuge Complex, Hawaii (p. 116)

Medicine Lake National Wildlife Refuge, Montana (p. 134)

Bosque del Apache National Wildlife Refuge, New Mexico (p. 164)

Santa Ana/Lower Rio Grande Valley National Wildlife Refuges, Texas (p. 172)

Everglades National Park, Florida (p. 200)

Edwin B. Forsythe National Wildlife Refuge, New Jersey (p. 240)

Iroquois National Wildlife Refuge, New York (p. 244)

A WETLAND CHORUS *Among the most common sounds heard in wetlands are the raucous calls of frogs. The green frog (above), found in eastern North America, varies in color and may even be blue.*

TRAVELING *the* COAST

Nowhere is there a greater diversity of habitats and a more fantastic array of wildlife than where the land meets the sea.

From the Florida Keys that shimmer in turquoise waters like a pearl necklace to evergreen-clad, mist-shrouded Vancouver Island, North America's coastal areas beckon with the promise of diverse wildlife and enchanting environments. Greater yellowlegs chase fish in marsh pools at Cape Cod. Sea otters crack open urchins while floating lazily on their backs in Monterey Bay. Thousands of hawks, eagles, and falcons wing

THE INTERTIDAL ZONE *is one of the richest of all habitats. Rock pools host an array of invertebrates, including giant spined sea stars (left). Waves deposit shells (right) and sea creatures on beaches, to the delight of waiting birds, such as the herring gull (right).*

over the New Jersey shore in fall. Sea turtles lay their eggs on Texas beaches.

Consider just a one-mile-wide section of coastline at Big Sur, California. Sorrel and redwoods line bubbling creeks. Turkey vultures soar over open fields of purple needlegrass. Mountain lions chase deer through chaparral.

SANDERLINGS *run after receding surf to gather washed up food, then scurry back up the beach ahead of the next wave.*

SEA OTTERS *spend much of their time in open water, even sleeping as they float on the sea.*

Sandpipers dash in and out of waves breaking on the beach.

Eighty-eight different species of algae and 192 species of invertebrate inhabit the intertidal zone. Roll up your pants and step onto the rocks. Look into the pools and you will find orange and purple sea stars, feathery anemones that look like flowers but whose petals are actually tentacles, and spiny urchins that resemble pincushions. Small purple shore crabs scuttle on the bottom, while sea palms and feather-boa kelp dance sinuously as the current ebbs.

Coastal areas are the most accessible outdoor destinations, and also the most popular. Though this makes for over-crowding in some areas, resourceful travelers can still find plenty of places

TRAVELING *in* WETLANDS

Wetlands play a crucial role in recharging and cleaning water systems, and provide homes for hundreds of bird, fish, reptile, and plant species.

GREAT BLUE HERONS *(left) are wetland inhabitants, ranging from areas of southern Canada, such as Point Pelee (right), to Mexico and the mangrove swamps of Florida (below). They normally nest in large colonies.*

Whether they're bogs, swamps, marshes, hog wallows, prairie potholes, or vernal pools, wetlands are among the most biologically bountiful habitats around. The water may be fresh, salty, or brackish; it is rarely deep, and is nearly always rich in nutrients. These watery foundations support a remarkable pyramid of life.

WETLAND COMMUNITIES

There are hundreds of types of wetland plant growing under, atop, or out of the water. Bladderworts are rooted beneath the surface and rarely venture above water, feeding on minute crustaceans and protozoans. Like ships without anchors, floating plants such as duckweed live wherever the wind blows them. Plants that grow up out of the water range in size from cattails

to mangrove bushes whose twisted roots look like nests of slithering water moccasins.

The combination of standing water and flowering vegetation provides ideal conditions for animals. Swarms of midges often cloud the skies above a marsh, water striders dance across the water surface, and backswimmers propel themselves with oar-like legs. The abundance of insects attracts many types of bird—surely the most conspicuous wetland creatures. Wood ducks, night herons, and orioles nest in shoreline trees while sedge wrens, swamp sparrows, and blackbirds feed and breed along the edges.

Rails, coots, egrets, and other shorebirds favor the shallows, with loons, grebes, and diving ducks taking to the deep.

Chirping crickets, croaking frogs, hooting owls, roaring alligators—these are the varied voices of the wetlands: an endless cacophony that is both harsh and beautiful.

Wetlands recharge water systems, act as buffers against storms, and serve as the planet's kidneys, using plants and bacteria to filter out contaminants. But despite all their strengths, wetlands are extremely fragile. In the United States, for example, more than half of the country's wetlands have been destroyed by diking, dredging, and draining. Government agencies and private groups are now

AMERICAN ALLIGATORS *can be distinguished from crocodiles by their broader, more rounded snouts.*

THE DESERT TORTOISE

The desert tortoise adapts wonderfully to climatic extremes. Active only 5 to 10 percent of the time, it spends most of its life in a burrow dug in the desert floor, where it lives on energy stored in its tissues as fat and on water recycled through its bladder.

During spring, when temperatures are mild and food abundant, the tortoise emerges to forage on wildflowers and grasses. It retreats to the cool of its burrow in the blistering heat of summer, emerging when the rains come to drink water in self-dug depressions and to eat dried broad-leaved plants. In the harsh winter, it hibernates.

Mountains complement desert as desert complements city, as wilderness complements and completes civilization.

Desert Solitaire,
EDWARD ABBEY (1927–89),
American writer

water you're pretty sure to find animals. Desert bighorns leave their rocky perches to drink. Look for the tracks of bobcats, coyotes, and desert kit foxes along the banks of oases. Keep an eye on the ground away from water, too, for each reptile species' track is as distinguishing as a fingerprint.

WHEN TO GO

Spring offers colorful scenery and the most comfortable temperatures. Wildflowers burst into life, with beauties such as purple sand verbenas, white dune evening primroses, and yellow desert sunflowers forming multicolored patterns. The spidery limbed ocotillo sprouts blossoms like

CALIFORNIA POPPIES *create a carpet of color on the uplands of the Mojave Desert (right).*

brilliant lipsticks. Migrant songbirds including warblers, sparrows, and flycatchers also add a splash of color. You'll find them among the bushes beside springs and water holes.

Summer heat discourages most travelers. In fall, the temperatures are more comfortable and wildlife is more active. Migrating waterfowl, including Canada geese, mallards, and cinnamon teals, fly in on their way from the tundra to the tropics. In winter, temperatures drop and, particularly in the high desert, snow leaves a mantle of white.

TOP DESERT AREAS

Death Valley National Park, California (p. 96)

Canyonlands National Park, Utah (p. 142)

Zion National Park, Utah (p. 144)

Grand Canyon National Park, Arizona (p. 158)

Saguaro National Monument, Arizona (p. 162)

Big Bend National Park, Texas (p. 168)

A DESERT GARDEN
Cholla (left), ocotillo (above right), and prickly pear cactus (below) grow among the rocks.

TRACKS *The sidewinder's unusual method of locomotion leaves a distinctive trail.*

where the only voices they'll hear are the calls of seabirds and the barks of seals.

SPECIAL EQUIPMENT

A sense of fun and wonder and a desire to explore are really all you need to enjoy an outing at the coast, but depending on where you're planning to go and what you want to do, certain items of equipment might add to the experience. If you have a sea kayak you can paddle out to offshore rocks and islets to take a close look at seabirds and marine mammals. In tropical waters, donning a mask, snorkel, and fins will enable you to enter a world of underwater wonders. Binoculars are a must, no matter where you go, but they're especially valuable on saltwater marshes and estuaries, for coastal wetlands support a staggering diversity of birds.

WHEN TO GO

Summer is the most popular season for people to visit the coast. After all, sun, sand, and sea is an unbeatable formula for

enjoyment. Fall brings cooler weather but there are more birds to be seen as migrants make their way south.

Winter brings some of the lowest tides. It is also a good time for spotting marine mammals. From late October through January, gray whales travel south along the Pacific

coast to breeding grounds in the lagoons of Baja California. At the same time, huge elephant seals congregate at Año Nuevo, south of San Francisco, to breed and whelp their pups. Birds also flock to the coast. Snow geese migrate south along the Atlantic Coast flyway (see p. 239) to spend the winter at refuges such as Pea Island National Wildlife Refuge in North Carolina.

Spring also sees wildlife on the move. Hundreds of falcons stop at Padre Island in Texas between late March and early May on their way to nesting grounds in the north. At Bush Key, off Florida, 100,000 sooty terns return in March to nest. And in late spring, fin and

The sea, once it casts its spell, holds one in its net of wonder forever.

JACQUES-YVES COUSTEAU, (b. 1910), French conservationist and marine explorer

humpback whales return from the south Atlantic to the waters off New England and Canada.

(see p. 239)

MIGRATION ROUTES

Traveling at the coast offers excellent opportunities to observe migrations. Humpback whales migrate south to their wintering grounds in the South Atlantic in fall, returning north in late spring. Canada geese (below) and American kestrels (bottom) are among the many species that migrate up and down the Atlantic Coast flyway.

TOP COASTAL AREAS

Point Reyes National Seashore, California (p. 102)

Olympic National Park, Washington (p. 120)

John Pennekamp Coral Reef State Park, Florida (p. 204)

Padre Island National Seashore, Texas (p. 170)

Acadia National Park, Maine (p. 226)

Gwaii Haanas National Park Reserve, British Columbia (p. 256)

Fundy National Park, New Brunswick (p. 260)

MARINE LIFE *The warm waters of Hawaii are filled with colorful tropical fish (above). Northern elephant seals (right) breed on the Pacific coast from the Baja to San Francisco.*

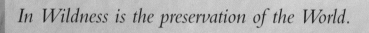

In Wildness is the preservation of the World.

HENRY DAVID THOREAU (1817–62),
American naturalist and writer

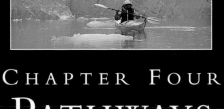

PUBLIC LANDS

A variety of government agencies is entrusted with the protection of our national parks, forests, and preserves.

OLD FAITHFUL *in Yellowstone National Park (right). Northern cardinals (left) can be seen in parks throughout the East.*

Public lands are the mountains, forests, prairies, deserts, wetlands, rivers, lakes, and seashores managed by the various government agencies entrusted with the protection of our natural resources, wildlife, and scenery. On these vast stretches of land you can pitch a tent, raft a river, look for eagles, hike a trail, climb a cliff, ride a horse, ski a slope, or just plain sightsee.

NATIONAL PARKS

National parks are the most popular and best known public lands. The United States National Park Service began life in 1872 with the creation of Yellowstone National Park. Today it manages over 70 million acres (28 million ha)

WHITE MOUNTAIN NATIONAL FOREST *(below) is one of the numerous regions administered by the United States Forest Service. A sign on the John Muir Trail in California (bottom).*

of land, including 53 national parks, 76 national monuments, 10 national seashores, 12 national preserves, 4 national lakeshores, and 17 national recreation areas. Environment Canada oversees that country's 34 national parks. In national parks you can usually expect facilities ranging from visitor centers, to lodges, to guided tours. Elaborate trail systems, helpful rangers, and a range of educational programs are hallmarks of the system.

Perhaps the most scenic public lands, national parks also tend to be the most crowded. Reservation systems, quotas, and traffic controls are now commonplace at such favorites as Yosemite and Grand Canyon. Still, plenty of wilderness opportunities remain for those willing to get off the beaten track, such as in

Canyonlands in Utah and Gates of the Arctic in Alaska. The national monuments also tend to be less crowded, though no less beautiful.

NATIONAL FORESTS

The United States Forest Service is in charge of over 191 million acres (77 million ha) of forests and grasslands, as well as monuments and recreation areas. There are 6 national forests in New England and 23 in the Southeast, but most of the nation's 156 federal woodlands are found from the Rockies west. Managed for multiple use, national forests mix wildlife protection with recreational opportunities and logging. The Forest Service maintains an extensive trail system, but visitor facilities tend to be minimal. Travelers must contact ranger offices about conditions and regulations before setting out into the backcountry.

In Canada, forests cover 1.5 million of the country's

3.8 million square mile (9.8 sq km) land mass. Forest tenure is the responsibility of the provincial governments.

PUBLICLY AND PRIVATELY OWNED PRESERVES *provide land for wildlife conservation throughout North America.*

NATIONAL WILDLIFE REFUGES

The National Wildlife Refuge System is managed by the United States Fish and Wildlife Service. More than 450 refuges covering more than 90 million acres (36 million ha) of land and water protect particular species of wildlife, many of which are rare or endangered. Unlike national parks, these refuges draw few crowds and visitor facilities are limited. In Canada, the Canadian Wildlife Service manages 46 national wildlife areas and 101 bird sanctuaries, covering a total of almost 4.7 million acres (1.9 million ha).

BUREAU OF LAND MANAGEMENT LANDS

The Bureau of Land Management administers the largest collection of public lands in the United States—over 270 million acres (109 million ha).

Comprised primarily of plains and desert areas in the West, BLM lands are managed for multiple use, in that mining, grazing, logging, and off-road vehicles are permitted in specific areas.

In recent years, the bureau has expanded its emphasis on outdoor recreation. Further information is available from local BLM offices.

STATE AND PROVINCIAL PUBLIC LANDS

Management of state and provincial public lands varies widely, the agencies going by such names as the State Department of Fish and Game, the Department of Natural Resources, the Division of State Lands, and the Department of Forestry. For Canada, check with the various provincial agencies, such as the Department of Environment and Lands and the Department of Lands and Forests.

All told, United States state wildlife agencies manage about 23 million acres (9 million ha) and state park and forest agencies administer another 30 million acres (12 million ha).

PRIVATELY OWNED PRESERVES

The many privately owned preserves cared for by such organizations as The Nature Conservancy and the National Audubon Society are often open to the public for hiking and wildlife viewing.

The Nature Conservancy manages more than 1,100 preserves nationwide, nearly all of which support rare and endangered species. The Nature Conservancy of Canada is the group's Toronto-based counterpart. The National Audubon Society and its state affiliates manage over 80 reserves and wildlife sanctuaries nationwide. Details of locations, opening times, and guided tours are available from local field offices.

This land is your land,

this land is my land,

From California to the

New York island,

From the redwood forest

to the Gulf Stream waters,

This land was made

for you and me.

WOODY GUTHRIE (1912–67),
American folk singer and songwriter

TALLGRASS PRAIRIE *preserved by The Nature Conservancy (right), where coyotes roam.*

THE NATIONAL SCENIC TRAILS

*What veins do for blood, this wonderful system of trails
does for hikers—carrying them throughout the country
and into the heart of the wilderness.*

The National Scenic Trails started as a young man's dream. Benton MacKaye spent his youth tramping around the backwoods near his Massachusetts home. After graduating from Harvard, he worked as a forester under Gifford Pinchot, the father of the United States Forest Service. In 1921, MacKaye wrote an article for the Journal of the American Institute of Architects outlining "a new approach to the problem of living". It was a blueprint for a hiking trail running the length of the Appalachian chain, a footpath that would allow people to leave the city and its pressures behind and "absorb the landscape and its influence as revealed in the earth and primeval life".

THE PACIFIC CREST TRAIL *includes the John Muir Trail, which crosses the Kern Plateau in the Sierra Nevada (right).*

THE APPALACHIAN AND THE PACIFIC CREST

It took 16 years and a colossal amount of effort—mostly by private citizens, helped by the Civilian Conservation Corps—but in August 1937 a six-man team carved out the last mile of the Appalachian Trail from Mount Katahdin in Maine to the tail of the Appalachians at Springer Mountain in Georgia. In 1968, the trail became the first in a series of specially designated national trails signed into law by President Johnson.

Passing through 13 states from Maine south to Georgia, the Appalachian Trail, covering

2,100 miles (3,380 km), gives hikers the chance to discover places that have altered little since the days of the Pilgrims. Mountains, lakes, streams, and ponds dominate its northern end. From the forest-covered Maine wilderness, the trail remains above the timberline through New Hampshire's White Mountains and cuts across the high, rugged woodlands of Vermont. After crossing the Berkshires in Massachusetts and the gentle rolling terrain of Connecticut and New Jersey, it heads south along the east range of the Alleghenies through Pennsylvania and the Blue Ridge Mountains. From Virginia south through North Carolina, Tennessee, and Georgia, it winds through pine forests and rhododendron gardens, offering majestic views from the rugged slopes of the Great Smokies.

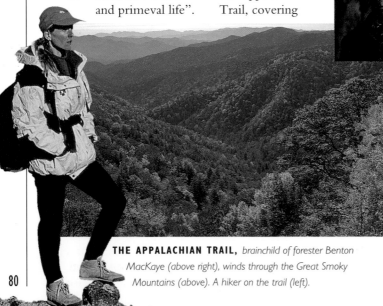

THE APPALACHIAN TRAIL, *brainchild of forester Benton MacKaye (above right), winds through the Great Smoky Mountains (above). A hiker on the trail (left).*

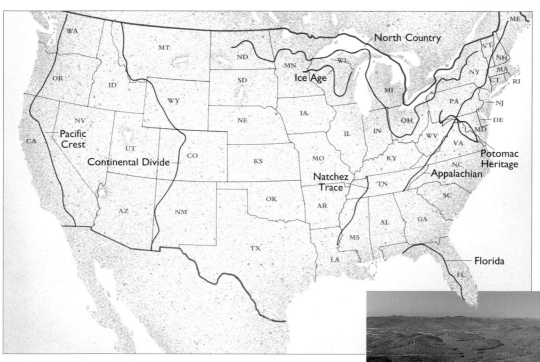

North Country

Ice Age

Pacific Crest

Continental Divide

Natchez Trace

Appalachian

Potomac Heritage

Florida

Ten years after MacKaye hatched his plan for this eastern footpath, Clinton Clarke of Pasadena, California, proposed a similar trail through the West Coast high country from Mexico to Canada. The Pacific Crest Trail took 60 years to complete and is 2,600 miles (4,200 km) long. It passes through 33 wilderness areas, 24 national forests, and 7 national parks. Highlights include a stretch through the Pasayten Wilderness in Washington's High Cascades region, the Sky Lakes Wilderness in Southern Oregon, and Castle Crags State Park in Northern California.

OTHER TRAILS

The Appalachian and the Pacific Crest trails, along with six other Scenic Trails, are now part of the National Trails System, administered

THE EIGHT NATIONAL SCENIC TRAILS *are part of the National Trails System, which also includes Historic and Recreation Trails. The North Country Trail passes through the Adirondacks (right).*

jointly by the National Parks Service, the Bureau of Land Management, and the Forest Service. Few trails have been completed so far, mainly because of inadequate funding, lack of government support, and negotiations over rights of way. Still, these trails, or parts of them, include paths blazed by Indians and pioneers, and to walk them is to follow in the footsteps of history.

THE FLORIDA TRAIL *starts in the Big Cypress National Preserve (above), where you could see a Florida panther (left).*

The almost-completed 1,300 mile (2,100 km) Florida Trail sweeps in an arc from the Everglades to the panhandle. It passes through Big Cypress National Preserve with its baldcypress swamp and sawgrass marsh—home of the endangered Florida panther.

When completed, the North Country Trail will meander for 3,200 miles (5,150 km). Starting at the Vermont border, it cuts west across New York's Adirondack and Finger Lakes regions and down through Pennsylvania and Ohio before heading north through Michigan's Upper Peninsula, Wisconsin, and central Minnesota.

The Continental Divide Trail follows the crest of the Rocky Mountains for 3,100 miles (5,000 km) between the Canadian and Mexican borders. It offers abundant wildlife, spectacular scenery, ghost towns, national parks, and wilderness areas.

CUSTODIANS *of* NATURE

Thousands of dedicated workers—paid and unpaid—care for public lands and private preserves and work for wildlife protection in a variety of other ways.

The people who work for local, state, and federal agencies, including the National Park Service, the Forest Service, the Fish and Wildlife Service, and the Bureau of Land Management, are nature's custodians. It's their job to manage critical habitat, operate parks, administer forests, maintain trails, and enforce game laws, among numerous other duties. Many of these agencies are huge employment centers for people who love the outdoors. The National Parks Service, for instance, has more than 12,000 full-time employees; the Forest Service has 33,000.

A PARK RANGER
on horseback with a young visitor.

A YELLOWSTONE GEOLOGIST
pushing his small craft out into the haze to check the depth of one of the park's hot springs.

Who hasn't dreamed of being a park ranger and spending a summer in a fire lookout deep in a forest or helping to pull endangered wildlife species back from the brink of extinction? If you're interested in a summer job in the great outdoors, or a lifetime career looking after wild places, you can obtain information regarding job prospects from the various agencies that are responsible for public lands.

Conservation organizations also have jobs for people who would like to devote their lives to protecting wildlife and natural areas. Biologists and ecologists work as

managers at the private wildlife preserves operated by The Nature Conservancy, and the National Audubon Society is staffed by scientists who spend time in the field.

VOLUNTEER VACATIONS

Many people work in the outdoors for free, during their vacations, generally either on research expeditions or service trips. On a research expedition, volunteers help scientists in the field. On a service trip, their work can vary from serving as campground hosts to rehabilitating damaged streams.

Dozens of agencies and non-profit groups help coordinate vacations of this sort (see p. 277 for a list of addresses). While volunteers usually have to arrange and pay for their own transport, most projects require nothing more of them than enthusiasm and a love of nature. Food and lodging are occasionally the volunteer's responsibility. Ask about these things in advance. Once you are accepted on a project, the sponsor usually lets you know what to bring and what will be expected of you.

The Student Conservation Association Inc. places students in volunteer positions with

STEPHEN MATHER (center), first director of the National Park Service. Carl Sharsmith (below) worked as a ranger in Yosemite for over 50 years.

government agencies through- out the country in jobs ranging from wildlife field surveys to park restoration, to academic research. The National Park Service takes on volunteers as visitor information aides and researchers in archaeology and natural science.

The Forest Service always needs people to serve as fire lookouts and wilderness aides, and to maintain trails and pick up litter. Volunteers with the Fish and Wildlife Service assist staff at ecological field stations, fish hatcheries, and wildlife management stations.

Many state park, forest, and wildlife agencies rely on unpaid workers, too. Duties range from campground host to trail builder. Volunteers are usually asked to make a four-week commitment.

North of the border, the Alpine Club of Canada has worked with the Canadian Parks Service to develop an extensive hut system for hikers, climbers, and skiers in the four Rocky Mountain parks (Banff, Jasper, Yoho, and Kootenay). Volunteers can work as custodians at these shelters during the summer months.

Many private conservation organizations also rely on volunteers. One of the oldest of these is the Appalachian Mountain Club. Established in 1876, it coordinates trail building and maintenance projects in various national parks and forests from Alaska to the Virgin Islands. The Sierra Club's ever-popular service trips, doing the same kind of work, have made its volunteer program the largest of its kind. Activities range from building check dams in California's Klamath National Forest to improving trout stream habitat in Colorado's South San Juan Wilderness.

Volunteer vacations with a more scientific bent are also available. Typically, volunteers assist scientists with a wide variety of tasks and pay a fee which helps to underwrite ongoing research. One such group is Earthwatch. This tax-exempt, nonprofit institution sponsors field research by finding paying volunteers to help scientists on expeditions throughout North America and around the world.

ALDO LEOPOLD'S LAND ETHIC

One of the first graduates of Yale Forestry School, Aldo Leopold became Supervisor of New Mexico's million acre Carson National Forest in 1911. At first believing that wilderness every- where should bow to the interests of western civilization, Leopold advocated extermination of wolves, mountains lions, and other predators.

When the deer in the Gila Wilderness, a hunting area in which all predators had been destroyed, became so numerous that they suffered a massive die-off, Leopold had second thoughts. "While a buck pulled down by wolves can be replaced in two or three years," he wrote, "a range pulled down by too many deer may fail of replace-ment in as many decades."

After leaving the Forest Service in the 1930s, Leopold spent the rest of his career developing his concept of the land ethic. In *A Sand County Almanac* he wrote: "All ethics so far evolved rest upon a single premise: that the individual is a member of a community of inter-dependent parts.

His instincts prompt him to compete for his place in the community, but his ethics prompt him also to cooperate (perhaps in order that there may be a place to compete for). The land ethic simply enlarges the boundaries of the community to include soils, waters, plants, and animals, or collectively: the land... In short, the land ethic changes the role of Homo sapiens from conqueror of the land-community to plain member and citizen in it."

TRAIL SIGNS *provide hikers with instructions as to how to behave in the wild.*

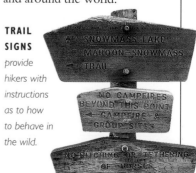

USING PATHWAYS *to* NATURE

Our guide to 70 North American nature areas, ranging from vast national parks to small but significant wildlife refuges, is the perfect place to begin planning your nature travel trip.

The entries in Pathways to Nature are organized into seven geographical groups, as indicated on the map on the opposite page. Within each region, states and preserves are listed alphabetically.

Each entry describes the landscape and wildlife of the nature area, and highlights particular species and natural features to look out for. Practical information is provided under the heading Traveler's Notes.

Each entry features a map showing the main access routes to the park and the location(s) of the principal visitor center(s). The following symbols are used:

🛣	*Canadian highway*
🛡	*Interstate freeway*
②	*US highway*
㉕	*State/provincial highway*
H58	*Secondary road*
●	*Visitor center*
----	*National boundary*
-- -	*State/provincial boundary*
....	*Ferry route*

TRAVELER'S NOTES

Information Having decided which nature area to visit, the next step is to contact the preserve and obtain further information. National parks publish excellent maps and guides and even small wildlife refuges normally provide basic maps and species lists.

Hours Many preserves remain open year-round, 24 hours a day. However, facilities and services will be limited outside visitor center opening hours.

Visitor center(s) Although visitor center facilities vary widely, the center is generally the best place to begin your visit to a nature area.

Fees Payment may be required for admission and for activities such as camping and backcountry travel. Some entry passes are valid for more than one day.

If you plan to visit a number of national parks, passes are available that entitle the bearer to a discount on admission fees. In the United States, the Golden Eagle Pass offers free admission for the bearer and accompanying person for one year. For senior citizens (over 62 years of age), the Golden Age Passport offers free entry and discounts on a range of facilities and services. Travelers with a permanent disability can obtain a Golden Access Pass. This too allows free admission and discounts on services. In Canada, all national parks sell one-day, four-day, and annual passes that are valid for the entire Parks Canada system.

The above passes can all be obtained at visitor centers or from the relevant parks service. See p. 277 for addresses.

Permits Activities such as boating, fishing, and back-country travel frequently require permits. In some areas there are long waiting lists for backcountry permits, so these should be obtained in advance of your trip. While the publishers of this book do not condone or wish to encourage hunting and fishing, these activities are available in some preserves. In the United States, a state license is normally required, although some parks allow fishing without a license. In Canada, permits are available at park offices.

Principal recreational activities available within each area are indicated by the following symbols: Boating Canoeing Climbing Cross-country skiing

Camping Fees are payable at most campgrounds and backcountry camping often requires a permit. If you are traveling during peak season, make sure you book well in advance or turn up early in the day at campsites.

Supplies Make sure you stock up with food and gas before heading into remote areas. Local population centers that provide these services are listed for each park.

Lodging Accommodation is usually available in nearby towns and villages. However, in more remote areas lodging may be restricted to purpose-built cabins or lodges within the preserve and demand for rooms may be high. It therefore pays to book your accommodation in advance, particularly if you plan to travel during peak season.

Access for people with disabilities An increasing number of parks offer facilities for travelers with disabilities, ranging from wheelchair-accessible trails to nature walks for the visually impaired. Many visitor centers and park headquarters have telephone devices for the deaf (TDDs) and some offer special tours.

Passes offering discounts on admission and services are available for travelers with disabilities—see Fees above.

When to visit Many parks are worth visiting year-round. In other areas, one season or month—during migration or wildflower seasons, for example—may be more rewarding than any other. At certain times, parks can be very busy. You can

help reduce overcrowding, and quite possibly have a more enjoyable experience, by visiting outside peak season.

Backcountry maps If you plan to venture into the back-country, you should obtain and learn how to use a compass and topographical maps (see p. 45). In the United States, topographical maps are available from the United States Geological Survey (USGS). Maps listed are generally 7.5 minute maps (1:24,000), except for the maps in the USGS National Park Series which are published in various scales. Index maps for each state are available free of charge. In Canada, topographical maps are available from the Surveys and Mapping Department of the Canadian Mapping Office (CMO). See p. 277 for addresses.

The Far West

The Far West

Canada

The Far West

The Mountain West

The Midwest and Great Plains

The Southwest

The Southeast

The Northeast

 Cycling   Downhill skiing   Hiking   Horse riding   Rafting   Scuba diving   Swimming

Gates of the
Arctic NPP

A L A S K A

Denali NPP   • Fairbanks

Anchorage

Tongass
NF

Olympic NP   ■ Seattle
                    ■ WA
                    • Mount Rainier NP

O R E G O N

| 0 | | 200 | | 400 | miles |
| 0 | 200 | 400 | 600 | km |

Redwood NP

Point
Reyes NS   Yosemite NP

San   Kings Canyon NP
Francisco
                            Sequoia NP

Monterey   Death
Bay NMS   Valley
                            NP

Kauai RC

Honolulu

H A W A I I

Haleakala NP

Los Angeles

C A L I F O R N I A

Hawaii
Volcanoes
NP

| 0 | 50 | 100 | | miles |
| 0 | 10 | 200 | | km |

The Far West

Denali National Park and Preserve

Alaska

The boundaries of Denali National Park and Preserve encompass and protect nearly 6 million acres (2.5 million ha) of rolling subarctic taiga and tundra, wide rivers, deep valleys, massive glaciers, and a range of jagged, snow-creased peaks crowned by mighty Mount McKinley—highest peak in North America. This is prime wildlife habitat and visitors are almost certain to see caribou, moose, even grizzly bears.

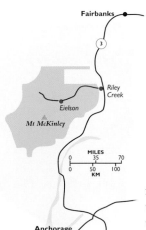

Fairbanks
3
Riley Creek
Eielson
Mt McKinley

MILES
0   35   70
0   50   100
KM

Anchorage

THE HIGH ONE

The Athapascan Indians knew Mount McKinley as Denali, or "the high one". On clear days, this 20,320 foot (6,200 m) mountain can be seen from Anchorage, 237 miles (380 km) to the south, but its peak is usually shrouded by cloud, especially in summer. McKinley has been a draw for mountaineers from all over the world ever since the first undisputed successful climb to the summit in 1913.

It dominates the Alaska Range—an awe-inspiring 600 mile (1,000 km) long crescent of mountain peaks that separate south-central Alaska from the state's vast interior.

The park is accessible by car, train, bus, and charter air. Summer is the main visitor season, although cross-country skiers and snowshoers come in winter. Plan on spending several days, if possible. No private vehicles are allowed past Savage River Bridge, about 15 miles (24 km) into the park on the 88 mile (140 km) long Park Road. Beyond this point, you must travel on the free park shuttle,

The glories of the northern lights, seen from the park.

Mount McKinley and the Alaska Range from the shore of Wonder Lake (above). Visitors enjoy a rare sighting of a gray wolf from one of the park's shuttle buses (left).

take a wildlife bus tour, pedal a bike, or walk. There are few trails: most hiking is in pathless backcountry.

There's no better way to enjoy the rich environment of Denali than by staying at one of the campgrounds or by backpacking into the wilderness. Summer days can last up to 20 hours, allowing plenty of time for visitors to go on extended walks and take advantage of one of the best places in North America to photograph wildlife.

TRAVELER'S NOTES

Information *Denali National Park and Preserve, Box 9, Denali National Park, AK 99755; tel. (907) 683-1266 in summer, (907) 683 2294 other months*

Hours *Always open*

Visitor centers *Riley Creek: daily in summer, 7 am–6 pm. Orientations, ranger-led programs, permits. Eielson: daily in summer, 9 am–7 pm. Ranger-led walks, wilderness instruction. For shuttle bus tickets, call (800) 622-7275*

Fees *Admission, camping*

Permits *Camping, backcountry access, fishing (state license)*

Camping *7 campgrounds (227 sites), plus 60 self-register backcountry sites at Morino. Reservations: call (800) 622-7275. Private camp-grounds near park entrance*

Lodging *Denali National Park Hotel; lodges and cabins at park entrance*

Supplies *Lynx Creek Campground, mile 238.6 George Parks Hwy, 1 1/2 miles north of park entrance. McKinley Mercantile, mile 1.4 on Park Road*

Access for people with disabilities *Visitor center, hotel, shuttle buses (arrange in advance)*

When to visit *Mid-May through Sept*

Backcountry maps *USGS Denali National Park*

Note *Plan backpacking carefully Consult park rangers at visitor center in advance of departure for advice on routes and equipment*

A red fox curled up among rock jasmine (above). A male willow ptarmigan atop a spruce tree (left).

CARIBOU: DENALI'S DWINDLING HERD

Once numbering in the tens of thousands, Denali's caribou herd has now diminished, for uncertain reasons, to just over 2,000. In fall, the caribou migrate from calving grounds high in the Alaska Range to their winter range in the northern regions of the park and preserve. This area of the park was enlarged substantially in 1980 in an effort to protect the herd's ancient domains.

Visitors traveling by shuttle bus often see these fine creatures foraging for grasses, sprouts, and willow near Sanctuary Flats and elsewhere along the road. Unlike the more solitary moose, caribou travel in groups of 20 or more, ever alert for wolves and grizzly bears. These predators constantly cull the caribou herd, usually taking newborn, old, or unhealthy animals.

Caribou have large hooves that provide good support on tundra and snow. Both males and females grow antlers, the only species in the deer family to do so. Male antlers are larger than female's, often growing into huge, multibranched arcs.

Park authorities ask that caribou-watchers stay at least 150 feet (46 m) away and use binoculars and telephoto lenses to observe or photograph these magnificent but truly wild animals.

Clouds enshroud the hills near Polychrome Pass (above). A bull caribou resting (below).

Be sure to bring long lenses, a tripod, and plenty of film! Bear in mind, though, that summer is also the time when most of the rain falls.

Taiga and Tundra

The park's lower elevations, called the taiga, or "land of little sticks" in Russian, are marked by scattered stands of white and black spruce, willow, dwarf birch, aspen, and alder. Berry bushes offer a harvest of blueberries, bearberries, crowberries, and cranberries—an important summertime food source for the region's animal and human populations.

In upland areas (above 2,700 feet [825 m]), there are no trees and the landscape becomes tundra—a collage of alpine flora hugging the earth. Here you find lichens, mosses, low-growing shrubs, and thick, colorful patches of wildflowers, such as moss campion and dwarf fireweed.

A sled team on the Stampede Trail in the far north of the park (above). In fall, berries, including bunchberry (right), add to the riot of color on the tundra.

As you explore the park, look out for caribou herds moving across the open land and moose grazing grassy lake bottoms or sheltering with their young under black and white spruce trees. Red foxes may be seen prowling for prey, and grizzly bears foraging for berries, particularly in the Sable Pass area. (Grizzlies, distinguished from rarely seen black bears by their humped backs and broad faces, sometimes weigh over 400 pounds [180 kg] and can present a danger to unprepared hikers. See p. 48 for advice on avoiding bears.)

As you take in this magnificent landscape, listen for the sharp warning calls of arctic ground squirrels; scan the high rocky regions for hoary marmots, pikas, and groups of white Dall sheep; and watch for small mammals such as lynx, wolverines, martens, and weasels scurrying about the tundra. You are unlikely to see any of Denali's wolves, however, as they tend to be wary.

Among the park's 159 bird species are migratory species from six continents, including waterfowl, shorebirds, songbirds, and birds of prey such as golden eagles and falcons. Year-round residents include jays, magpies, ptarmigans, and ravens.

Just outside the park, you can take raft rides on the glacier-fed Nenana River, flightsee over Mount McKinley by airplane or helicopter, or go horseback riding on wilderness trails. **BD**

Fall colors reflected in the waters of Wonder Lake (left). Mount McKinley offers climbers adventure and challenges (above).

Gates of the Arctic
National Park and Preserve

Alaska

Wolves howl and grizzlies prowl in the sprawling Alaskan wilderness high above the Arctic Circle. Gates of the Arctic National Park and Preserve covers some 8 million acres (3.24 million ha) of this dramatic country.

The park was named by explorer and conservationist Bob Marshall (see p. 25). Back in the 1930s, he followed the North Fork of the Koyukuk River up to its headwaters. As he made his way across the rugged Brooks Range he

The Dall sheep's huge curled horns may be up to 3 feet (1 m) long.

spied two facing peaks he named Frigid Crags and Boreal. The pair now serves as the gateway to this rugged, roadless park.

Getting here is no easy task. While you can reach the southeastern corner of the park via the Dalton Highway and an access road through Coldfoot and Wiseman, most visitors fly to the village of Bettles 150 miles (240 km) north of Fairbanks, then charter a bush plane to take them the remaining 50 miles (80 km). There are few established airstrips in the arctic expanse, but experienced pilots can land on lakes, gravel bars, even rivers. This allows travelers to choose their own destination, designate a pick-up time and place, and strike off into the Alaskan wilderness for an unforgettable backcountry experience. Precautions are required, however, as this is an extremely remote natural area. Make sure you pack a first aid kit and emergency supplies.

ARCTIC WILDLIFE

The terrain in the park ranges from treeless tundra to ragged peaks etched by glaciated valleys. Despite being inside the Arctic Circle, 400 different species of plant grow here. Wildlife

The granite walls of the Brooks Range (above). A summer snowstorm dusts a valley in the northeast of the park (right).

abounds. Besides grizzlies and wolves, there are Dall sheep clinging to windswept mountainsides and moose feeding in the lower elevation muskeg bogs. Each year, during July and August, the great Western Arctic caribou herd migrates through the area, which lies between their calving grounds to the north and their winter range in the south. The thunder of a thousand hooves often fills the air. Other large mammals include black bears, wolverines, and lynx. Eagles and falcons rule the skies, and waterfowl, such as tundra swans and snow geese, are found on the lakes.

Hikers can choose their own routes, but most opt to stick around the lakes, such as Summit, Redstar, Karupa, Hunt Fork, and Chimney. Trails link some of the lakes but most of them lie far apart. Isolation rules supreme.

One of the best ways to explore is to float down one of the park's many rivers. You can choose between various sections on the Alatna, John, North Fork, Nigu-Etivluk, and the Kobuk. A popular trip takes rafters 100 miles (160 km) down the North Fork, from the shadow of the Gates to Bettles. While the rapids are gentle—they're graded Class I–II—the scenery is anything but. DH

TRAVELER'S NOTES

Information *Gates of the Arctic National Park & Preserve, 201 First Avenue, Fairbanks, AK 99701; tel. (907) 456-0281*

Hours *Always open*

Visitor center *Park service office in Bettles open in summer; tel. (907) 692-5494*

Fees *None*

Permits *Fishing, hunting (state licenses)*

Camping *Backcountry camping*

Lodging *Bettles Lodge, Bettles, AK 99726; tel. (907) 692-5111*

Supplies *Bettles*

Access for people with disabilities *None*

When to visit *Summer is nightless and when it's at its warmest. Winter is dayless and freezing*

Backcountry maps *USGS Killik River, Chandler Lake, Philip Smith Mtns, Ambler River, Survey Pass, Wiseman, Chandalar, Hughes*

Wolves are seldom seen but occasionally heard.

93

Tongass National Forest

Alaska

No national forest is bigger than Tongass. Covering 16 million acres (6.5 million ha) and nearly the entire Alaskan panhandle, it encompasses vast glaciers, whole islands, and dozens of wild rivers. Sections of the Tongass' temperate rain forest have suffered severely from clear-cut logging, but many areas remain untouched, uncharted, and unexplored.

Tongass is so huge that deciding where to go can be a problem. The ideal place to start is the Mendenhall Glacier Visitors Center, north of Juneau. It not only provides a stunning view of this frozen river of ice, but is the starting point for several trails. There is also a relief map to use for plotting trips to other parts of the forest.

To the south lies Admiralty Island National Monument. Blanketed by old-growth forest, it is home to a considerable population of brown bears and has one of the largest nesting sites of bald eagles in the world. Taking the Cross Admiralty Canoe Route, which cuts across the southern end of the island, is an adventurous and rewarding way to explore this wooded wilderness.

Northwest of Admiralty Island is Glacier Bay National Park—a dazzling, world where tongues of ice stream down from the heights of the

Waterfalls in Misty Fjords National Monument (left). A totem pole from Totem Bight State Park, on the Inside Passage (right).

Icebergs in the still water of Mendenhall Lake (above).
An Alaskan brown bear catching salmon (right).

Fairweather Range and which can only
be explored by kayak, chartered yacht, or
cruise ship. Here you can witness the
spectacular sight of slabs of ice breaking from
the faces of glaciers and crashing into the sea.

FJORDS AND WILDERNESS
Tracy Arm–Fords Terror Wilderness lies
to the east, where tidal flats, wildflower-filled
meadows, forests, and ice fields surround an icy
blue fjord. Fords Terror is a chasm, filled with
rapids and swirling whirlpools.

To the south is Misty Fjords National
Monument. Boat or kayak is the only way
to reach this breathtaking wilderness that lies
between two enormous fjords—Behm and
Portland canals. At its heart is a region of
dense forest dotted with lakes and rimmed
by jagged peaks. Brown and
black bears lumber through
the trees and along the shores,
while Sitka black-tailed deer
bound across the meadows.
King, silver, red, chum, and
pink salmon are all found here.
Sea lions and harbor seals haul
out along the coast and orcas
and Dall's porpoises swim the
deeper waters.

Tongass straddles the Inside
Passage, the scenic marine
highway that connects Alaska
to the lower 48 states, and the
ferries that travel from Seattle
to Juneau offer some of the best
wildlife viewing anywhere. DH

TRAVELER'S NOTES

Information *Forest Supervisors:
Chatham Area, 204 Siginaka Way,
Sitka, AK 99835-7316; tel. (907) 747-
6671. Ketchikan Area, 648 Mission
Street, Federal Building, Ketchikan, AK
99901-659, tel. (907) 228-6202.
Stikine Area, PO Box 309, Petersberg,
AK 99833-0309, tel. (907) 772-3841*

Hours *Always open*

Visitor center *Mendenhall Glacier, 13
miles (21 km) north of Juneau:
Mon–Sun, 9 am–4 pm (Sat–Sun only in
winter)*

Fees *None*

Permits *Fishing, hunting (state
licenses); backpacking*

Camping *Developed, primitive, and
wilderness campgrounds and campsites*

Lodging *Forest Service cabins; motels
and lodges scattered throughout
southeast Alaska*

Supplies *Major towns in southeast
Alaska*

Access for people with disabilities
*Mendenhall Glacier Overlook, boat tours
of Misty Fjords*

When to visit *Summer for wildflowers.
Winters are wet*

Backcountry maps *USGS Mt
Fairweather, Juneau, Sitka, Sumdum,
Petersburg, Craig, Ketchikan*

Note *Ferry information: Alaska Marine
Highway System, Box 25535, Juneau,
AK 99802–5535; tel: 1-800-642-0066*

Death Valley National Park

California

Death Valley National Park covers an immense area of rugged landscape, from the lowest point on the continent at 280 feet (85 m) below sea level near Badwater, to 11,049 feet (3,370 m) at Telescope Peak. It is a land of sand dunes and mountain hikes, geological wonders such as Ubehebe Crater and Titus Canyon, fine birding at the oases, and wildflowers in spring.

The Shoshone Indians lived a nomadic life in Death Valley, hunting and gathering in the mountains spring through fall, and spending winter on the desert floor. In 1849, during the California gold rush, a group of prospectors became lost in the valley and ran out of water.

Before they found a way out, one member of the party died, giving rise to the name Death Valley.

The climate is exceedingly hot and dry, with temperatures reaching over 100 degrees Fahrenheit (38° C) in summer and up to 75 degrees (24° C) in winter. Average rainfall is less than 2 inches (5 cm) a year. Mornings and evenings afford wonderful views in crystal-clear air; middays shimmer with heat.

DESERT FLORA

Despite the harsh environment, over 900 kinds of plant grow within the park. Wildflowers, cacti, creosote bush, and mesquite are found in the desert, and pinyon and bristlecone pines grow in the mountains. Bristlecones, which have been carbon-dated to over 4,500 years old, are among the oldest living things in the world. They are found only on a few peaks in the mountains of the western desert, and grow very slowly under extremely harsh conditions.

Badwater Salt Flats, the lowest point in the United States, lies 280 feet (85 m) below sea level. Desert iguanas (left) inhabit creosote bush desert and dry stream beds.

Sunrise at Zabriskie Point near Furnace Creek (above). The oasis at Scottys Castle (right) is a hot spot for reptiles and birds.

The mammals of Death Valley are nocturnal, but they can sometimes be spotted at dawn or dusk. They include kit foxes, coyotes, mountain lions, bobcats, black-tailed deer, black-tailed jack rabbits, kangaroo rats, and desert bighorn sheep. The best time for finding reptiles, such as the chuckwalla and the desert iguana, is in the early morning, or out driving at night.

Birding is rewarding at the oases at Furnace Creek Ranch, Scottys Castle, and Mesquite Spring throughout the year. You will see desert species such as the greater roadrunner, and migratory land and water birds such as the yellow-rumped warbler, lazuli bunting, and various ducks. Death Valley has become a hot spot for finding rare visitors, such as eastern warblers, which home in on the lush oases when they become lost in the desert. May and November are the best months to look for rarities such as the scissor-tailed flycatcher, Mississippi kite, painted bunting, and hooded warbler. You never know what you might find here. SM

TRAVELER'S NOTES

Information Death Valley National Park, PO Box 579, Death Valley, CA 92328-0570, tel. (760) 786-2331

Hours Always open

Visitor center Furnace Creek: 8 am–6 pm daily

Fees Admission, camping, tours of Scottys Castle

Permits Backcountry travel

Camping 9 campgrounds (1,200 sites)

Lodging Furnace Creek Inn, Furnace Creek Ranch tel. on-site reservations, (760) 786-2345 central reservations, (800) 236 7916; PO Box 187, Death Valley, CA 92328; Stovepipe Wells Village, Highway 190, Death Valley, CA 92328, tel. (760) 786-2387

Supplies Furnace Creek, Stovepipe Wells, Scottys Castle (limited services May–Oct)

Access for people with disabilities Visitor center, pullouts, Scottys Castle (lower level)

When to visit Nov–May (desert floor); Mar–Apr for wildflowers; Nov, May for birding; May, Sept for high-country hiking

Backcountry maps USGS Death Valley National Monument and Vicinity

Note Always carry water for hiking. If your car breaks down in summer, stay with the car. Do not set out on foot to seek help

A decorated backcountry road sign.

Kings Canyon and Sequoia National Parks

California

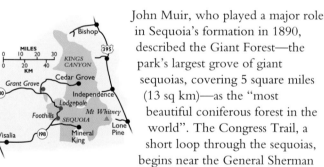

Kings Canyon and Sequoia—two adjoining parks in the southern Sierra Nevada—preserve groves of *Sequoiadendron giganteum*, the giant sequoia, the largest tree in the world (redwoods being the tallest). The parks cover more than 1,300 square miles (3,350 sq km) of lakes, gorges, rushing rivers, and towering granite peaks, including Mount Whitney—the highest peak in the lower 48 states. Some of the parks' sights can be reached by car, but there are few roads. The best way to see this wonderful wilderness is to hike, and you can choose from more than 700 miles (1,130 km) of trails.

GIANT SEQUOIAS

In warmer times, giant sequoias covered much of North America, but now they are restricted to the western slopes of the Sierra Nevada between 5,000 and 7,000 feet (1,525 to 2,135 m). They grow in mixed coniferous forest, with a dogwood and rhododendron understory.

John Muir, who played a major role in Sequoia's formation in 1890, described the Giant Forest—the park's largest grove of giant sequoias, covering 5 square miles (13 sq km)—as the "most beautiful coniferous forest in the world". The Congress Trail, a short loop through the sequoias, begins near the General Sherman Tree—one of the world's largest living organisms. At least 2,300 years old, this superb tree is 275 feet (84 m) tall and 103 feet (31 m) in circumference.

Nearby Moro Rock offers panoramic views to the west. The Crescent Meadow and Log Meadow Loop Trail are bright with wildflowers in summer. Other Sequoia attractions include Crystal Cave (a marble cavern) and the fairly strenuous 3½ mile (5.5 km) round-trip hike to Tokopah Falls.

For the keen backpacker, the High Sierra Trail leads from Crescent Meadow into the high country and joins the John Muir Trail along the Sierra crest. A steep, winding road,

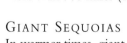

Douglas' squirrels are commonly known as chickarees.

Moonrise from the John Muir Trail on Mount Whitney (above). Pileated woodpecker (left).

open only in summer, leads to the Mineral King trailhead, providing access to alpine lakes and amazing Kern Canyon.

From Sequoia, the Generals Highway leads to Grant Grove in Kings Canyon National Park, where the huge General Grant Tree grows. Kings Canyon Highway offers views of two of America's deepest gorges, where the south and middle forks of the Kings River meet, and then leads to Cedar Grove, the center of Kings Canyon. Further on, the road offers views of glacial domes and an awesome granite monolith at Grand Sentinel Viewpoint. From Roads End, trails lead to the Rae Lakes area and east to the high Sierra peaks.

Black bears, chipmunks, and chickarees can be seen in the sequoia groves, and marmots and pikas in the high country. Western tanagers and hermit thrushes are found among the sequoias, while rosy finches inhabit alpine areas. SM

A car being driven through a redwood in 1910. This misuse of the park's trees is no longer permitted.

TRAVELER'S NOTES

Information *Superintendent, Kings Canyon and Sequoia National Parks, 47050 Generals Highway, Three Rivers, CA 93271-9651, tel. 559-565-3341*

Hours *Always open*

Visitor centers *Foothills, Lodgepole, and Grant Grove: daily, 8 am–4.30 pm, closed Dec 25*

Fees *Admission, camping*

Permits *Backcountry use, fishing (state license)*

Camping *3 campgrounds open year-round, 11 campgrounds open mid-May through mid-Oct; backcountry by permit*

Lodging *Giant Forest, Grant Grove,*

and Cedar Grove lodges, tented cabins at Bearpaw High Sierra Camp; reservations 559-561-0410

Supplies *Giant Forest, Lodgepole, Grant Grove, Cedar Grove*

Access for people with disabilities *Visitor centers, Trail for All People, Grant Grove, pullouts*

When to visit *Sequoia groves year-round, high country mid-May to mid-Oct (Kings Canyon Hwy closed mid-Oct to mid-May)*

Backcountry maps *USGS Sequoia and Kings Canyon National Parks*

Monterey Bay
National Marine Sanctuary

California

The Monterey Bay area has long been known for its picturesque coastline and its rich marine life, and in 1992, Monterey Bay National Marine Sanctuary was formed to protect this region. The sanctuary covers 5,300 square miles (13,727 sq km), extending from the Gulf of Farallones west of San Francisco, south some 300 miles (480 km) to Cambria, and up to 50 miles (80 km) offshore. One of the Pacific's richest marine environments, Monterey Bay has huge underwater kelp forests and one of North America's deepest submarine canyons. Because the continental shelf is so close to shore, the park provides divers with the chance to see deep ocean habitats. Its coastline includes a rocky shoreline that is excellent for tidepooling, coastal dunes, sandy beaches, mud flats, and estuaries.

The Monterey coastline is blessed with a Mediterranean-like climate. In winter, stormy weather alternates with warm, clear days. In spring and summer, high pressure builds off the coast ushering in cool, fog-laden air. The warmest and clearest days are in fall.

OCEAN TRIPS

The sanctuary's rich waters provide food for a large resident population of marine mammals and seabirds, and act as a fueling station for migratory birds. Nearly hunted to extinction, California's marine mammals are now protected under the Marine Mammal

Sea otters cleverly use rocks to open their favorite shellfish. Otters can be seen in kelp forests from Monterey to San Luis Obispo.

Forests of eel grass and elk kelp sway lazily in Monterey Bay (above). The coast at Point Sur (left). Spanish shawl, a nudibranch (right).

Protection Act. They fall into three groups: cetaceans (whales, dolphins, and porpoises), pinnipeds (seals and sea lions), and sea otters. On any day of the year, sea otters, California and Steller's sea lions, and harbor seals can be seen along the Monterey coastline. On ocean trips from Monterey, you can observe seabirds such as albatrosses, shear-waters, alcids, and storm–petrels, and marine mammals including the Pacific white–sided dolphin and Dall's porpoise, as well as whales. Gray whales migrate through the area in winter and spring, and blue and humpback whales can be seen in August.

Migratory shorebirds and ducks winter at Elkorn Slough at Moss Landing and at the mouth of the Carmel River. Peak seasons are fall and spring for rarities and winter for large numbers. Point Pinos is good for viewing sea otters, sea lions, shorebirds, and huge waves. Carmel and Asilomar beaches are ideal for swimming. North of Monterey, on the San Mateo coast, James Fitzgerald Marine Reserve is a great place for tidepooling. At Año Nuevo State Reserve you can see an elephant seal rookery and seabird colonies. South of Monterey, the coastlines of Point Lobos State Reserve and Big Sur are popular for their coves, underwater marine reserves, seabird colonies, and hiking trails. SM

TRAVELER'S NOTES

Information Monterey Bay National Marine Sanctuary, 299 Foam Street, Suite D, Monterey, CA 93940; tel. (408) 647-4201

Hours Always open

Visitor center Mon–Fri, 8 am–5 pm, closed national holidays

Fees Camping

Permits Fishing (state license)

Camping Sunset State Beach, Andrew Molera State Park, Pfeiffer Big Sur State Park

Lodging Monterey, Pacific Grove, Carmel, Santa Cruz, San Francisco

Supplies Monterey, Pacific Grove, Carmel, Santa Cruz, San Francisco

Access for people with disabilities Pullouts

When to visit Year-round. Sep–Oct warmest months

Note Tide tables, useful for tidepooling and shorebirding trips, are available from sporting goods stores

Point Reyes National Seashore

California

I f you can visit just one place in the San Francisco Bay Area, visit Point Reyes. This area offers year-round access to coastal wilderness, with pounding surf, tide pools, dramatic cliffs, miles of beaches and trails to hike, spectacular views, and a rich diversity of habitats, ranging from sea level to 1,407 feet (430 m) atop Mount Wittenburg. The weather is invigorating: summers are cool and foggy, while winter days are alternately sunny and rainy. On any given day, you're likely to encounter fog and wind along the western shoreline and mild, calm weather on the eastern side of the peninsula.

EARTHQUAKE COUNTRY

A peninsula jutting into the Pacific Ocean, the bedrock of Point Reyes is completely different from that of the land to the east, matching up

geologically with the Tehachapi Mountains, 300 miles (480 km) south. The point rests on a portion of the Earth's crust known as the Pacific Plate, which is creeping northwest at the rate of 2 inches (5 cm) a year. The rest of the continent lies on the American Plate, which is creeping westward at a slower rate. The San Andreas Fault, the rift zone where the two plates meet, runs in a northwest direction through Tomales Bay and south through Olema Valley, where the Bear Valley Visitor Center is located. Here you can see a working seismograph measuring earth movements along the fault. Along the nearby Earthquake Trail you can see the effects of the 1906 earthquake, when the pressure of the two plates upon each other thrust the peninsula almost 20 feet (6 m) northwestward.

Inverness Ridge traverses the peninsula north-south, its slopes covered with forests of Bishop pine, Douglas fir, and mixed evergreens. This woodland is home to woodpeckers, owls,

Point Reyes Lighthouse (left) is a prime lookout for whales, with elephant seals, harbor seals (right), and seabirds frequenting the rocks below.

salamanders, squirrels, raccoons, and deer. A network of trails crisscrosses the ridge from Bear Valley and Palomarin, leading through coastal scrub on the downslope to secluded beaches and backpacking campgrounds in the south. The northern half of the peninsula is primarily pastoral country, with dairy farms on the headlands. The coastline is characterized by long beaches with soaring cliffs, and huge estuaries bordered by marshes.

From September through May, Limantour and Drakes esteros are major wintering and migratory grounds for numerous waterbirds. A spectacular birding hike is to walk the length of Limantour Spit along a trail in the dunes and return to the trailhead via the beach. Canoeing or kayaking in the esteros will enable you to see the wildlife even more clearly.

Birding is terrific year-round at the point, with over 360 species recorded in the area. In spring and fall it is a hotspot for vagrant landbirds—ones that drop into the islands of cypresses on foggy nights when their navigation skills fail them.

Drakes Beach is one of the most spectacular beaches on the continent (above). Brown pelicans (right) can be seen along the coast from June to January.

Mammals include mountain lions, bobcats, gray foxes, black-tailed deer, sea lions, seals, and a reintroduced population of tule elk. In winter and spring, people come to watch migrating gray whales. These great creatures head south in the winter months and return in April and May with their young.

The coastal wildflower season lasts from February through July. California poppies dot the roadways, Indian paintbrush and wallflowers cling to the cliffs, blue-eyed grass grows in the meadows, and bush lupine and Douglas iris cover the slopes down to the sea. SM

TRAVELER'S NOTES

Information Point Reyes National Seashore, Point Reyes Station, CA 94956-9799, tel. (415) 663-1092

Hours Always open

Visitor centers Bear Valley: tel. (415) 663-1092, Mon–Fri, 9 am–5 pm, Sat–Sun, 8 am–5 pm. Lighthouse: tel. (415) 669-1534; Ken Patrick Visitor Centre: tel. (415) 669-1250

Fees None

Permits Backcountry camping, fishing (state license)

Camping 4 backcountry campgrounds, reservations advised; campground at Samuel P. Taylor State Park

Lodging Inverness, Olema, Point Reyes Station

Supplies Point Reyes Station, Inverness, Olema, Bolinas, Stinson Beach

Access for people with disabilities Visitor centers, Earthquake Trail, and trails to Limantour, North and South Beaches; assisted listening device at Bear Valley Visitor Center; audio programs for Earthquake Trail

When to visit Year-round

Backcountry maps USGS Point Reyes National Seashore

Redwood National Park

California

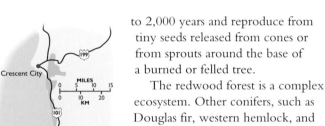

On the wet north coast of California, Redwood National Park preserves large stands of the earth's tallest tree, *Sequoia sempervirens*, the redwood, which grows to over 300 feet (90 m). The park is a United Nations World Heritage Site and Biosphere Reserve of 40,000 acres (16,200 ha) of old-growth redwoods and another 60,000 acres (24,300 ha) of watershed, wildlife corridors, and coastline. It encompasses Jedediah Smith Redwoods, Del Norte Coast Redwoods, and Prairie Creek Redwoods state parks.

ABOUT REDWOODS

Some 60 million years ago, 40 species of sequoia covered much of North America, but now only two species remain—the redwood and the giant sequoia (see p. 98). Redwoods are now restricted to California's temperate north coast, where they receive up to 100 inches (250 cm) of moisture a year—rain in winter and fog in summer. These slow-growing giants live up to 2,000 years and reproduce from tiny seeds released from cones or from sprouts around the base of a burned or felled tree.

The redwood forest is a complex ecosystem. Other conifers, such as Douglas fir, western hemlock, and Sitka spruce grow among the redwoods. The understory consists of rhododendron, madrone, alder, maple, oak, azalea, and many varieties of fern. You can find arboreal, California slender, Del Norte, and Pacific giant salamanders by looking carefully on the forest floor and under fallen branches and logs.

The birdlife is wonderfully varied, including northern specialties such as gray jays, old-growth species such as the spotted

Wild rhododendrons grow throughout the redwood forest.

Redwoods (above) are the tallest trees in the world. The Pacific giant salamander (left), at up to 6 inches (15 cm) long, is the largest North American salamander. Spotted owl (below).

owl, and marvelous songsters, such as winter wrens and hermit thrushes.

The marbled murrelet is a tiny seabird whose nesting site remained a mystery until recently, when a logger found a nest high in the redwood forest.

Land mammals include river otters, flying squirrels, black bears, and Roosevelt elk. Harbor seals and California and Steller's sea lions populate coastal waters year-round. You can see gray whales migrating south January through February and returning north in April and May.

REDWOOD CONSERVATION

The three parks that form the core of Redwood National Park were bought by the Save-the-Redwoods League in 1918 and became state parks. In 1968, the national park was established, after a survey found that only 15 percent of the state's original redwood forests remained. Ten years later it was expanded to protect and replant the watershed around the park boundaries that had been devastated by timber harvesting. Controversy still rages over protection of old-growth forest, as lumber companies seek to continue logging the region. SM

TRAVELER'S NOTES

Information Superintendent, Redwood National Park, 1111 Second Street, Crescent City, CA 95531; tel. (707) 464-6101

Hours Always open

Visitor centers Redwood: daily, 9 am–5 pm. Prairie Creek: daily, 10 am–2 pm. Crescent City: daily, 8 am–5 pm. All closed Thanksgiving, Dec 25

Fees Admission, camping

Permits Backcountry camping, fishing (state license)

Camping Jedediah Smith, Del Norte, Coast, and Prairie Creek Redwoods state parks (reservations [800] 444-7275)

Lodging Crescent City, Arcata, Eureka

Supplies Crescent City, Klamath, Orick, Trinidad, Arcata, Eureka

Access for people with disabilities Visitor centers, nature trail in Prairie Creek State Park

When to visit Year-round; May–Sep peak, rainy season Nov–Mar

Backcountry maps USGS Orick, Bald Hills, Holter Ridge, Fern Canyon

Note Summer shuttle service from Redwood Information Center to Tall Trees Trailhead to view redwoods

Yosemite National Park

California

Situated in the Sierra Nevada Mountains, to the east of San Francisco, Yosemite National Park contains the incomparable Yosemite Valley, magnificent waterfalls, a rich diversity of animal and plant species, towering giant sequoia trees, and extensive hiking trails through vast expanses of mountain wilderness.

The Miwok Indians inhabited the Yosemite area until 1851, when white settlers moved into the Sierra. Yosemite's fame soon spread and in 1864 the Mariposa Grove of Giant Sequoias and Yosemite Valley were set aside as state parklands. John Muir, founder of the Sierra Club, wrote eloquently about Yosemite and lobbied to preserve the area. In 1890, Yosemite National Park was formed.

As you ascend the western foothills of the Sierra, towering pines herald the entrance to the park long before its striking

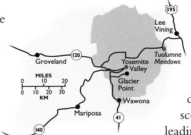

geological features appear.

Yosemite Valley lies at 4,000 feet (1,220 m), in a forest of black oaks, incense cedar, yellow and sugar pine, western azalea, and California dogwood. A one-way drive leads around the valley, with scenic pullouts and hiking trails leading to Bridalveil Falls, El Capitan, Yosemite Falls, Half Dome, Mirror Lake, and Vernal and Nevada falls.

WALKING IN THE VALLEY

As you walk along the trails in the valley, keep an eye out for the rare peregrine falcon, and the dipper, a curious landbird that nests under waterfalls and walks underwater to feed on aquatic insects. Black-tailed deer and Merriam's chipmunks are common and at nightfall you may see flying squirrels gliding silently from tree to tree or hear the call of a northern pygmy-owl.

Northern flying squirrels (far left).
An ancient giant sequoia (left).

Yosemite Valley and El Capitan (above). Upper Yosemite Falls and the Merced River in spring (right).

Wawona Road leads to the south of the park and the Mariposa Grove of Big Trees, where you can wander among the giant sequoias. Glacier Point, leading off Wawona Road (which is open June through September) provides visitors with one of the most awe-inspiring views in the world. Cliffs drop 3,200 feet (980 m) to Yosemite Valley, vast Half Dome looms at eye level, the Merced River cascades down granite cliffs at Vernal and Nevada falls, and a panoramic vista sweeps into the high country, with its snow-covered peaks.

Black bears and calliope hummingbirds can sometimes be seen in the meadows that surround the Bridalveil Creek Campground on the Glacier Point Road.

Pikas live on steep, boulder-covered slopes in the high country.

TRAVELER'S NOTES

Information Superintendent, PO Box 577, Yosemite National Park, CA 95389; tel. (209) 372-0200

Hours Always open. Tioga Road Entrance closed Nov–May

Visitors centers Yosemite Valley: daily, 9 am–6 pm. Tuolumne Meadows: June–Sept, 9 am–5 pm. Information centers at Wawona (daily, 8 am–5 pm) and Big Oak Flat (daily, 9 am–5 pm)

Fees Admission, camping

Permits Backcountry access, fishing (state license)

Camping 3 campgrounds open year-round; 10 open last weekend of May to Oct. Reservations recommended, tel. 800-436-7275. Backcountry sites: June–Aug apply for permit in advance

Lodging Ahwahnee Hotel, Yosemite Lodge, Curry Village, Wawona Hotel. Tented accommodation at Tuolumne Meadows Lodge, White Wolf, High Sierra trail camps. Reservations recommended: lodges tel. (559) 252-4848

Supplies Yosemite Valley, Crane Flat, Tuolumne Meadows, Wawona

Access for people with disabilities Yosemite Valley Visitor Center, Indian Cultural Museum, Ansel Adams Gallery, Happy Isles Nature Center, some trails

When to visit Yosemite Valley year-round; June–Aug best for backpacking and birding; Dec–Mar for snowshoeing

Backcountry maps USGS Yosemite National Park

THE HIGH COUNTRY

The Big Oak Flat Road leads north from Yosemite Valley to Crane Flat, home to weasels and the great gray owl. From here, the Tioga Road leads into the High Sierra, passing red fir forests where grouse and porcupines live. There are outstanding scenic pullouts at Olmsted Point and Tenaya Lake, where massive granite domes loom and yellow-bellied marmots peek at visitors from rock piles.

Tuolumne Meadows at 8,800 feet (2,680 m) is surrounded by snow-covered peaks. Keep an eye open for northern goshawks and mountain bluebirds in the meadows and surrounding lodgepole pine forest.

The road continues over Tioga Pass at 9,945 feet (3,033 m), giving hikers access to trails that lead to alpine meadows edged by whitebark pine forests at the foot of Mount Conness, and, in mid-July, carpets of wildflowers on Mount Dana. Pikas (tiny mammals of the high country) can be seen among the rocky debris at the bottom of cliffs. From the pass, the road continues out of the park, plunging down Lee Vining Canyon, leading to the Sierra's magnificent eastern escarpment, the high sagebrush desert of the Great Basin, and Mono Lake National Tufa Reserve.

Even though millions of people make their way to Yosemite each year, it's possible to get away from the crowds by visiting at off-peak times and by hiking. There are 800 miles

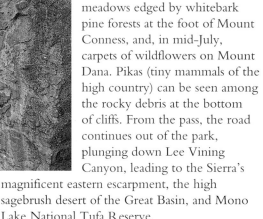

Yosemite Valley from Inspiration Point (top). Climber on Elephant Rock (center). Porcupine (above). Northern pygmy-owl (right). Tenaya Canyon (far right)

108

(1,290 km) of trails to explore, in addition to the
John Muir Trail, popular with backpackers, that
starts at Happy Isles and winds its way along the
Sierra crest 188 miles (300 km) south to Mount
Whitney in Sequoia National Park. SM

*Sunset at Half Dome (above). Intrepid
visitors standing on Balanced Rock
at Glacier Point (below).*

THE CREATION OF YOSEMITE

Yosemite was formed by great
glaciers during the ice age.
Nowhere is this more apparent
than in Yosemite Valley, eroded
by the Merced River and then
shaped by the 3,000 foot
(900 m) deep Yosemite Glacier.
The glacier created a classic
U-shaped valley with sheer walls,
and other grand geological
features such as El Capitan and
Royal Arches, and the dramatic
cliffs at Glacier Point.

As the ice melted, water
cascaded from hanging gardens
and collected in a terminal
moraine near El Capitan, forming
Lake Yosemite. The lake gradually
dried up into a fertile valley floor,
clothed in pines, oaks, and
meadows, through which the
Merced River still flows. Four
major waterfalls add to the valley's
magnificence and continue to cut
into its granite walls.

Examples of
glacial processes can
be seen on the granite
throughout the park, including
glacial polish, cirque formations,
smoothings (great lines made
by the ice), and glacial erratics
(boulders strewn by the
glaciers). Remnants of the
glaciers, such as the mini-glacier
at the base of Mount Lyell, can
still be seen.

In northern Yosemite, the
Tuolumne River and glaciers
carved the Hetch Hetchy
Canyon—a valley similar to
Yosemite. Despite the efforts
of John Muir and others, who
campaigned vociferously
against its construction,
a dam was built at
Hetch Hetchy in 1914,
flooding the area to
provide water for
San Francisco.

Haleakala National Park

Hawaii

Though the last eruption here occurred in 1790, Haleakala volcano is dramatic proof of the Hawaiian islands' fiery origins. Hawaiian for "House of the Sun" (the demigod Maui is said to have held the sun prisoner here in order to provide more daylight for his people), Haleakala National Park features an immense crater, magical-looking silverswords that grow nowhere else, and upland rain forest.

Haleakala was once a great mountain of lava formed by numerous volcanic eruptions. About 100,000 years ago, when volcanic activity had lessened, erosion from massive amounts of rain formed the vast natural bowl that we see today, now filled with cinder cones and lava flows from subsequent eruptions.

Silversword leaves are thickly covered in a lustrous silver-gray down.

The road to the summit climbs 10,023 feet (3,057 m) in just 40 miles (64 km), the vegetation changing dramatically the higher you go. Not far from the entrance lies Hosmer Grove where there is a fascinating collection of exotic trees such as eastern red cedar, Douglas fir, lodgepole pine, eucalyptus, spruce, and juniper that were planted in 1910 to prevent erosion. At the nearby Waikamoi Preserve you can go on guided hikes and birding expeditions through forests to a lush gulch where ohia lehua trees surround a babbling stream. Look for iiwis and apapanes—two members of the colorful Hawaiian honeycreeper family.

TOWARD THE CRATER RIM

As the road makes its way up to the crater rim, there are several places where you can stop and take a look at the extraordinary landscape, notably at Kalahaku Overlook, where you can see gleaming silverswords dotted here and there among the cinders. These distant relatives of the sunflower, with their silvery leaves, are found only on the volcanic heights of Maui and Hawaii. They bloom

A cinder cone in Haleakala Crater (above). Pandanus trees frame Oheo Gulch Cascade in Kipahulu Valley (right)—accessible from the Hana road, in the south. An apapane in an ohia lehua (below).

The park road continues up to the visitor center on the rim of the crater—a fabulous point from which to look across the crater floor to surrounding peaks and cinder cones. A series of trails crosses the crater, enabling visitors to trek through this weird and barren landscape. Weather conditions can change rapidly, and freezing temperatures on the volcano are not uncommon, so make sure you are properly equipped. A short trail from the visitor center climbs White Hill, passing the ruins of ancient stone windbreaks used by Hawaiians during their pilgrimages.

only once in their lifetime—usually between May and November—and then they die. Nenes, native geese, brought back from the brink of extinction through a captive breeding program, can be seen making their way across the sparsely vegetated lava flows.

The road eventually reaches the crater summit at Puu Ulaula Overlook. From here, you can sometimes spy Molokai, Lanai, and the Big Island of Hawaii in the distance. Occasionally, you might even see Oahu, 130 miles (210 km) to the northwest. DH

TRAVELER'S NOTES

Information Superintendent, Haleakala National Park, Box 369, Makawao, Maui, HI 96768; tel. 808-572-4400, 808-572-4410

Hours Always open

Visitor center House of the Sun: 7.30 am–4 pm. Exhibits on volcanoes

Fees Admission, campsites, cabins

Permits Backcountry camping

Camping Developed site at Hosmer Grove; undeveloped at Kipahulu; backcountry camping (permit required) at Holua and Paliku

Lodging 3 cabins in park; lottery held first day of each month for reservations 2 months ahead

Supplies Kahului, Makawao

Access for people with disabilities Headquarters and visitor center. Overlooks on scenic drive

When to visit Year-round. Early morning for spectacular sunrises

Backcountry maps USGS Lualailua Hills, Kaupo, Kilohana, Kipahulu, Hana

Hawaii Volcanoes National Park

Hawaii

P ele, the Hawaiian goddess of volcanic fire, rules the Big Island of Hawaii with a fiery fist. The most volatile part of this youngest of the Hawaiian islands is encompassed by Hawaii Volcanoes National Park, where two of the most active volcanoes on earth—Kilauea and Mauna Loa—provide a bizarre and fascinating terrain.

Kilauea Crater, Pele's legendary home on the southeastern slope of Mauna Loa, is the island's liveliest volcano. Its eruptions are recorded in early Hawaiian legends and have continued periodically to the present day. Evidence of a 1790

As lava spills into the sea (above), it creates mountainous clouds of steam.

eruption is visible on the park's Footprint Trail, where the footprints of native people, caught unawares by the huge explosion, are preserved in hardened volcanic ash.

An 1840 outburst was the first to destroy a village; a more recent volcanic eruption in 1990 on the east rift zone of Kilauea destroyed the entire town of Kalapana, on the coast, including more than 200 homes and other structures.

Amaumau ferns are among the various ferns and tree ferns that thrive in the park (left). Figures chipped in the lava at Puuloa by early Hawaiians (right).

RISING FROM THE ASHES

The park's 344 square miles (890 sq km) include deep craters, calderas, steam vents, lava tubes, sulfur banks, and even an ongoing effusion of fiery magma, at the end of the Chain of Craters Road, that can be viewed from up close. Despite this harsh, gas-spewing landscape, a number of native plant species flourish here, including the hardwood acacia koa; the ohia lehua tree with its characteristic red pompon blooms; and the mammane, which boasts clusters of bright yellow flowers.

If you follow the Thurston Lava Tube Trail, you will pass through a lush forest of giant tree

ferns known as hapuu. This fern grows as high as 20 feet (6 m) and was one of the first plants to arrive on the islands after they were formed.

Before the Polynesians discovered Hawaii, there was already an astounding diversity of plant and animal life, much of it descended from the few species that managed to drift by air or sea to this remote archipelago. A thousand kinds of flowering plant had evolved from a few hundred colonizers; over 70 kinds of native bird had evolved from as few as 15 original species.

TRAVELER'S NOTES

Information *Superintendent, PO Box 52, Hawaii Volcanoes National Park, HI 96718-0052; tel. 808-985-6000*

Hours *Always open*

Visitor center *Kilauea Visitor Center: year-round, 7.45 am–5 pm, tel. (808) 967-7311. Films of recent eruptions hourly 9 am–4 pm, maps and guides. Nearby Jaggar Museum has displays on types of lava*

Fees *Admission*

Permits *Backcountry camping*

Camping *2 basic campgrounds, 1 with showers*

Lodging *Volcano House Hotel, PO Box 53, Hawaii Volcanoes National Park, HI 96718; tel. (808) 967-7321. Rustic camper cabins, same address and phone*

Supplies *Volcano Village*

Access for people with disabilities *Visitor facilities, pullouts on Crater Rim Road and Chain of Craters Road, several pathways*

When to visit *Nov–March. Kilauea's summit can be rainy and chilly at any time of year, but the coastal area is usually dry and warm*

Backcountry maps *USGS Hawaii Volcanoes National Park*

Note *A 24 hour hotline provides information on the latest eruptions in the park—call (808) 985-6000*

Lava flowing from the Kilauea Puu Oo cinder cone in 1993 (above). The brilliant red pompon flower of the native ohia lehua tree (left).

PELE'S FIERY WORLD

Lava may emerge from a volcano in a steady gush or, more dramatically, as a fiery fountain caused by a build up of gases. There are two types of lava flow, known in Hawaii as pahoehoe and aa, which differ in appearance but are chemically alike. Pahoehoe flows quickly and has a smooth, ropy surface. It is hotter and contains more gas than aa, which flows slowly and carries rough chunks of pumice.

When lava emerges as a powerful spray (often exceeding 2,000 degrees Fahrenheit [1,143° C]), the molten rock is hurled into the air to form either fine glassy filaments (known as Pele's hair) or small black droplets (Pele's tears).

Park travelers take note: lava rock is regarded as sacred by the Hawaiians. Not only is taking rock souvenirs from the park illegal, it would also, according to legend, invite the wrath of Pele.

Fine examples of Pahoehoe lava (below) can be found along many of the park's trails.

Even today, over 90 percent of Hawaii's native flora and fauna is endemic—found nowhere else on Earth. But the detrimental effects of introduced plants and animals have led to the extinction of many of these species and continue to threaten others.

Hawaii Volcanoes' most celebrated native bird is the nene, a ground-nesting goose, which barely escaped being wiped out by hunters and predators such as non-native rats and mongooses. A breeding program begun in the 1950s has successfully bolstered the nene population and groups are often seen in the Kilauea area and on the Mauna Loa Strip Road. Other native birds in the park include the elepaio (Hawaiian flycatcher) and three colorful kinds of Hawaiian honeycreeper.

The endangered nene (left), a species of goose unique to Hawaii, is now a common sight around Kilauea.

Fiery tracers of lava erupt from Kilauea (left). The black sands of Kamoamoa Beach (above), and some of the park's many volcanic craters (right).

TOURS AND TRAILS

Visitors can follow a variety of roads, trails, and paths to explore this exotic landscape. Crater Rim Drive circles Kilauea's summit and craters, passes through rain forests and desert, and provides access to scenic stops and short walks. The 3 mile (5 km) Halemaumau Trail crosses the scarred floor of Kilauea to the rim of smoky Halemaumau Crater, where, according to local lore, two lovers jumped to their deaths during an explosion in 1932. Trails also lead to the Sulphur Banks, where volcanic fumaroles belch gases and vapors, and to Steaming Bluff, where vents release steam from deep cracks. The Devastation Trail, a short boardwalk atop volcanic cinders, takes you through a skeleton forest charred by a 1959 eruption. One of the park's finest walks is the Kilauea Iki Trail, a two-hour hike descending 400 feet (120 m) through rain forest into a crater and across steaming lava flows.

For an unforgettable backcountry trip, you can hike the 18 mile (29 km) trail to the summit of Mauna Loa. This will take three or four days. Hikers must be in good physical condition and properly equipped for winter mountaineering, for snow is common near the summit in winter.

The Chain of Craters Road runs from Crater Rim Drive and descends 3,700 feet (1,130 m), to where a recent lava flow blocks the road. (Surface flows may be visible here at night.) Points of interest along this route include Lua Manu and Pauahi craters, Mauna Ulu Lava Shield, Kealakomo Overlook, Puuloa Petroglyphs Trail, and Holei Sea Arch. BD

Giant ferns line the Thurston Lava Tube Trail.

Kauai National Wildlife Refuge Complex

Hawaii

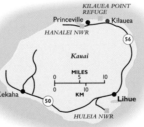

Hawaii has the dubious distinction of having had more birds become extinct than anywhere else in the United States. Of the 70 species found here when Captain James Cook arrived in 1778, 25 have disappeared forever and 28 are in danger of following suit. Fortunately, three preserves on the spectacular north and east coasts of Kauai provide protection for many of Hawaii's remaining endemic species. Together, these preserves make up the Kauai National Wildlife Refuge Complex.

Seabirds fill the skies over the rocky promontory at Kilauea Point. Among the birds to be seen are wedge-tailed shearwaters, red-footed boobies, white-tailed tropicbirds, and frigatebirds. From December through March, Laysan albatrosses can be seen wheeling overhead. This is one of the few places in North America where you can see these long-distance flyers, their 7 foot (2 m) wingspans making them hard to miss. Fledgling brown-footed and red-footed boobies perch around the lighthouse, involved in gangly antics as they learn to fly. Shearwaters gather at dusk from March through November. Common introduced landbirds include mynahs, Japanese white-eyes, and laughing thrushes.

The promontory on which the lighthouse stands provides an excellent view of the picture-

Hanalei (above) is a sanctuary for many of Hawaii's endangered waterfowl species. The remarkable display of the male great frigatebird (left) involves inflating its bright red throat pouch.

postcard shoreline and is a good point from which to look out for Hawaiian monk seals, green sea turtles, spinner dolphins, and occasional whales passing by.

PROTECTED WETLANDS
Nearby, 917 acre (370 ha) Hanalei National Wildlife Refuge is made up of taro patches that have been cultivated for over 1,200 years. In a unique arrangement with the US Fish and Wildlife Service, taro farmers combine cultivation with wetlands habitat protection, resulting in a haven for nearly 50 different species of bird, including endangered Hawaiian stilts and ducks. Kauai remains the last stronghold for the endemic Hawaiian duck.

An overlook on Highway 56 provides display boards and a fine view of this lush valley. If you bring binoculars or a spotting scope, you'll be able to observe such residents as golden plovers, tattlers, coots, and gallinules.

More wetland habitat has been preserved at the 238 acre (96 ha) Huleia National Wildlife Refuge. Consisting of wooded slopes and grassy bottomlands along the Huleia River, this lovely preserve supports 31 species of bird, including 13 endemics. Next to the refuge is the Menehune Fishpond, also known as Alakoko.

The coastline at Kilauea Point (above), where red-footed boobies (below) and frigatebirds nest in huge colonies.

The Menehune Overlook off Highway 58 provides an elevated spot from which to look for birds feeding in this quiet patch of paradise. DH

TRAVELER'S NOTES

Information Kilauea Point, Hanalei, and Huleia National Wildlife Refuges, P.O. Box 1128, Kilauea, Kauai, HI 96754; tel. (808) 828-1413

Hours Always open

Visitor center Kilauea Lighthouse, off Hwy 56: Mon–Fri, 10 am–4 pm

Fees Admission at Kilauea

Permits None

Camping None

Lodging Hanalei, Princeville

Supplies Hanalei, Princeville

Access for people with disabilities Roadside overlooks

When to visit Seabirds plentiful Nov–Mar; most other birds year-round

Mount Rainier National Park

Washington

Few mountains in North America can match the majesty of Mount Rainier. The huge bulk of this dormant volcano seems to hover over the lowlands of Puget Sound, its distinctive glacier-clad double summit changing color as the sun illuminates it throughout the day.

Years of campaigning by local newspapers and conservation groups led to the creation of Mount Rainier National Park in 1899.

Even then, when travel was difficult, the mountain's awesome natural splendor drew thousands of visitors. Today, the park's 300 miles (480 km) of trails are heavily used and mountaineering parties wishing to tackle the summit must make reservations.

Perhaps the best perspective of the park comes from walking all or part of the Wonderland Trail, a 93 mile (150 km) circumnavigation of the mountain which passes through alpine meadows and valley forests. The trail provides a stunning view of the 27 major glaciers on Rainier's slopes—the largest collection of glaciers on one peak in the lower 48 states. A result of the summit's heavy snowfalls and year-round freezing temperatures, these rivers of ice drape the mountain on all sides, melting gradually as they encounter higher temperatures at lower altitudes.

Hikers crossing the suspension bridge over Carbon River (left). Small mammals, such as the Columbia ground squirrel (right), often visit campgrounds, but they should never be fed.

ALPINE FLOWERS AND ANIMALS

Once the snow has melted from the alpine meadows, the rich soil supports a multi-hued carpet of wildflowers which bloom in successive waves. Indian paintbrush, avalanche lilies, Sitka valerian, marsh marigolds, and purple shooting stars grow in riotous profusion.

Fifty-four species of mammal roam the park's 235,612 acres (95,420 ha), but most of the large ones, such as black bears and black-tailed deer, are seldom seen. Campers are likely to encounter Townsend chipmunks and chattering ground squirrels, and hikers on alpine trails may hear the whistles of hoary marmots and spot black-horned mountain goats grazing on sedge grasses.

Over 120 types of bird call Rainier home at various times of the year, most of them migrating to warmer climates once the snow falls. Campers are harassed by gray jays, blue jays, and Clark's nutcrackers looking for a food handout. Woodpeckers, flickers, chickadees, and juncos are found in the forest. Golden eagles, ravens, and red-tailed hawks soar on thermals above the meadows. And high on the slopes of Rainier, the rock ptarmigan's feathers change from speckled brown to white as winter appoaches. **ST**

TRAVELER'S NOTES

Information *Superintendent, Mount Rainier National Park, Tahoma Woods, Star Route, Ashford, WA, 98304-9751; tel. 360-569-2211*

Hours *Always open*

Visitor centers *Paradise: mid-May to Sept 11, daily, 9 am–7 pm; Sept 12–Oct 10, 9.30 am–6 pm; Oct 15 to mid-May, Sat, Sun and hols 10 am–5 pm. Exhibits, information. Sunrise: July 1 to mid-Sept, daily, 9 am–6 pm. Displays, naturalist walks. Ohanapecosh: mid-June to Oct 10, daily, 9 am–7 pm. Exhibits, information. Also hiker centers at Longmire and White River: June–Sept, daily, 8 am–4.30 pm.*

Fees *Admission, camping*

Permits *Backcountry camping, mountain climbing*

Camping *5 campgrounds, (569 sites). Call 1-800-365-CAMP (2267)*

Lodging *Inns at Paradise, Longmire—contact Mount Rainier Guest Services, Box 108, Ashford, WA 98304, tel. 360-569-2275; Hotels, motels in Enumclaw, Packwood, Elbe, Eatonville*

Supplies *Food at Paradise Visitor Center, Sunrise Lodge, National Park Inn, Paradise Inn. Gas at Enumclaw, Ashford, Elbe, Packwood, Eatonville*

Access for people with disabilities *Visitor centers, Longmire Museum, Cougar Rock campground. Trails near Paradise Visitor Center paved but steep*

When to visit *July–Aug, particularly for wildflowers, but busy. Weekends crowded mid-May to mid-Sept. Roads often closed by snow in winter*

Backcountry maps *USGS Mount Rainier National Park*

Mount Rainier viewed from Reflection Lake (top). In spring and summer, meadows are filled with wildflowers, including blue lupine and magenta paintbrush (above).

Olympic National Park

Washington

The earliest European visitors to the coastline of northwestern Washington were deterred from making landfall by the pounding surf and rocky headlands. From his vantage point safely offshore, British Naval Captain John Meares noticed a gleaming white summit towering over the dense forest and exclaimed, "If that be not the home where dwell the Gods, it is beautiful enough to be, and I therefore call it Mount Olympus".

Prevailing westerly winds, the moderate Japanese current, and rugged mountains jutting 1^1/$_2$ miles (2.5 km) above sea level produce more rainfall in this remote corner of Washington State than anywhere else in the United States. The fog-enshrouded beaches, misty rain forests, and serrated, glacier-clad summits of Olympic National Park overwhelm the senses. Jagged barnacles and abrasive sea stars cling to sandstone boulders rounded

by the surf. When high pressure stills the air, shafts of sunlight illuminate water droplets on every fern and pine needle in the rain forest.

Olympic's coastal strip is especially rich in birdlife and the many peculiar invertebrates that dwell in tide pools. These pockets of salt water, best viewed at low tide, contain sea stars, sea cucumbers, and sea anemones. Snails, limpets, periwinkles, and mussels cling to the rocky ocean shelf, where they are relentlessly pounded by waves. There are birds everywhere. Bald eagles watch patiently from atop old-growth Sitka spruce, then swoop down for offshore salmon. Sandpipers flit to and fro, while cormorants, scoters, and murres probe the ocean's surface for fish. Gulls pick up clamshells and open them by dropping them on the rocks, where they neatly split in two.

FOREST DWELLERS

The forests are crisscrossed by hundreds of miles of trails. Two large ungulates are of particular interest to visitors. Roosevelt elk thrive in rich pastures on the rain forest floor and move to subalpine meadows for summer.

Olympic marmot.

A hiker looks across to the Olympic Mountains from Boulder Peak (above). Many of the park's valleys are filled with dense temperate rain forest (left).

During the ice age, the Olympic peninsula lay locked beneath huge glaciers, effectively cut off from the rest of the continent. Some species that are common elsewhere in western mountain ranges, including the grizzly bear, red fox, and bighorn sheep, either failed to survive this period or never managed to reach the peninsula. A number of other species evolved in isolation and to this day are found nowhere else in the world. They include the Olympic marmot, Olympic chipmunk, snow vole, Flett's violet, and two species of trout— the Beardlsee and the Crescenti.

On the higher slopes, the mountain goats that prowl the rocky precipices were actually introduced earlier this century. They have become so prolific that park authorities have had to implement a goat-removal program.

A sea star on the rocks.

TRAVELER'S NOTES

Information *Olympic National Park, 600 East Park Ave, Port Angeles, WA 98362-6798; tel. 360-452-4501. TDD for visitor center 360-452-0306*

Hours *Always open*

Visitor centers *Olympic Park: daily, 9 am–4 pm (extended in summer), exhibits. Hoh: daily, 9 am–4 pm (extended in summer), exhibits. Hurricane Ridge: daily, 9 am–4 pm, exhibits. Storm King: daily, June–Sept. Hood Canal: mid-May to mid-Sept, 8 am–4.30 pm, permits and information*

Fees *Admission, camping*

Permits *Backcountry camping*

Camping *17 campgrounds (925 sites)*

Lodging *Lodges and cabins in park.*

Motels and inns at Forks, Port Angeles

Supplies *In park: Fairholm General Store, Kalaloch Lodge. Food at Sol Duc Hot Springs Resort, Log Cabin Resort. Outside park: Forks, Port Angeles*

Access for people with disabilities *Visitor centers, mini-trail in Hoh Rain Forest, Madison Falls Trail at Elwha. Hurricane Ridge guide on tape.*

When to visit *July–Aug for hiking, camping, but busy. Nov–Mar wet but good for beachcombing*

Backcountry maps *USGS Olympic National Park*

Kootenai
NWR
Glacier NP   Medicine Lake NWR ■

MONTANA

Billings ●

Yellowstone NP ■

IDAHO
Boise ●   Grand Teton NP ■
        Craters of the
        Moon NM ■   WYOMING

                                    Cheyenne ●

                    Salt Lake   Rocky
                    City   Mountain NP ■
NEVADA   ● Denver
        Great Basin NP ■   UTAH   COLORADO
                    Canyonlands NP ■
        Bryce Canyon NP ■
            ■ Zion NP
Red Rock
Canyon NCA ■
        ● Las Vegas

        0   100   200   miles
        0   200   400   km

The Mountain West

Rocky Mountain National Park

Colorado

The Rockies are among America's highest mountains, and Rocky Mountain National Park is their showcase. The view from Moraine Park, one of the park's spacious valleys, provides an awesome sense of scale. The ponderosa pines, with their vanilla-scented bark, are massive; 600 foot (183 m) high moraines (ridges of debris left by retreating glaciers) snake along the sides of the valleys; winding rivers are flanked by sweeping marshy meadows. Yet, all is dwarfed by the surrounding mountains. Sun reflects from their

soaring, wind-polished rock. Thunderclouds snag on their peaks, before lowering into the valleys. Even in summer, snow fills many of the glacier-carved basins, known as cirques.

It is this high world—the roof of the Rockies—that Rocky Mountain National Park was established to protect. Although its forests and river valleys are of great importance, most of all the park tells an alpine story, for one-third of its 266,000 acres (108,000 ha) is above the timberline. Because it protects such a large amount of fragile alpine environment, the park has been designated an International Biosphere Reserve by UNESCO.

AN ALPINE WORLD

In terms of geological time, the Rockies are young mountains—only 50 to 70 million years old. Although ice-age glaciers primarily shrouded the upper Midwest, they also covered alpine areas of the Rockies. The weight of these massive, slow-moving layers of ice ground out mountain valleys, softening sharp V-shapes into gentler curves. The semi-circular headwalls

Much of Rocky Mountain National Park is above the timberline.

Longs Peak, seen from Trail Ridge Road (above). Two young hoary marmots (right), wrestling among the rocks.

and rock-rimmed alpine lakes at the base of most peaks are also the work of glaciers.

The park affords many opportunities to see this alpine world up close. Trail Ridge Road, famous as one of the nation's few great alpine highways, switchbacks up to 12,000 feet (3,660 m), providing views of meandering, oxbowed rivers far below and ranges with names such as Never Summer Mountains beyond. Trail Ridge Road also leads to the park's Alpine Museum and tundra trails. Tundra means "land of no trees" in Russian, and it is easy to understand why no trees grow in this wind-scoured environment, where the views seem to roll on forever.

The plants that do survive amid the tundra's rocks have made dramatic adaptations. Most, like the pink-flowered moss campion, hug the ground, taking advantage of the few inches of air warmed by the earth. Some produce red pigments that protect their leaves from sunburn.

TRAVELER'S NOTES

Information *Superintendent, Rocky Mountain National Park, 1000 Highway 36, Estes Park, CO 80517-8397; tel. 970-586-1206, fax 970-586-1310*

Hours *Always open*

Visitor centers *Headquarters, Kawuneeche: year-round. Alpine Center: June–Sept. Lily Lake: May–Sept. All 9 am–5 pm. Publications, permits*

Fees *Admission, camping*

Permits *Backcountry camping, fishing (state license)*

Camping *5 campgrounds (589 sites),*

200+ backcountry sites

Lodging *Estes Park, Grand Lake*

Supplies *Estes Park, Grand Lake*

Access for people with disabilities *1 backcountry campground, 3 trails, visitor centers*

When to visit *Summer, but busy; winter for cross-country skiing; fall for aspen colors*

Backcountry maps *USGS Rocky Mountain National Park*

Solitary and secretive, mountain lions range throughout the Rockies but are seldom seen.

The best way to see the park, however, is to get off the roads and travel on foot, along some of the 355 miles (570 km) of hiking trails. In spring, Wild Basin offers shimmering lakes, rippling cascades, bright yellow arnica daisies, and, hidden in dim, damp spots, exquisite pink calypso orchids, for which Calypso Cascades is named. In fall, mountain ash trees at Bear Lake and along other waters are hung with brilliant orange-red berries and acres of gold-leafed quaking aspens light up stretches of dark Douglas fir. In winter, conifers bend under the snow, and all is evergreen, white, and silent but for the rhythmic swish of cross-country skis and, perhaps, the chattering of a midnight-blue Steller's jay.

MOUNTAIN MAMMALS

Boardwalks pass through beaver-pond habitat, though it is rare to see these nocturnal builders during the day. Native green cutthroat trout, threatened by introduced trout species, are being propagated in state fisheries and

A cross-country skier climbs through aspens (above left). The Steller's jay (right) is widespread in the West.

Others have waxy leaves so that they lose less moisture to the constant winds. Against vast panoramas, this is a world of miniature beauties.

During summer, when it is rarely closed by snow, Trail Ridge Road connects the east and west sides of the park. Quite different from the lusher, open valleys of the eastern portion, the west has its own rugged attractions. It borders Grand Lake, the area's largest natural alpine lake, and it is the birthplace of that great river of the West, the Colorado.

126

Hallett Peak from Bear Lake in winter (above left) and on a September morning (above). Calypso orchids (below) bloom in damp, shady areas.

ELK WATCH

Most of the year, elk are rarely seen, other than at dawn and dusk when they forage in small bands at the forest's edge, and even then their soft coloring allows them to blend in with the grasses and the bark of ponderosa pines.

In early fall, however, biological drives take precedence over caution and bull elk bugle their challenges to one another. The valleys ring with the sounds of their calls and their crashing antlers as they fight for the right to mate with huge harems of cow elk.

The dominant elk then sort out their herds, dozens or even hundreds of cows milling around them in the evenings.

With all the park's grizzlies and wolves destroyed decades ago, mountain lions are the only remaining predators strong enough to kill a mature elk. As a result, the elk population now numbers 2,000 to 3,000, and their browsing on shrubs and young trees is destroying parts of the park's plant population.

Bull elk can weigh up to half a ton.

restored to the park. Moose, reintroduced to public lands north of the park, have made their way to Rocky Mountain and are occasionally seen in the Kawuneeche Valley. Other mammals, including bighorn sheep, mountain lions, black bears, weasels, elk, and marmots, live in the rich range of habitats between valley floor and mountain top. MS

Craters of the Moon National Monument

Idaho

The terrain at Craters of the Moon lives up to its name. Vast expanses of lava flows peppered with caves and cinder cones give this 83 square miles (215 sq km) of central Idaho the appearance of Earth's closest neighbor.

The visitor center at the park entrance is the best place to start as it features informative displays and a short film about the volcanic activity that took place in the region. The lava only stopped flowing here 2,000 years ago and geologists say it will start again some day. There are two types of lava, known by the Hawaiian terms aa and pahoehoe. Aa is jagged-edged rubble capable of shredding all but the stoutest-soled boots into ribbons. Pahoehoe

The turkey vulture is a common summer visitor. It soars for long periods with its wings held in a distinctive V-shape.

(meaning "ropy") flowed from the ground in a more fluid form, and is smooth and silky. Also common are "lava bombs"—distinctive round rocks that originally formed when blobs of molten lava were thrust upward into the air, cooling and hardening as they fell to the ground.

A 7 mile (11 km) auto tour runs from the visitor center and stops include Big Craters, where rangers conduct guided walks. They also hold educational programs in the amphitheater near the campground, both morning and evening, from mid-June to Labor Day.

A short walk leads to the top of Inferno Cone, offering a stunning view, to the southeast, of a line of cinder cones. These cones, situated in the adjacent Craters of the Moon Wilderness Area, mark the Great Rift, a 65 mile (105 km) long fissure up to 800 feet (245 m) deep that opened up in the Earth's surface 15,000 years ago, triggering the beginning of the lava flows.

CRATERS AND CINDER GARDENS

Another key stop is the Cave Area, where a short trail from the parking lot will take you to a series

A hiker climbs the black lava slopes of Inferno Cone (above). In spring, occasional rain and snowmelt provide moisture for wildflowers, including monkeyflowers and eriogonums (right).

of caverns, ice caves, and lava tubes. Make sure to bring a flashlight and fresh batteries with you, because artificial light is needed to see these geological wonders.

At first glance, the park may seem devoid of life, but no fewer than 200 species of plant have managed to gain a foothold in this rocky, forbidding landscape. They are well spaced, to share the little moisture that does not drain away through the porous lava. If you take the Devils Orchard or Tree Molds trails you will have a chance to see some of these plants up close.

Wildflowers are a delight in spring, with bitterroot lewisias, dwarf monkeyflowers, and eriogonums creating "cinder gardens". Low-growing shrubs, such as sagebrush, rabbitbrush, and antelope bitterbush, have colonized the open areas, while limber pines have taken root on the wetter, north-facing slopes.

There are songbirds ranging from warblers to bluebirds in the vegetation, while sharp-shinned hawks, turkey vultures, and northern harriers patrol the skies. Red foxes and coyotes prey on pocket mice, white-tailed jack rabbits, and woodrats. Mule deer are a common sight. **DH**

TRAVELER'S NOTES

Information *Superintendent, Craters of the Moon National Monument, Box 29, Arco, ID 83213; tel. (208) 527-3257*

Hours *Year-round, 8 am–4.30 pm*

Visitor center *At park entrance; year-round, 8 am–4.30 pm, closed Thanksgiving, Dec 25*

Fees *Camping*

Permits *For overnight trips into Craters of the Moon Wilderness*

Camping *Developed sites but no sewage. Open May–Oct*

Lodging *Arco*

Supplies *Arco*

Access for people with disabilities *Visitor center, Devils Orchard Trail*

When to visit *Spring for wildflowers; in winter, park road ideal for cross-country skiing*

Backcountry maps *USGS Craters of the Moon*

Kootenai National Wildlife Refuge

Idaho

In the far north of the Idaho Panhandle, just 20 miles (30 km) south of the Canadian border, thousands of ducks and geese congregate in spring to breed at the Kootenai National Wildlife Refuge in the Kootenai Valley—a rich, spreading mosaic of ponds, marshes, grasslands, grain fields, forests, and uplands lying in the shadow of the mighty Selkirk Range of the Rocky Mountains. By summer, the air is filled with the sound of quacking ducklings and honking goslings.

Waterfowl aren't the only wildlife that thrive at Kootenai. Although the refuge is small, covering only 2,775 acres (1,250 ha), it provides protection for a striking range of plants, birds, mammals, and reptiles.

MIGRATING BIRDS

More than 215 bird species have been spotted at Kootenai, with springtime producing the greatest variety. Waterfowl, including tundra swans, gadwalls, mallards, northern shovelers, redheads, herons, grebes and a variety of teals, start filling the ponds in March. They're joined in April by songbirds such as yellow-rumped warblers, common yellowthroats, American goldfinches, and red-eyed vireos. By June, the hatchlings start to make their appearance.

The fall migration begins early, with shorebirds and a variety of birds of prey stopping off to rest and feed while on their southward trek. Besides red-tailed and rough-legged hawks, keep an eye out for bald and golden eagles, northern harriers, and ospreys.

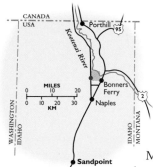

Beavers use their incisor teeth to cut through plants and trees, which they use for food and for building their lodges.

Looking across the refuge (above). Coyotes (left) are more likely to be heard than seen. A visiting osprey (below).

Though most visitors come to see the birds, there is also a good chance of spotting a number of mammal species. Both mule and white-tailed deer are common sights, and sometimes visitors will catch a glimpse of a moose or an elk. Coyotes can be heard calling, but are seldom seen, and though mountain lions are known to prowl in the reserve, the chances of seeing these secretive big cats are slim.

Wildflowers paint the landscape brilliant colors in spring and later in the year fruit-bearing plants, such as Oregon grapes, thimbleberries, elderberries, and huckleberries attract a host of wildlife, including the occasional black bear.

For an overview of the refuge, you can take the 4¹/₂ mile (7 km) auto tour, which travels through all the major habitat types. You can then park the car and set out on foot along various trails. The Island Pond Nature Trail is an easy one-hour self-guided loop around a cattail marsh. Here you can see wood ducks, common goldeneyes, and hooded mergansers using nesting boxes.

The footpath to Myrtle Falls provides a welcome respite in summer, when temperatures are high, leading through stands of tamaracks and cedars. Yellow-pine and red-tailed chipmunks chatter from the tree branches and an assortment of lush ferns and mosses carpet the forest floor. DH

Huckleberries are a favorite food of birds and black bears in summer and fall.

TRAVELER'S NOTES

Information Superintendent, Kootenai National Wildlife Refuge, HCR 60, Box 283, Bonners Ferry, ID 83805; tel. (208) 267-3888

Hours Year-round, daylight hours

Visitor center Refuge office, 2 miles past the entrance: Mon–Fri, 8 am–4.30 pm

Fees None

Permits Fishing and hunting (state licenses)

Camping None

Lodging Bonners Ferry, Coeur D'Alene

Supplies Bonners Ferry, Coeur D'Alene

Access for people with disabilities Chickadee Trail, Moose Overlook Photoblind, refuge office wheelchair accessible

When to visit Mar–May for waterfowl; Apr–June for songbirds; fall for migrants

Glacier National Park

Montana

Glacier National Park crowns northern Montana, its ice fields sparkling like diamonds throughout the year. Bejeweled by sapphire-colored lakes and strung with hundreds of miles of rivers and streams, Glacier's empire encompasses more than 1 million acres (405,000 ha), including two ranges of the northern Rocky Mountains, glacier-carved valleys, spreading pine forests, and plentiful wildlife.

Together, Glacier and its Canadian neighbor, Waterton Lakes National Park, are known as the Waterton–Glacier International Peace Park.

Amtrak's Empire Builder stops daily at both West Glacier and East Glacier late April through late October, although most visitors tour the park on its stunning scenic auto

Floating ice on Iceberg Lake.

Heavens Peak, one of the many dramatic sights along Going-to-the-Sun Road.

route—Going-to-the-Sun Road. This cuts across the park, crossing the mighty Continental Divide 6,664 feet (2,033 m) above sea level. It offers stupendous views, opportunities to see the abundant wildlife, and plenty of places to leave the car and explore on foot.

First stop from the west entrance is Lake McDonald, where an old-world lodge and a nature walk provide a perfect introduction to the park. A couple of miles further on are the massive, roaring McDonald Falls and, as the road winds on, towering mountain cliffs crowd in on all sides. Keep an eye out for moose feeding in the marshy ponds along McDonald Creek.

A mountain goat resting on the crags of Mount Clements (above). Rafting on the white water of Flathead River (right).

As the road makes its way through upper McDonald Valley, alpine views grow increasingly dramatic and cascades splash the road. At the summit, Logan Pass, trails lead through meadows bright with wildflowers in summer. Try the route to Hanging Gardens or the Hidden Lake Overlook Trail. Mountain peaks range in all directions, the rocky faces of mounts Clements, Oberlin, Pollock, and Reynolds offering extensive challenges to climbers. Look closely at any white spots on the rock faces as they may be mountain goats.

TAKING TO THE TRAIL

The park boasts more than 700 miles (1,100 km) of trails. Hikers can choose between easy ambles through spruce and pine forests to arduous treks over rock and ice. Everywhere you go, there is wildlife, from small creatures such as ground squirrels and pikas to elk, bighorn sheep, and mule deer. There are also sizeable populations of black and grizzly bears.

Birdwatching is excellent, with more than 200 species either resident or visiting. There are spruce grouse in the forests; Canada geese and harlequin ducks on the waterways; white tailed ptarmigan in the alpine regions; and hundreds of golden and bald eagles feed on spawning salmon on lower McDonald Creek in fall. DH

TRAVELER'S NOTES

Information Superintendent, Glacier National Park, P.O. Box 128, West Glacier, MT 59936-0128; tel. 406-888-7800

Hours Always open

Visitor centers St Mary: late May to mid-Oct. Logan Pass: mid-June to mid-Sept

Fees Admission, camping

Permits Backpacking

Camping 13 campgrounds, both developed and primitive

Lodging Hotels, lodges, and chalets in park and adjacent areas

Supplies In park and adjacent areas

Access for people with disabilities Some areas. Taped brochure for visually impaired

When to visit Summer for most access, wildlife. Fall for colors. Winter for cross-country skiing

Backcountry maps USGS Glacier National Park

Golden-mantled ground squirrel.

133

Medicine Lake
National Wildlife Refuge

Montana

Tucked in the remote northeastern corner of Montana, Medicine Lake National Wildlife Refuge has 31,457 acres (12,760 ha) of lakes, ponds, uplands, and meadows. These provide food, water, and nesting sites for hundreds of thousands of waterfowl, shore-birds, raptors, and songbirds.

The refuge's star attraction is a colony of thousands of white pelicans that come here to breed and rear their young. With wings that spread 9 feet (3 m) in flight, these huge fish–eaters arrive en masse every spring. By summer their numbers have increased by thousands more, as chicks hatch and fledge. Determined parents fill the skies, swooping back and forth to feed their boisterous young.

Canada geese also arrive in droves during spring and fall migration, as do thousands of sandhill cranes, and large flocks of whistling swans, shovelers, teals, mallards, pintails, and gadwalls.

The breeding season brings eared, western, and horned grebes by the thousands. Noisy California, Franklin's, and ring-billed gulls will have you believing you're standing on the beach rather than beside a landlocked lake many hundreds of miles from the nearest ocean.

An 18 mile (30 km) auto tour takes visitors along the water's edge, bringing them close to dozens of different species of shorebird, including Wilson's phalaropes, avocets, black terns, great blue herons, egrets, and sandpipers.

In the upland areas, look out for chestnut-collared longspurs, lark buntings, Le Conte's sparrows, and prairie falcons. Northern harriers fly over wet regions and short-eared owls patrol the dryer areas. Other raptors attracted by the

White pelicans on Medicine Lake (above). A female white-tailed deer (left).

abundance of prey include Swainson's and ferruginous hawks, and bald and golden eagles.

Besides birds, there are coyotes, pronghorns, and white-tailed deer to be seen. Does and their spotted offsprings are quite common throughout the refuge.

Along the auto route you will find an observation tower, photo blinds, and picnic spots. Or you may prefer to go exploring by canoe. You can then paddle along the shore, out to the islands, or through the bulrushes where many birds nest and feed.

Expect to be scolded by the territorial red-winged blackbirds that perch atop the cattails. Their chattering will set the American coots to braying.

TRAVELER'S NOTES

Information *Medicine Lake National Wildlife Refuge, 223 N. Shore Rd, Medicine Lake, MT 59247-9600; tel. (406) 789-2305*

Hours *Year-round, sunrise to sunset*

Visitor center *Office at refuge*

Fees *None*

Permits *Fishing, hunting (state licenses)*

Camping *25 miles north in Plentywood*

Lodging *Culbertson, Plentywood*

Supplies *Culbertson, Plentywood*

Access for people with disabilities *Auto tour route*

When to visit *May–Oct*

A walk through the uplands will flush pheasants and gray partridges. On spring mornings, male sharp-tailed grouse gather at their dancing grounds—flattened out dirt patches in the meadows and prairies—to stomp and inflate their lavender gular sacs in a bid to attract mates. This is a wonderful ritual to watch. DH

Male sharp-tailed grouse performing their intricate mating dance.

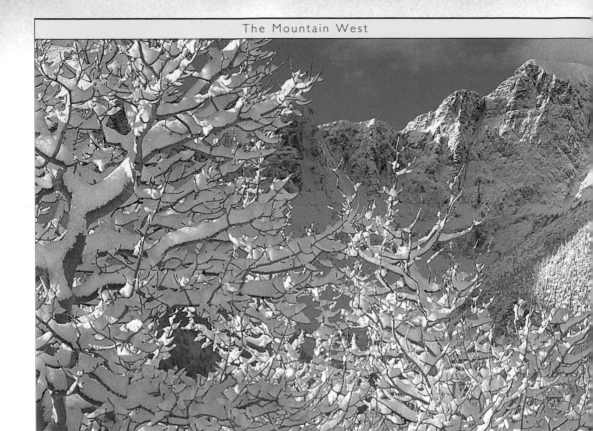

Great Basin National Park

Nevada

An island of mountains in a sea of desert, Great Basin is a welcome sight for travelers driving "America's loneliest highway"—US Highway 50. The park has one of the largest limestone caverns in the West, Lehman Caves, and a 13,063 foot (3,984 m) glacier-covered peak with a road winding almost to its summit. In between lie sagebrush flats, aspen forests, alpine meadows, glacial lakes, and stands of 4,000-year-old bristlecone pines.

Lehman Caves are richly decorated with stalactites, stalagmites, draperies, and flowstone. The limestone is formed from what was once a 1,000 foot (305 m) thick layer of shells and bones from creatures that lived in the warm, shallow sea that covered this region around 500 million years ago. Among the striking mineral deposits that adorn the caves are helectites that resemble noodles and popcorn, and clusters of snow-white needles called aragonite.

On its way up Wheeler Peak, the scenic drive passes through a variety of habitats. You can stop to enjoy the creamy yellow cliff roses that smell like orange blossom, and take in the view of Great Basin spread out below you. As the road climbs, pinyons and junipers give way to aspens which line Lehman Creek. During

Bobcats (left) are nocturnal, but you may find their tracks around the park. Some of the remarkable limestone formations found in Lehman Caves (right).

Wheeler Peak in winter (above). Lexington Arch (right) lies in the wild southern region of the park. Red-tailed hawks (below) are often seen soaring high on rising air currents.

spring, this glacier-fed stream swells with runoff, becoming a boisterous ribbon of white water as it tumbles down its rocky bed. Deer are plentiful here. Keep an eye out, too, for bobcat tracks.

After passing through thickets of shrubby mountain mahogany and manzanita dotted with pink-and-yellow-flowered prickly pear cactus, the road enters a deep forest of Englemann spruce and Douglas fir. It finally winds up at the campground in a subalpine forest of limber pine and spruce, an ear-popping 9,950 feet (3,035 m) above sea level.

HIGH TRAILS

You can leave the car here and take to the trails to view Wheeler Peak. During winter, snow drapes around it like a monarch's ermine robe. In summer, a sheet of ice clings fast within the folds of its north-facing cirque, a legacy of the ice age. In spring and summer, flower-spangled meadows carpet the mountain at treeline. Among the more showy species are buttercups, violets, blazing stars, monkey-flowers, and pussytoes. Turkey vultures, golden eagles, and other raptors soar overhead, while northern orioles, evening grosbeaks, lazuli buntings, pine siskins, and yellow-breasted chats are busy in the vegetation below. DH

TRAVELER'S NOTES

Information Superintendent, Great Basin National Park, Baker, NV 89311; tel. 775-234-7331

Hours Always open

Visitor center Year-round, 8 am–5 pm, longer in summer. Maps, booklets; café, gift shop, cave tours

Fees Cave tours and developed campgrounds

Permits Fishing (state license)

Camping 4 developed, 2 primitive campgrounds

Lodging Motel in Baker

Supplies Baker

Access for people with disabilities Visitor facilities, pullouts on Wheeler Peak Scenic Drive

When to visit May–Oct. Winter for cross-country skiing. Snow can keep Wheeler Peak Road closed through June

Backcountry maps USGS Wheeler Peak

137

Red Rock Canyon National Conservation Area

Nevada

If you are staying in Las Vegas and want to have a really wild time, head west on Charleston Boulevard for the red sandstone rocks of the Spring Mountain Range that are visible from the edge of town. A short drive from the pleasure palaces of Vegas will plunge you into 170,000 acres (68,850 ha) of spectacular desert wilderness, with cliffs towering 2,000 feet (610 m) above canyon floors, lush oases fed by underground springs, abundant birds, and several species of large wild mammal.

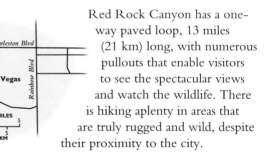

Red Rock Canyon has a one-way paved loop, 13 miles (21 km) long, with numerous pullouts that enable visitors to see the spectacular views and watch the wildlife. There is hiking aplenty in areas that are truly rugged and wild, despite their proximity to the city.

PINYON PINES TO MESQUITE

Lying near the conjunction of the Mojave and Great Basin deserts, Red Rock comprises a mosaic of plant communities that are typical of both. In the wettest higher elevations you will find a mix of pinyon pines and junipers, with scattered sagebrush. Below, where the rainfall is slightly lower, grow a large number of Joshua trees. Low-alkali soils in washes support a community characterized by scrubby rabbitbrush, whereas desert shrubs, such as sagebrush, Spanish bayonet, and needlegrass, grow in shallow soils that receive little rainfall.

The loggerhead shrike (left) impales its prey on a thorn before eating it.

138

Some of the region's red rocks (above). A Mojave yucca in bloom (left). A feral burro (below).

Near springs and creeks, the vegetation includes cattails, mesquite, rushes, and desert willows, providing excellent spots for birding.

One of the best places to see many of Red Rock's 100 plus bird species is Lost Creek Canyon, a short hike from the road. Look for golden eagles, red-tailed hawks, Cooper's hawks, and the aggressive loggerhead shrike, which impales its prey—usually insects and small lizards—on thorns before eating it. The loggerhead shrike and the ubiquitous roadrunner live throughout Red Rock, as does the cactus wren, which builds football-shaped nests of stems and stalks in the spiny branches of cholla cacti.

More than 45 species of mammal inhabit Red Rock, although most are secretive and therefore difficult to spot. Even so, knowing that you are in country where mountain lion, bighorn sheep, mule deer, bobcats, and kit foxes roam makes for an exciting outdoor experience. Look for bighorn at Willow Springs, just off the Loop Road, and in the canyons.

Red Rock Canyon is a refuge for the imperiled desert tortoise, whose habitat is fast being destroyed by development in many parts of its range, including the rapidly growing Las Vegas urban area.

Off Route 160, (which connects with Route 159), there is always a good chance of seeing some of Red Rock's small herd of feral horses, descendants of animals once owned by miners and ranchers. Along 159, you are also likely to come across feral burros. These seem tame and will approach your car, sometimes even poking their muzzles through a window. Don't attempt to pet or feed them, though, as they tend to bite and kick. ER

TRAVELER'S NOTES

Information Red Rock Canyon National Conservation Area, HCR 33, Box 5500, Las Vegas, NV 89124; tel. (702) 363-1921

Hours Year round, 7 am to dusk

Visitor center Daily, 8 am–5 pm summer, 8 am–4.30 pm winter. Closed Dec 25

Fees Admission and camping

Permits None

Camping 1 primitive campground (15 sites)

Lodging Las Vegas

Supplies Las Vegas

Access for people with disabilities Visitor center, three pullouts

When to visit Any time. Take plenty of water if going off road. Beware of dehydration in summer

Backcountry maps USGS La Madre Spring, La Madre Mountain, Mountain Springs, Blue Diamond

Bryce Canyon National Park

Utah

Bryce Canyon National Park is an astonishing amphitheater of red rock spires and eroded canyon walls, rimmed by woods of spruce and fir. Ebenezer Bryce, a Mormon settler who lived in the area, summed it up by saying, "It's a hell of a place to lose a cow!"

The towering limestone spires (called hoodoos), arches, and cliffs that embellish Bryce's interlinked canyons represent some 50 million years of geological activity. Some of the park's oddest features have acquired fanciful names, such as Thors Hammer, Silent City, and the Hat Shop. You might think of a few names of your own as you wander Bryce's 50 miles (80 km) of trails.

The 13 overlooks on the park's roads provide spectacular views, but on day hikes into the canyon you'll encounter shapes so fantastic, colors so rich, and terrain so bewildering that you may think you're no longer on planet Earth.

CANYONS AND HOODOOS

A short descent from the canyon rim on the Navajo Loop Trail brings you into Wall Street, a deep, narrow canyon that dazzles the senses. Another favorite trail is the 8 mile (12 km) loop through Fairyland Canyon—a wonderland of hoodoos and rock sentinels. And, for a spectacular overview, hike the Rim Trail at sunrise, when the canyon glows eerily in golds, reds, and purples.

In spring and early summer, Bryce erupts in a spectacular display of wildflowers, including sego lilies (Utah's state flower), star lilies, bellflowers, blue columbine, yarrow, asters, clematis, skyrocket gilias, penstemons, Indian paintbrush, evening primrose, and wild

The short-horned lizard (left) is one of the few reptiles able to tolerate Bryce's cold climate. Wall Street on the Navajo Loop Trail (right).

Map labels:
12
Hatch
89
14 Long Valley Junction
Cannonville
MILES 0 5 10
0 5 10 15 KM

Bryce Amphitheater viewed from Bryce Point (above). Fresh snow cloaks the canyon at Sunrise Point (right).

iris. In all, over 400 plant species are found in the park—enough to delight any botanist.

Mule deer, porcupines, skunks, gray foxes, and coyotes can often be seen browsing or prowling in the park's meadows. Scan the ground and you might see chipmunks, ground squirrels, marmots, and, possibly, Utah prairie dogs a threatened species. Elk can sometimes be spotted, grazing, at dawn and dusk. Mountain lions and pronghorns are rarer.

Over 160 species of bird visit the park each year. Watch for swifts and swallows along cliff faces, and nighthawks, hummingbirds, northern flickers, meadowlarks, bluebirds, and robins in the meadows and woods. Most of the park's bird species migrate in fall, but hardy Steller's jays, pygmy nuthatches, ravens, eagles, and owls remain throughout the long, snowy winter.

Thors Hammer is one of the park's most distinctive hoodoos.

Winter in the park is a magical time. There are few visitors, and Bryce's elevation, ranging from 6,000 to 9,000 feet (1,800 to 2,700 m), ensures a good snowpack for cross-country skiing and snowshoeing. **DD**

TRAVELER'S NOTES

Information *Superintendent, Bryce Canyon National Park, PO Box 170001, Bryce Canyon, Utah 84717-0001; tel. (435) 834-5322, fax (435) 834-4102*

Hours *Year-round, except Dec 25*

Visitor center *Main road, 1 mile (1.5 km) from park boundary, 8 am–4.30 pm in winter, extended hours rest of year; closed federal holidays. Interpretative programs, ranger-led hikes*

Fees *Admission, camping*

Permits *Backcountry camping*

Camping *2 campgrounds (218 sites)*

Lodging *For reservations write to: Amfac, 4001 East Iliff Ave, Suite 600, Aurora, CO 80014; tel. 303-297-2757; fax. 303-237-3175*

Supplies *Store near Sunrise Point*

Access for people with disabilities *Trail between Sunrise and Sunset points, viewpoints, park buildings, campsites*

When to visit *Apr through Oct. Winter for skiing, snowshoeing*

Backcountry maps *USGS Bryce Canyon National Park*

Canyonlands National Park

Utah

Rugged and remote, Canyonlands lies at the heart of one of the most fascinating desert landscapes in the continent. This austere country, dissected by two mighty rivers, the Green and the Colorado, has a deep sense of timelessness about it.

The park covers over 500 square miles (1,295 sq km) of rock spires, canyons, mesas, and buttes carved from the Colorado Plateau, and is divided into three districts: the high elevation Island in the Sky, the Needles (the most developed area), and the remote Maze. Some roads are paved, but most are suitable for four-wheel-drive vehicles only. To really explore, it's best to go on mountain bike, river raft, or on foot.

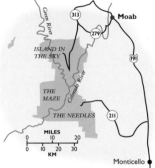

Angel Arch and Molar Rock in the Needles (left). Desert bighorn sheep (above).

From mid-April to mid-June, wildflowers such as evening primrose and Indian paintbrush bloom in the canyons and meadows, but for most of the year the arid conditions keep plant and animal life in check. Because there is little water, grasses grow in clumps and trees and bushes are well spaced. Smaller animals, such as ground squirrels, usually obtain their water through seeds, stems, and insects, while larger mammals, such as mule deer, coyotes, and bighorn sheep seek out springs, washes, streams, or rain-filled potholes.

Deep within the canyons, it's a much wetter world. Here, seeps in the rock support hanging gardens of grasses, ferns, columbine, orchids, and other plants. Lining the river banks are cottonwoods, willows, and tamarisk—an exotic species.

The view from Elephant Hill (above). A mountain biker surveys the Colorado River from the White Rim Road (right).

THE THREE DISTRICTS

Island in the Sky lies over 6,000 feet (1,800 m) above sea level. Over 17 miles (27 km) of paved roads lead to various trails and overlooks. From Grand View Point you can take in the vast desert landscape and the two rivers. The Mesa Arch Trail is a short hike through woodland to a sandstone arch perched above the Colorado River and the White Rim Road—a popular route for bikes and four-wheel-drive vehicles.

The Needles offers 12 miles (19 km) of paved roads, extensive four-wheel-drive tracks, and over 55 miles (70 km) of hiking trails. These routes lead to an amazing world of sandstone monoliths (needles), towers, arches, and canyons.

To the west is the Maze—30 square miles (78 sq km) of labyrinths and weird rock formations. Entering this district is a challenge as there is only one established trail, and access is via a 59 mile (95 km) dirt road that may be impassable in bad weather. Deep within the Maze's twisting canyons lie remarkable Anasazi ruins and petroglyphs. ᴮᴰ

TRAVELER'S NOTES

Information Superintendent, Canyonlands National Park, 2282 S. West Resource Blvd, Moab, UT 84532-3298; tel. 435-259-7164

Hours Always open

Visitor centers Main and Center Sts, Moab, UT 84532; tel. (800) 635-6622. Winter, 8 am–5 pm; extended hours rest of year. Other visitor centers in the three districts: winter, 8 am–4.30 pm; extended hours rest of year

Fees Admission, camping

Permits Backcountry camping, rock climbing, river rafting

Camping Squaw Flat (26 sites); Willow Flat (12 sites)

Lodging Moab, Green River, Monticello, Blanding

Supplies Moab, Green River, Monticello, Blanding

Access for people with disabilities Visitor centers; overlooks at Island in the Sky, the Needles

When to visit Spring and fall

Backcountry maps USGS Canyonlands National Park

Newspaper Rock, near the Needles District, bears petroglyphs recording 1,000 years of human habitation.

143

Zion National Park

Utah

Named for the heavenly city of God by nineteenth-century Mormon settlers, Zion Canyon and its surroundings illustrate the way in which wind and water can shape stone into the most fantastic forms. Zion National Park, Utah's most visited park, was established in 1919 to protect this amazing world of brilliantly

colored canyons, geological wonders, and complex desert and forest ecosystems.

The central feature of the 147,000 acre (59,500 ha) park is Zion Canyon—cut by the Virgin River over a period of 13 million years. A scenic drive runs beside the river for 6 miles (10 km), snaking between the canyon's 2,000 to 3,000 ft (600 to 900 m) walls of sedimentary rock, which glow in shades of crimson, tan, and orange, and form massive rock monoliths, such as the Temple of Sinawava. Along the banks of the river grow cottonwood, box elder, willow, and ash, providing welcome shade for summer picnics and a glorious display of brilliantly colored foliage in fall.

The Zion–Mount Carmel Highway—a breathtaking feat of engineering—switchbacks steeply up from the canyon floor and passes through two tunnels to a landscape of white, pastel, orange, and red Navajo sandstone plateaus and massive petrified sand dunes, such as the Checkerboard Mesa—its gridlike patterns formed by vertical cracks in its horizontal strata.

The Virgin River winds toward the Watchman rock formation.

SEEING THE SIGHTS ON FOOT

Most visitors see Zion solely from their cars, but the park is truly a place for hikers. Even short hikes from the main road lead to enchanting spots, such as Emerald Pools, fed by waterfalls, and Weeping Rock, where the moist cliffs are thick with wildflowers, ferns, and mosses. The easy 2 mile (3 km) round trip Riverside Walk, Zion's most popular trail, leads to the Narrows, where the canyon's great walls begin to close in.

Experienced hikers can explore the Narrows, where the canyon walls are, at times, a mere hallway width apart, but you should only do this in dry weather, and you must register with the visitor center first. The route runs for 16 miles (26 km), and you sometimes have to wade through thigh-deep sections of the river. (During spring runoff, and following summer storms, the river turns into a raging torrent and the route is closed.) Equally

Zion Canyon's massive rock walls (above), illuminated by the morning sun, greet a hiker near the park's south entrance. Day hikers explore one of Zion's many water-worn side canyons (right).

arduous are the trails that climb to Angels Landing, Observation Point, and the West Rim, but the breath-taking views they give over this "land of the rainbow canyons" are ample reward.

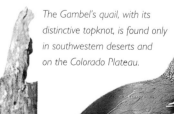

The Gambel's quail, with its distinctive topknot, is found only in southwestern deserts and on the Colorado Plateau.

TRAVELER'S NOTES

Information *Superintendent, Zion National Park, Springdale, UT 84767; tel. (435) 772-3256*

Hours *Always open*

Visitor centers *Zion Canyon: summer, 8 am–8 pm, winter, 8 am–5 pm, tel. (435) 772-3256. Kolob Canyons: daily, 8 am–5 pm, tel. (435) 586-9548*

Fees *Admission, camping*

Permits *Backcountry hiking, camping*

Camping *South Campground (140 sites), Watchman (270 sites); 6 primitive campsites at Lava Point*

Lodging *Zion Lodge, Zion National Park, Springdale, UT 84767; tel. (303) 297-2757. Reservations advised at least 6 weeks in advance. Hotels, bed-and-breakfasts in Springdale*

Supplies *Springdale*

Access for people with disabilities *Visitor center, some trails*

When to visit *April though Nov. Spring for wildflowers; Fall for foliage colors*

Backcountry maps *USGS Zion National Park*

145

KOLOB CANYONS AND LAVA POINT

Two other areas well worth exploring are Kolob Canyons and Lava Point, in the northwest of the park. Kolob Canyons Road takes you 5 miles (8 km) into red rock "finger" canyons, where the lower slopes are forested with bigtooth maple, and pinyon and juniper grow on the plateaus. Hikers and backpackers can make a strenuous 14 mile (23 km) round-trip to Kolob Arch which, with a span of 310 feet (95 m), is one of the largest natural arches in the world.

The road to Lava Point climbs steeply from Kolob Terrace Road. At the point, which is at an elevation of 7,896 feet (2,400 m), you are rewarded with vast views of Zion's plateaus.

GREENERY

Zion boasts the richest diversity of plants in Utah—almost 800 species. This amazing array has evolved in response to a wide range of micro-environments created by differences in elevation, sunlight, water, and temperature.

In the lower regions, prickly pear and cholla cacti, desert sage, and mesquite trees withstand climatic extremes and scant moisture, whereas in the canyon bottoms, where water is abundant, sandbar willow and water birch thrive. On rocky overhangs and canyon walls, seeps create hanging gardens of golden and cliff columbine, scarlet monkeyflowers, and maidenhair ferns. Stands of juniper, ponderosa pine, pinyon pine, live oak, manzanita, white fir, Douglas fir, and quaking aspen grow in side canyons and on high plateaus and isolated mesas.

Checkerboard Mesa (top) is one of the park's extraordinary sandstone formations. A desert tarantula (above right). Waterfalls cascade at Lower Emerald Pool (left).

In spring and early summer, the canyon floors are dotted with wildflowers—sand buttercups, Indian paintbrush, violets, orchids, and lilies. These day-blooming species are followed, in July and August, when the weather is hotter, by night-blooming plants such as sacred datura, with its large, white trumpet-shaped flowers, and evening primrose.

The Watchman, near the South Entrance (above). Indian paintbrush (left). Greater roadrunner (below).

TADPOLE SHRIMP

After short but torrential thunderstorms, rainfall gathers in pools and puddles in the sandstone terrain of the Colorado Plateau. As the water collects, tiny tadpole shrimp hatch from eggs lying in the silt at the bottom of these depressions in the rock. These freshwater crustaceans are descendants of shrimp that lived here more than a million years ago, when there was plenty of water and lakes dotted the region. It is thought that the eggs may remain dormant for up to 100 years, until brought to life by rainwater.

Racing to complete their reproductive cycle before the pools evaporate, the shrimp grow to ½ inch (1 cm) within 6 days. All are female and they reproduce rapidly by cloning themselves. Later, as the pond dries, males are produced and normal reproduction takes place, ensuring that the species has the genetic advantages of sexual reproduction. The shrimp feed on minute organisms that also appear following rainfall.

Inhabiting Zion's lowest, rocky elevations are animals that have adapted to the hot summer sun, cold winters, and arid environment. These include the kangaroo rat, which obtains water from the food it eats, and the chuckwalla, Zion's largest lizard.

Roadrunners are common, and Gambel's quail can be seen scurrying about the wooded washes on the desert edge.

In the canyon bottoms, where there is more moisture and running water, mule deer, beaver, and birds such as the American dipper are found. If you scan the canyon walls, you may see canyon wrens flitting about and peregrine falcons nesting. Golden eagles soar above the park's highest elevations. Rarer are bobcats, mountain lions, and Mexican spotted owls. Zion snails—a species unique to the region—can be found in the canyon's hanging gardens. BD

147

Grand Teton National Park

Wyoming

With a visitor center in a town called Moose, it's not surprising that Grand Teton National Park is a prime spot for observing wildlife. Roaming the 310,000 acre (125,500 ha) park is a 7,500 strong elk herd, some of which overwinters just south of the park in the National Elk Refuge. Other large mammals include black and grizzly bears, antelope, bison, and, of course, the occasional moose. Small herds of Rocky Mountain bighorn sheep range isolated mountain areas; and beavers, martens, mink, weasels, and coyotes frequent the marshes, meadows, and woods.

In spring, wildflowers, including balsamroots (below), bloom in profusion throughout Jackson Hole.

Encompassing the broad, flat valley of Jackson Hole, the park is framed by the jagged, glacier-draped Teton Range. It is surrounded by pristine national forests and three wilderness areas: Teton Wilderness, Jedediah Smith Wilderness, and Winegar Hole Wilderness. The Snake River meanders through the park, feeding 20 mile (30 km) long Jackson Lake. South of Jackson are two smaller, equally pristine lakes—Leigh and Jenny. Bald eagles and ospreys are common along the shores of the Snake River and Jackson Lake. Blue herons, killdeer, trumpeter swans, mallards, and Canada geese reside in wetland areas. More than 200 species of bird have been identified in the park.

There are nearly 900 species of wildflower in Grand Teton. After the snow melts, an exquisite floral mix starts to appear, beginning in lower elevations with sage buttercups, spring beauties, and yellowbells. In early summer, the valley is covered in blue-purple lupines, scarlet gilias, yellow arrowleaf balsamroots, yellow mountain sunflowers, pink mountain hollyhocks, and blue upland larkspur. By midsummer, hikers are greeted by fields of white columbine, pink daisies, bluebells, red

Grand Teton (above), at 13,770 feet (4,200 m), is the highest peak in the Teton Range and a popular destination for climbers (left). Black bear cubs (below).

paintbrush, and lavender asters. Above the treeline, alpine forget-me-nots—the park's official flower—grace the meadows.

THE BACKCOUNTRY

Grand Teton has swarms of summer visitors, but few venture into the backcountry. There are over 200 miles (320 km) of hiking trails, ranging from easy strolls on the valley floor to arduous climbs into the mountains. Jackson Lake, at the base of 12,605 foot (3,844 m) Mount Moran, acts as a barrier between the wilderness and the tourist hordes. A delightful way to see these wild regions is on a guided kayak trip on the lake. These overnight and multi-day camping trips explore the shoreline, and provide access to some of Grand Teton's more remote corners. BD

TRAVELER'S NOTES

Information *Superintendent, Grand Teton National Park, Drawer 170, Moose, WY 83012; tel. (307) 739-3300. TDD phone for Moose Visitor Center: 307-739-3400*

Hours *Always open*

Visitor centers *Moose: late May to early Sept, 8 am–7 pm; rest of year, 8 am–5 pm, tel. (307) 739-3399. Colter Bay: early June to early Sept, 8 am–8 pm; though early Oct, 8 am–5 pm; closed rest of year, tel. (307) 739-3594. Both have daily programs*

Fees *Admission (also valid for Yellowstone), boating, camping*

Permits *Backcountry camping, rock climbing, rafting; fishing (state license)*

Camping *Colter Bay (310 sites), Gros Ventre (360), Jenny Lake (49), Lizard Creek (60), Signal Mountain (86)*

Lodging *Park lodges and cabins, Jackson; Teton Village*

Supplies *Colter Bay, Flagg Ranch, Moose Junction, Signal Mountain, Jackson*

Access for people with disabilities *Visitor centers, campfire programs, pullouts*

When to visit *Spring, summer, fall*

Backcountry maps *USGS Grand Teton National Park*

Yellowstone National Park

Wyoming

Established in 1872, Yellowstone was the first national park in the world. It preserves a huge area of wilderness (2.2 million acres [0.9 million ha]) in the northwestern corner of Wyoming, plus slivers of land along the Montana and Idaho borders. Each summer, more than 3 million visitors flood through the park's five entrances to explore the 370 miles (600 km) of looping roadways and numerous trails that weave through the region.

Yellowstone's greatest attraction is its remarkable array of geothermal wonders: gushing geysers, fuming fumaroles (steam vents), polychrome paint pots, and mucky mudpots—a landscape so bizarre that the area's first European explorer, mountain man and trapper John Colter, was ridiculed as a teller of tall tales when he tried to describe the wonders he had seen.

GUSHING GEYSERS

The park's 250 active geysers—the densest collection of geysers in the world—are concentrated in five geothermal basins: West Thumb, Old Faithful (Upper), Midway, Lower, and Norris. The most famous geyser is Old Faithful, which erupts for two to five minutes at intervals varying from 33 to 120 minutes. Spectacular spouting can also be found in the Lower Geyser Basin, where the Great Fountain Geyser erupts with bursts that are up to 200 feet (60 m) high and lasting from 45 to 60 minutes. Some small geysers erupt constantly,

Yellowstone has the most concentrated collection of geysers in the world (left).

A bison rests in the snow near Old Faithful (above). Minerva Hot Springs (left). Mudpots at Pocket Basin and a young yellow-bellied marmot (below).

or every few minutes, and some of the large ones remain inactive for periods of months or even years at a time.

Geysers occur when surface water seeps through porous rock, is superheated and pressurized, then rises to the surface, erupting through steaming vents. When heated waters rise under less pressure, they form hot springs.

One of the most dramatic springs in the park is Mammoth Hot Springs, where hot water laden with minerals constantly bubbles up, depositing up to 2 tons of limestone on the surface every day. Over the past 8,000 years, this process has created a massive stone terrace.

TRAVELER'S NOTES

Information PO Box 168, Yellowstone National Park, WY 82190-0168; tel. (307) 344-7381. TDD (307) 344-2386

Hours Closed early Nov to mid-Dec, and from mid-March for a month

Visitor centers Albright (Mammoth Hot Springs): early June to Labor Day, 8.00 am–7.00 pm. Old Faithful: early June to mid-Aug, 8.00 am–8.00 pm. Canyon: early June to late Aug, 8.00 am–7.00 pm. Fishing Bridge: early June to mid-Aug, 8.00 am–6.00 pm. Grant Village: early June to mid-Aug, 8.00 am–6:00 pm. For hours during rest of year call (307) 344-2386

Fees Admission, camping, boating

Permits Backcountry camping, boating, fishing (state license)

Camping 11 campgrounds (1,864 sites). Reservations (307) 344-7311

Lodging Lodges at Old Faithful, Grant Village, Lake, Canyon; Mammoth Hot Springs Hotel. Reservations (307) 344-7311

Supplies Old Faithful, Canyon, Grant Village, Lake, Mammoth Hot Springs

Access for people with disabilities Visitors centers, walkways, lodging within park, some campsites

When to visit May through Aug. Winter for skiing, snowshoeing

Backcountry maps USGS Yellowstone National Park

Aside from this geothermal landscape, Yellowstone is mostly a vast plateau of pine forest and sprawling meadows. There are over 80 species of wildflower, springtime blooms including monkeyflower, lupine, fireweed, mountain bluebell, and Rocky Mountain fringed gentian (the park's official flower).

Much of Yellowstone's rich vegetation was wiped out in the huge firestorms that raged during the summer of 1988, but the wildlands are regenerating with vigor—a dramatic example of the role fire plays in the ecosystem. The impact of these fires on the park's landscape will be evident for many years to come.

IN THE MEADOWS AND FORESTS

There are 279 bird species in the park and checklists can be obtained from any of the visitor centers or by writing to the park. Bald eagles, ospreys, trumpeter swans, white pelicans, ducks, and Canada geese are commonly seen, especially in Hayden Valley and along the shores of Yellowstone Lake.

The park boasts the greatest concentration of mammal species in the lower 48 states—some 60 species—which explains why the area was prime hunting ground for Native American tribes. (Archeological evidence has revealed that humans have lived on the Yellowstone plateau for over 8,000 years.)

Bison can be seen in summer in the Hayden Valley and in spring and fall in the Lower Geyser Basin. Elk graze in meadows throughout the park, moose nibble forage near Pelican Creek, pronghorns browse the flats near the North Entrance, and bighorn sheep frequent the slopes of Mount Washburn in summer. Black bears are common; rarer, and more unpredictable, are the park's

Excelsior Geyser (top). Morning Glory Pool (center). Feeding a black bear in earlier days (right)—an example of what park visitors should never do.

152

200 to 300 resident grizzly bears. Smaller mammals, such as squirrels, chipmunks, beavers, badgers, marmots, muskrats, and snowshoe hares can often be seen scurrying about.

PEAKS AND MEANDERING RIVERS

Mountain ranges, many with peaks rising to over 10,000 feet (3,500 m), surround the park. They include the Gallatin Range to the west and north, the Absaroka and Beartooth ranges to the north and east, and the Tetons to the south. Runoff from these ranges feeds the park's waterways, including the meandering Madison and Lewis rivers, the thermally heated Firehole River, and 20 mile (30 km) long Yellowstone Lake, where kayakers and canoeists can paddle their way to boat-in campgrounds at several

The Lower Falls in the Grand Canyon of the Yellowstone (above) are twice as high as Niagara. The fringed gentian (right) is the park's official flower.

points along the 100 mile (160 km) shoreline. The lake feeds into the Yellowstone River, which tumbles and roars for 24 miles (38 km) through the golden-hued Grand Canyon of the Yellowstone. On its journey through this deep gorge, the river plummets 417 feet (127 m) down Upper and Lower Yellowstone Falls. BD

YELLOWSTONE IN WINTER

Yellowstone attracts more than 3 million visitors each summer. Far fewer—about 140,000—come in winter, yet this is a magical time. The park's management makes great efforts to accommodate winter visitors, offering wildlife viewing tours by snowcoach, comfortable winter lodging, and guided cross-country ski tours.

Except for snowmobiles, the park is hushed—clad in its thick winter cloak. In the geyser basins, steam billows from the fumaroles, wreathing nearby trees and shrubs in ice. Winter-coated bison use their massive heads as snowplows to reach the snow-covered grass. Elk forage in windswept meadows or graze on the perennially green grass close to the thermally heated waterways. Sharing their struggle for survival are over-wintering birds such as trumpeter swans, various ducks, Canada geese, and bald eagles.

The park offers winter visitors all sorts of activities and wonderful sights.

153

Grand Canyon NP

ARIZONA   NEW MEXICO

Albuquerque

Phoenix

Bosque Del Apache NWR

Saguaro
NM   Coronado NF

Carlsbad
Caverns NP

El Paso

Dallas

TEXAS

Houston

San Antonio

Big Bend NP

Padre Island NS

0   100   200   miles
0   200   400 km

Santa Ana / Lower Rio
Grande Valley NWR

The Southwest

Coronado National Forest

Arizona

Situated in the rugged mountain ranges of southeastern Arizona, Coronado National Forest covers an exceptional variety of habitats from the desert floor to altitudes over 10,000 feet (3,050 m). The forest encompasses 1.7 million acres (0.7 million ha) in 12 mountain areas, of which the Santa Catalinas, the Santa Ritas, the Huachucas, and the Chiricahuas are the major attractions. Two of America's top birding spots—Madera and Cave Creek canyons—are within Coronado's boundaries, and the forest is also a wonderful place for camping, hiking, and skiing. There are also areas of historical interest, such as the Cochise Stronghold—a natural fortress used by the Apaches.

ISLANDS IN THE SKY

The Santa Catalinas and surrounding ranges mark the southern tip of the Rockies, and the Santa Ritas, Huachucas, and Chiricahuas are an extension of the Mexican Sierra Madre. Surrounding these "islands in the sky" are two great deserts—the Sonoran to the west and the Chihuahuan to the southeast.

Naturalists flock to see the specialties of these "Mexican mountains"—the many birds and animals that are drawn by the steep-walled canyons and year-round streams. The mountains are a riot of color in summer, with wildflowers and bright tropical birds, and offer respite from the desert's heat. The vegetation changes from cacti at the base of the ranges to grasslands, then cottonwoods and sycamores in the canyons, upward to mixed

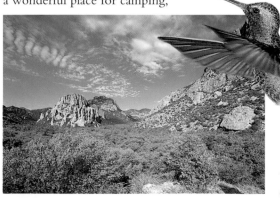

The Chiricahua Mountains (left) offer dramatic mountain scenery and lush vegetation. A male broad-billed hummingbird (above).

oak and pine forests, and finally to conifers and mountain meadows. Red-faced and Grace's warblers can be seen at high altitudes in summer.

Cave Creek Canyon in the Chiricahua Mountains (above). The Arizona barrel cactus (left). The Sonora mountain kingsnake (below left) is a harmless mimic of the poisonous coral snake.

The Santa Catalinas, north of Tucson, feature spectacular Sabino Canyon with towering cliffs, ski slopes on Mount Lemmon, and wonderful views. Directly south of Tucson, the Santa Ritas are famous for Madera Canyon, where broad-billed, blue-throated, and magnificent hummingbirds come to feeders around Santa Rita Lodge. To the east, a network of steep trails in the Huachucas takes you into Ramsey, Carr, and Miller canyons, with interconnecting trails along the crests. Scores of hummingbirds can be seen at the Ramsey Canyon Preserve and ringtails can be spotted at night.

Hummingbirds can be seen throughout the Chiricahuas, from Portal to the high mountain meadows of Rustler Park. In the lower elevations, Cave Creek Canyon provides striking wildlife walks, with a chance to see the elegant trogon, one of North America's most beautiful birds, and perhaps a mountain lion early in the morning. SM

TRAVELER'S NOTES

Information *Coronado National Forest, 300 W. Congress, Tucson, AZ 85701; tel: (520) 670-4552*

Hours *Always open*

Visitor centers *Santa Catalina Ranger Station (RS): tel. (520) 749-8700, Mon–Fri, 8am–4.30 pm; Sat–Sun, 8.30 am–4.30 pm. Nogales RS: tel. (520) 281-2296, Mon–Fri, 8 am–4.30 pm. Sierra Vista RS: tel. (520) 378-0311, Mon–Fri, 8 am– 5 pm. Douglas RS: tel. (520) 364-3468, Mon–Fri, 8 am–5 pm. Safford RS: tel. (520) 428-4150, Mon–Fri, 8 am–5 pm*

Fees *Camping*

Permits *Backcountry use, fishing (state license)*

Camping *Campgrounds*

in Catalinas, Santa Ritas, Huachucas, Chiricahuas; backcountry by permit

Lodging *Tucson. Lodges within the forest include Santa Rita Lodge, Madera Canyon 520-625-8746; The Nature Conservancy Mile Hi/Ramsey Canyon Preserve 520 378 2785; Cave Creek Ranch 520-558-2334*

Supplies *Tucson, Sierra Vista, Portal*

Access for people with disabilities *Sabino Canyon Visitor Center and lower canyon; turnouts*

When to visit *Year-round, Jun–Aug peak wildlife and wildflower seasons*

Backcountry maps *USGS Sabino Canyon, Mount Lemmon, Mount Hopkins, Miller Peak, Portal, Rustler Park*

Grand Canyon National Park

Arizona

Nothing approaches the Grand Canyon in terms of form, scale, and glowing color. It is the grandest example of erosion anywhere—a chasm 285 miles (460 km) long, 18 miles (30 km) wide, and over a mile (1.6 km) deep.

Assisted by uplift of the land, the Colorado River has carved the canyon through layers of multicolored sandstone, shale, limestone, and metamorphic formations, down to Vishnu schist —some of the oldest exposed rock in the world.

Wind, rain, snow, and frost have combined with the river over several million years in the ongoing erosion process.

Indian cultures have inhabited the region for some 4,000 years. The first white person to fully explore the area was John Wesley Powell. The canyon became a national park in 1919, which was expanded in 1975.

THE SOUTH RIM

The South Rim, the main part of the park, lies at 7,000 feet (2,135 m). Tall ponderosa pines grow near the rim, but because rainfall is light, stunted pinyon pine and juniper cover the plateau. Mountain bluebirds, mountain chickadees, and Abert's tassel-eared squirrels frequent the trails. In summer, wildflowers such as cliff rose and penstemon bloom in abundance.

The view of the canyon is stunning from Yavapai Observation Station. From here you can walk the Rim Trail to Hermits Rest, an 18 mile (29 km) round trip that passes the main lookouts, or you can take a bus along West Rim Drive. East Rim Drive leads to Tusayan

The Colorado River at Nankoweap Rapid (far left).
Goldenrod (left).

158

A morning fog rolls over the South Rim (above). Native American pictographs (right) are found throughout the park.

Archeological Museum, at the site of an ancient pueblo; Lipan Point, overlooking the San Francisco Peaks; and Desert View, where the Watchtower offers a fine view of the canyon and the Painted Desert.

THE NORTH RIM

Only 9 air miles (14 km) from the South Rim but over 200 miles (320 km) by road, the Kaibab Plateau, on the North Rim, is also 1,000 feet (300 m) higher. The climate is cooler and wetter here and this part of the park is closed from November to mid-May because it is blanketed in snow.

Back from the rim, there are forests of yellow and ponderosa pine and mountain meadows where asters bloom and weasels dart during summer. At higher elevations, there are forests of blue spruce and aspen. Mule deer and woodpeckers live among the trees, as does the Kaibab tassel-eared squirrel—a white-tailed close relative of the Abert's squirrel found on the South Rim.

Fewer people visit the North Rim because of limited road access, which benefits those who do make the trip.

TRAVELER'S NOTES

Information *Superintendent, Grand Canyon National Park, PO Box 129, Grand Canyon, AZ 86023; tel. (520) 638-7888.*

Hours *South Rim open year-round, North Rim open mid-May through Oct*

Visitor centers *South Rim: visitor center and Yavapai Observation Station, open daily, 8 am–5 pm; Desert View Museum open daily 9 am–5 pm; North Rim: information desk at Grand Canyon Lodge open mid-May through Oct*

Fees *Admission; camping*

Permits *Backcountry camping, fishing (state license)*

Camping *South Rim: Mather Campground open year-round, reservations recommended, Desert View summer only. North Rim campground summer only. Backcountry sites*

Lodging *South Rim: El Tovar Hotel, Bright Angel, Thunderbird, Kachina, Maswik, Yavapai, and Moqui Lodges; tel. 303-297-2757. Inner Canyon: Phantom Ranch, tel. 303-297-2757. North Rim: Grand Canyon Lodge, tel. 303-297-2757*

Supplies *Grand Canyon Village, Desert View, North Rim Store*

Access for people with disabilities *Visitor center (wheelchairs available), Yavapai Observation Station, West Rim Drive, Mather Campground, pullouts*

When to visit *Apr–Oct for hiking, rafting*

Backcountry maps *USGS Grand Canyon National Park*

The rising sun lights up a rock pinnacle below Cape Royal on the North Rim.

Grand Canyon Lodge stands on Bright Angel Point, a spectacular promontory jutting into the canyon. Cape Royal Drive takes you to Point Imperial, overlooking Marble Canyon and the Painted Desert, and to Cape Royal, offering magnificent lookouts along the way.

THE INNER CANYON

You can only visit the Inner Canyon on foot, on a mule, or on a raft. If you're fit and have the time, hiking into the canyon is by far the best way to see it, but the trails are only for those unafraid of heights. As you make your way down, you descend from present-day topsoil on the rim to the canyon floor's 2 billion-year-old rocks.

The Bright Angel Trail and the South Kaibab Trail both lead down to the Colorado River from the South Rim, each taking two days to complete the round trip.

MAJOR JOHN WESLEY POWELL

In 1869, the last significant blank spot on the map of the United States was filled when Major John Wesley Powell (1834–1902), a Civil War veteran who had lost an arm in combat, successfully led a party of nine men down the Colorado River and through the Grand Canyon.

Powell made a second trip to the canyon in 1871 and thereafter headed up expeditions into areas encompassed by today's Capitol Reef, Canyonlands, Bryce, and Zion national parks. His diary of the first expedition, published in 1875, and his studies of the canyon country remain classics.

Powell's involvement with Native Americans led him to serve for 23 years as director of the Bureau of Ethnology, a federal agency set up to study Indian culture. As director of the United States Geological Survey, Powell initiated topographical mapping of the country and made proposals for the conservation of the arid canyon country. Ironically, with the construction of Glen Canyon Dam and the formation of Lake Powell in 1963, one of Powell's favorite areas of the Colorado Plateau was lost.

Major John Wesley Powell

The canyon and the plateau seen from Navajo Point (top). The Colorado River below Toroweap Point (above).

The Bright Angel Trail winds down a rugged and precipitous 9¹/₂ mile (15 km) path. It passes through Indian Garden, a welcome cottonwood oasis, before descending a series of switchbacks called the Devils Corkscrew to the Kaibab Suspension Bridge, which leads to Bright Angel Campground and Phantom Ranch. Mule rides return via the steeper 6¹/₂ mile (10 km) South Kaibab Trail to Yaki Point.

From the North Rim, the 14 mile (23 km) North Kaibab Trail circuit requires three days to complete, or you can link up with one of the South Rim trails for a cross-canyon hike.

When hiking in summer, carry at least 1 gallon (4.5 l) of drinking water per person per day, for temperatures reach over 100 degrees Fahrenheit (38° C) in the Inner Canyon. Reservations are required for Bright Angel Campground and Phantom Ranch, and for mule rides into the canyon.

As you descend into the canyon, desert plants become more plentiful. Rock gardens of cacti, agave, and creosote bush are common along the canyon walls. For most of the day, apart from golden eagles or ravens circling overhead, and warblers and hummingbirds flitting around canyon oases, wildlife is hard to see. At dawn and dusk,

A mule train climbing the South Kaibab Trail in the Inner Canyon (above). An Abert's tassel-eared squirrel sitting in a ponderosa pine (left).

however, the canyon comes alive, and chuckwallas, rattlesnakes, bighorn sheep, and, occasionally, mountain lions may be seen making their way along the ledges.

WHITEWATER RAFTING

For many, the ideal way to experience the canyon is on a whitewater river rafting trip. Licensed concessionaires operate trips April through October, starting at Lees Ferry in Marble Canyon, just below Glen Canyon Dam. Most trips end 225 miles (360 km) downriver, at Diamond Creek. Trips vary from 7 to 18 days, depending on whether they are motor or oar powered, and you camp on sandy beaches along the river. A list of operators is available from the park.

SM

The Colorado offers some of the most exciting river rafting in North America.

Saguaro National Monument

Arizona

Saguaro National Monument comprises two sections separated by the city of Tucson. Saguaro East is in the dramatic Rincon Mountains, with 75 miles (120 km) of trails ranging from the desert floor up to forests at altitudes of 9,000 feet (2,750 m). Saguaro West is in the Tucson Mountains, near the Tucson Desert Museum and Old Tucson, where many westerns have been filmed. The country here is studded by thousands of stately saguaros.

THE GIANT SAGUARO
The saguaro cactus is the senior member of this desert community. One saguaro fruit contains up to 2,000 seeds, but the odds are against their survival because they're a major source of food for many animals, particularly ants and mice.

Saguaros mature slowly, measuring only 1/4 inch (2.5 mm) at one year, sprouting their first arm at 75 years, and taking 150 years or more to reach 30 feet (10 m). Seedlings grow in the shade of rocks or trees such as mesquite or palo verde, where they are protected from extremes of temperature

and are hidden from animals. The accordion-like pleats store moisture in a gelatin-like substance and allow the plant to expand quickly to take in water through the roots. Waxy skin reduces moisture loss and thorns discourage animals from biting into the plant for moisture.

Mature saguaros bloom once a year, in May or June, each flower opening in the evening and wilting by the next afternoon. During the night, bats, birds, and insects pollinate the flowers.

The saguaro provides shelter for many desert inhabitants, much like an apartment building. Red-tailed hawks nest in branching arms and Gila woodpeckers excavate nesting holes, which are also used by owls and honeybees. These holes are markedly cooler in summer than the temperature outside, and warmer in winter.

The native Papago Indians depended on the saguaro for shelter, using the sturdy inner ribs for building, and they marked the beginning of their year by harvesting the fruits, which

A western rattlesnake preparing to strike.

they ate and from which they made jam, syrup, and wine.

The flora of this rich community has special adaptations for living in extreme temperatures. The ocotillo, for example, leafs out and flowers within hours of receiving rain. Other plants include creosote bush, and barrel, fishhook, and prickly pear cacti. Birds such as white-winged doves, Gambel's quail, Abert's towhees, and Costa's hummingbirds are active at dawn and dusk, but take cover from the midday heat. Most mammals and reptiles are active only at night, although they can sometimes be seen at dawn and dusk.

Saguaros in bloom (above). North America's tiniest owl, the elf owl (left).

They include bobcats, jack-rabbits, coyotes, cactus mice, sidewinders, Gila monsters, and many varieties of lizard.

Natural causes, such as freezing temperatures and high winds, are thought to be the main reasons for the decline of saguaros in the Tucson area, where the cacti are at the extreme northern and eastern edge of their range. In areas where saguaros are not protected, grazing is a major reason for the decline of saguaro forests because the cattle compact the ground with their hooves and trample seedlings. Unfortunately, vandalism and cactus rustling for gardens also continue to take a toll. SM

The Gila wood-pecker (left) makes its nest in mature saguaros.

TRAVELER'S NOTES

Information *Saguaro National Monument, 3693 South Old Spanish Trail, Tucson, AZ 85730-5601; tel. Visitor information 520-733-5153, Business offices 520-733-5100*

Hours *7 am–7 pm. Walk-in access 24 hours*

Visitor centers *Saguaro East and West: year-round, 8 am–5 pm. Information, permits*

Fees *Admission*

Permits *Backcountry camping*

Camping *5 backcountry campsites by permit; developed campsites in adjacent Coronado National Forest and Tucson Mountain County Park*

Lodging *I-10 Miracle Mile, Tucson*

Supplies *Tucson*

Access for people with disabilities *Wheelchair access at Saguaro E. visitor center, pullouts on Cactus Forest Drive and Desert Ecology Trail (Saguaro E.), Desert Discovery Trail (Saguaro W.)*

When to visit *Year-round, Mar–May peak wildflowers, Jun–Sept hot but excellent for wildlife at dawn and dusk*

Backcountry maps *USGS Tanque Verde, Mica Mountain, Avra*

Note *Always carry water when driving or hiking in the desert*

Bosque Del Apache National Wildlife Refuge

New Mexico

Birds are the great attraction at Bosque del Apache. Lying 90 miles (145 km) south of Albuquerque along the Rio Grande River, the refuge serves as the major wintering ground for thousands of snow geese, sandhill cranes, and ducks.

Spanish traders who traveled along El Camino Real, the historic route from Mexico to Santa Fé, named the region for the Apaches who used to camp in the woods that bordered the river. The refuge was established in 1939, preserving significant wetlands and woodlands in the Rio Grande Valley and high desert wilderness areas in the cactus-covered Chupadera and San Pascual mountains adjacent to the river valley. The climate is dry and relatively moderate year-round. Within the refuge's 57,000 acres (23,000 ha) some 320 species of bird, 51 kinds of mammal, 60 reptiles and amphibians, and 24 native fish have been recorded.

In this region of open country, each season brings its highlights. Summer is the breeding season, a time to observe teals, western painted turtles, spadefoot toads, whiptail lizards, and great horned owls. Spring and fall bring thousands of birds along the major migratory route of the Rio Grande River. Parades of sandpipers come through, and rufous and broad-tailed hummingbirds can be seen at the feeders outside the visitor center. Mule deer and coyotes are around throughout

Whooping cranes perform a courtship "dance" by jumping into the air and gracefully floating down.

In winter, red-winged blackbirds can be seen in huge flocks (above) and large numbers of sandhill cranes (below) come to the refuge.

TRAVELER'S NOTES

Information Refuge Manager, Bosque del Apache National Wildlife Refuge, PO Box 1246, Socorro, NM 87801; tel. (505) 835-1828

Hours Auto tour route open one hour before sunrise to one hour after sunset daily, year-round; Seasonal Tour Road Apr–Sep (same hours)

Visitor center Mon–Fri, 7.30 am–4 pm, Sat–Sun 8 am–4.30 pm, year-round

Fees Admission

Permits Fishing, hunting (state licenses)

Camping Primitive campsites for educational and volunteer groups only

Lodging Socorro, San Antonio

Supplies Socorro, San Antonio

Access for people with disabilities Visitor center, auto tour route

When to visit Year-round. Nov–Mar for huge numbers of waterbirds

the year, as well as roadrunners—a southwestern favorite.

Winter is the season when the refuge truly comes alive. At dawn, thousands of snow geese can be seen rising from the marshes and dropping into nearby fields. The 15 mile (24 km) auto tour takes you around marshes and ponds filled with ducks, cranes, ibis, herons, and shorebirds. Nearby black willow and cottonwood bosques serve as perches for numerous species of wintering birds of prey, including bald eagles.

ON THE BRINK OF EXTINCTION

You may be lucky enough to see the rare whooping crane among the many thousands of gray sandhill cranes. Many consider the whooping crane the most magnificent bird on the continent—a pure white bird with black wingtips, standing 5 feet (1.5 m) tall, and with a wingspan of 7 feet (2 m). At the time the refuge was created, only 17 sandhill cranes wintered there. Now as many as 17,000 sandhills and a small number of whooping cranes come for the winter.

These whooping cranes are offspring from an experiment that was begun in 1976, in which a number of whooping crane eggs were placed in sandhill crane nests in Idaho. At that time there were fewer than 100 whooping cranes and the species was on the verge of extinction. The protected lands of Bosque del Apache provide the critical wintering ground for this new population of whooping cranes.

If you visit in February, you may be fortunate enough to see both species of crane practicing their ritualized courtship dances for their northern breeding grounds. SM

165

Carlsbad Caverns National Park

New Mexico

Lying in the Chihuahuan Desert in the foothills of the Guadalupe Mountains, Carlsbad Caverns National Park contains the largest and most spectacular cavern system on the continent. Native Americans knew the cavern more than 1,000 years ago, but it wasn't until late in the nineteenth century that white settlers, curious about clouds of bats in the area, came across it. There are 80 caves within the park's nearly 47,000 acres (19,035 ha), but only Carlsbad Cavern and New Cave are open to the public.

UNDERGROUND MARVELS

The caverns are situated within a reef system (now fossilized) that existed over 250 million years ago in a huge inland sea. After the area was uplifted a few million years ago, forming the Guadalupe Mountains, rainwater seeped into the reef, forming passages in the lime- stone that eventually

Englemann's prickly pear (left).

became the vast chambers we see today. In turn, the dissolved lime- stone was deposited by the dripping water on the ceilings and floors of the caves, forming a wondrous array of decorations.

The size of Carlsbad Cavern is overwhelming. The full tour begins at the natural entrance, passing a huge cave where Mexican free-tailed bats sleep during the day. You then descend 830 feet (253 m) below the Earth's surface for about 1 mile (1.6 km), passing through a number of ornately decorated chambers. These lead to the Big Room, which can also be reached the easy way—by elevator from the visitor center.

The Big Room is immense. It has a ceiling as high as a 60-story building and a floor area that is equal to 14 football fields. There are elaborate decorations everywhere—stalagmites, stalactites, columns, draperies, flowstone, popcorn formations, cave pearls, twisting helictites, needle-like aragonite formations, and crystal lily pads floating on a cave pool.

In order to preserve these delicate treasures, you must not touch formations or step off the trails. Be sure to wear rubber-soled shoes and take a sweater, as the temperature year-round is 56 degrees Fahrenheit (13° C).

The Hall of Giants in the Big Room (above). Mexican free-tailed bats at the mouth of the cave (left).

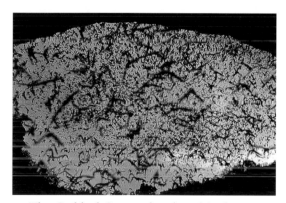

The Carlsbad Caverns bats breed in the region from May through October and migrate to Mexico for the winter. Their numbers have decreased over the years from a staggering 8 million to 300,000, but they still make an impressive dusk flight from the cavern. Their predawn return is equally striking, as they fold their wings and plummet into the cave from several hundred feet up. Look for cave swallows among the bats—uncommon migrants that also breed in the caverns.

The park has much to offer above ground as well. In this rich desert habitat, over 60 cactus varieties grow, along with desert shrubs and creosote bush. Higher up, on Guadalupe Ridge, the vegetation changes to agaves and ocotillos and then junipers and pines. There are 50 miles (80 km) of hiking trails in the mountains; make sure you have a map and carry plenty of water.

Mule deer, jack rabbits, rattlesnakes, and lizards can be seen along park roads at dawn and dusk. The Rattlesnake Springs oasis attracts colorful landbirds, such as the painted bunting. SM

TRAVELER'S NOTES

Information Superintendent, Carlsbad Caverns National Park, 3225 National Parks Highway, Carlsbad, NM 88220; tel. (505) 785-2232

Hours Carlsbad Cavern: daily, closed Dec 25 (Natural Entrance: 8.30 am–2 pm. Big Room: 8.30 am–3.30 pm). New Cave: ranger-led tour only, daily in summer, Sat–Sun rest of year

Visitor center Daily, 8 am–5.30 pm, closed Dec 25

Fees Admission, guided tours

Permits Backcountry
Camping Backcountry, Whites City
Lodging Whites City, Carlsbad
Supplies Whites City, Carlsbad
Access for people with disabilities Visitor center, Big Room, Bat Flight Amphitheater, Rattlesnake Springs
When to visit Year-round
Backcountry maps USGS Carlsbad Caverns, Serpentine Bends

Visitors to Carlsbad Caverns in the 1920s were lifted in and out in bat guano buckets. 167

Big Bend National Park

Texas

Spread over 1,250 square miles (3,200 sq km) in a remote corner of West Texas, Big Bend National Park is known for its spectacular geological formations and vast untouched desert and mountain habitats. It is named for the bend in the Rio Grande River which marks its southern border (and the border with Mexico). This mighty river has carved three magnificent limestone canyons within the park and three more downriver, which whitewater experts can travel through on rafting trips.

An inland sea once covered the area, and as the water receded, the layers of sediment hardened into rock, in which traces of shells and fossils have been preserved. (The most famous fossil is pterosaur—a huge flying dinosaur—found here in 1975.) Then came volcanic and mountain building activity, followed by erosion, and the region gradually assumed the form we see today.

AN ISLAND OF VEGETATION

The Chisos Mountains are an island of mountain vegetation surrounded by the Chihuahuan Desert. Many "south-of-the-border" species are found here and many endemic species have developed in the mountains. Biologists come here to study the desert and the rich wildlife: over 1,000 plant species, 435 species of bird, 78 species of mammal, and 66 species of reptile and amphibian have been recorded in the park.

The rare Lucifer hummingbird (above). Clumps of prickly pear line the banks of the Rio Grande in Santa Elena Canyon (left).

The Rio Grande at Hot Springs (above). A claretcup cactus in full bloom in the Chisos Mountains (left).

Rains in late summer and mild winter temperatures create lush vegetation around Rio Grande Village and rare Mexican bird species often stray here from over the border. The spectacular canyons adjacent to the floodplain echo with the song of the canyon wren and the call of nesting peregrine falcons.

The road to the mountains crosses the desert, where agaves, ocotillo, and many types of cactus grow. At dawn and dusk you might see a herd of collared peccaries (wild pigs), or a rattlesnake. At about 3,500 feet (1,060 m), the vegetation changes to yuccas, grasses, and tall shrubs, their flowers attracting Scott's orioles and the rare Lucifer hummingbird. South of Persimmon Gap, Dagger Flat is a spectacular sight, filled with giant dagger yuccas, which are even more striking when crowned with flower stalks.

High in the park's heart lies the Chisos Basin, and from the Window Trail (named for the V-shaped notch in the west side) you can see towering peaks and spires and spot varied buntings and gray-breasted jays in the pinyon pines and junipers. In summer, the basin is bright with wildflowers.

Trails lead from the basin into the higher mountains, where moist woodlands of big-tooth maple and ponderosa pine grow in the canyons. The 11 mile (18 km) loop trail to Boot Springs is popular with birders, who come looking for nesting Colima warblers—the only spot in which they're found north of Mexico. SM

TRAVELER'S NOTES

Information Big Bend National Park, PO Box 129, Big Bend National Park, TX 79834; tel. (915) 477-2251

Hours Always open

Visitor center Panther Junction, year-round, 8 am–6 pm. Facilities also at Rio Grande Village, The Basin, and Persimmon Gap; same hours

Fees Admission, camping

Permits Backcountry camping, river rafting

Camping Chisos Basin (62 sites); Rio Grande Village (99 sites); Cottonwood (primitive); 1 RV park, Rio Grande Village; backcountry campsites

Lodging Chisos Mountains Lodge (915) 477-2291; Study Butte, Marathon

Supplies Panther Junction, Chisos Basin, Rio Grande Village, Castolon

Access for people with disabilities Visitor center at Panther Junction, Window View Trail

When to visit Year-round. Peak season Rio Grande Village Nov–Apr, Chisos Basin Jun–Aug

Backcountry maps USGS Big Bend National Park

Padre Island National Seashore

Texas

The Gulf coast of Texas is bordered by a string of long, narrow barrier islands. Padre Island is the most magnificent of these, extending 80 miles (130 km) along the central and lower Texas coast from Corpus Christi to Port Mansfield. Padre Island National Seashore preserves one of the longest stretches of pristine ocean beach on the continent, backed by majestic windswept sand dunes, 30 to 40 feet (9 to 12 m) high. Grasslands and tidal flats border the western shores of the island, which is separated from the mainland by a long, shallow lagoon—Laguna Madre. A deep canal for boat traffic (the Intracoastal Waterway) runs through the lagoon, and there is limited access to the island for boats, bicycles, and cars. However, most of Padre Island can only be explored on foot.

The climate here is hot and humid in summer, cooler in winter. The weather

Black-tailed jack rabbit

of the Gulf of Mexico constantly shapes Padre Island. Winds sculpt the dunes, waves bring in new shells daily, and storms sometimes form new channels through the island. In fact, the island is slowly growing toward the mainland. Pioneer plants, such as sea oats, take root, then sand is blown toward them, gradually forming huge dunes. By degrees, other plants begin growing on the dunes, and, in time, beach grasslands are formed.

The various habitats that make up Padre Island are home to a fascinating array of wildlife. Bottlenose dolphins and many species of saltwater fish live in

Sea oats grow among the sand dunes.

The pristine sands along the ocean shoreline of Padre Island (above). A bottlenose dolphin (left). In April, sea turtles (below) come ashore to lay their eggs on the beaches.

the gulf waters. The beaches are inhabited by ghost crabs and Wilson's plovers, and loggerhead sea turtles return to the shore each April to lay their eggs. A surprising number of species, including coyotes, jack rabbits, lizards, and western diamondback rattlesnakes are found in the grasslands and dunes. The lagoon is a fertile breeding ground for saltwater fish and its tidal flats are feeding grounds for shorebirds. Its spoil islands (islands formed from material dredged from the canal) provide nesting and resting sites for skimmers, gulls, herons, and pelicans.

SPRING ACTIVITY

In spring, waterbirds perform courtship dances, and waves of migrating shorebirds pass through the area, fueling up on Laguna Madre's tidal flats. Tiny landbirds that winter in Central and South America and breed in eastern and midwestern North America migrate across the gulf in April

and May. If storms occur, as they usually do, large numbers of colorful warblers, tanagers, and other landbirds take refuge in the island's vegetation—a phenomenon known as "fallout"

The dunes and beach grasslands are fragile and can easily be destroyed, so hiking or driving on them is prohibited. You are allowed to drive along the hard, wet sand on the beach, but be sure to check the conditions with the visitor center before setting off. **SM**

TRAVELER'S NOTES

Information *Padre Island National Seashore, P.O. Box 181300, 20301 Park Road 22, Corpus Christi, TX 78480; tel. 361-949-8068., Corpus Christi Information Center, tel. (800) 678-6232*

Hours *Always open*

Visitor center *Malaquite Beach, Padre Island: daily, 9 am–4 pm, closed Thanksgiving, Dec 25, Jan 1; tel. (361) 949-8068*

Fees *Admission, camping*

Permits *Backcountry use, fishing (state license)*

Camping *Malaquite Beach Campground (40 sites); Yarborough Pass (primitive)*

Lodging *Corpus Christi*

Supplies *Corpus Christi*

Access for people with disabilities *Visitor center, beaches*

When to visit *Year-round; spring–summer peak; tropical storms Jun–Oct*

Backcountry maps *USGS Padre Island National Seashore*

Santa Ana/Lower Rio Grande National Wildlife Refuges

Texas

The Lower Rio Grande Valley is the fertile floodplain of the Rio Grande River. Its boundaries extend south from Falcon Dam to the Gulf of Mexico and northward to Raymondville. Most of the area is now farmed, but remnants of native habitat are preserved in Santa Ana and Lower Rio Grande Valley National Wildlife Refuges and adjacent parks. Many tropical and subtropical species reach their northern limit here.

Giant toads are up to 6 inches (15 cm) long.

BIOLOGICALLY MEXICAN
Lying in the center of the valley, Santa Ana National Wildlife Refuge is 2,080 acres (840 ha) of subtropical gallery forest—a mature forest of huge Texas ebonies and jungle-like thickets of willows and mesquite— that was set aside in 1943. There are also three lakes within its boundaries. More Mexican than North American biologically, the refuge acts as a magnet for naturalists.

Over 370 species of bird have been recorded here, and because of the subtropical climate there is a large resident population. The Mississippi and Central flyways (see p. 239) converge north of the valley, funneling thousands of migrating hawks into the area in March and April. In spring and summer, colorful tropical birds breed in the refuge, including green jays, buff-bellied hummingbirds, altamira orioles, and green kingfishers. The dawn chorus is unlike any other north of the border, with turkey-like

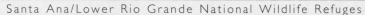

plain chachalacas calling loudly. Fall and winter bring mild temperatures, additional wintering birds, and wandering Mexican rarities.

Mammals and reptiles include jaguarundis, nine-banded armadillos, ocelots, Texas tortoises, and coral snakes. After summer rains, you will find amphibians everywhere, including the giant toad—North America's largest toad.

A REFUGE IN THE MAKING
Introduced species, such as house sparrows and starlings, and expanding species, such as cowbirds, are now common in the valley's agricultural areas, and the habitat for native species has shrunk to islands of vegetation. The Lower Rio Grande Valley National Wildlife Refuge has been set up to protect some of these remaining patches of habitat in Starr, Hidalgo, Willacy, and Cameron counties, and currently these areas are not open to the public. A refuge in the making, the aim is to acquire 132,400 acres (53,600 ha) of land to represent the various kinds of native habitat in

An observation blind (above). Mexican mammals, such as the ocelot (below), wander into Santa Ana, but are difficult to see.

the valley, ranging from palm forest to tidal flats, and to establish wildlife corridors between them.

A number of nearby reserves are also worth visiting, including the National Audubon Society's Sabal Palm Grove Sanctuary, the Laguna Atascosa National Wildlife Reserve, the Bentsen–Rio Grande State Park, and the Falcon Dam area (where Mexican brown jays can sometimes be seen below the dam). SM

TRAVELER'S NOTES

Information Refuge Manager, Santa Ana/Rio Grande Valley National Wildlife Refuges, Route 2, Box 202A, Alamo, TX 78516; tel. (956) 787-3079

Hours Pedestrian and bicycle access daily, sunrise to sunset; closed Thanksgiving, Dec 25, Jan 1. Contact refuge manager to obtain details about private vehicle access and the times when the tram is operating

Visitor center Mon-Fri 8 am–4.30 pm; Sat, Sun, and holidays 9 am–4.30 pm; closed Thanksgiving, Dec 25, Jan 1

Fees Interpretive tram tour

Permits None

Camping Bentsen–Rio Grande State Park (fee), Falcon State Park (fee)

Lodging Brownsville, McAllen

Supplies Brownsville, McAllen

Access for people with disabilities Visitor center and Trail A leading to Willow Lake are wheelchair accessible. Wheelchair birding tours are run during the winter months

When to visit Year-round. Breeding season spring and summer. Fall and winter excellent for viewing resident species and Mexican rarities

Green jay.

173

Isle Royale
NP

Voyageurs NP

Pictured Rocks NL

N D A K O T A

Theodore
Roosevelt
NP
Bismarck

M I N N E S O T A

W I S C O N S I N

M I C H I G A N

S D A K O T A

Minneapolis

Chicago

Indiana
Dunes NL

I O W A

O H I O

NEBRASKA

Des Moines

I L L I N O I S

I N D I A N A

Kansas City

St Louis

K A N S A S

M I S S O U R I

Shawnee NF

Ozark NSR

Tallgrass Prairie P

O K L A H O M A

Oklahoma City

Wichita Mountains
NWR

0	100	200	miles
0	200	400	km

The Midwest and Great Plains

Shawnee National Forest

Illinois

In southern Illinois, cradled in the arms of the Mississippi and Ohio rivers, lies Shawnee National Forest. Here, quite abruptly, the incessant sun and distant horizons of the prairie give way to shade, intimate spaces, and dramatic precipices.

The 270,000 acres (110,000 ha) of the forest sprawl across a bulwark of sandstone ridges overlooking an area once covered with swamp forest. More than 95 percent of these lowlands have been drained for agriculture, but significant remnants, such as LaRue Swamp and Heron Pond, are protected.

DRY HILLS AND SWAMPS

Shawnee is a plant lover's paradise. You can stand on high, dry hills amid shortleaf pines, then drive a few miles to an emerald-green swamp picketed with tupelo and baldcypress.

The 2,000 acre (810 ha) LaRue Swamp–Pine Hills area, not far from the town of Wolf Lake, harbors 43 percent of all the known plant species found in Illinois.

There are 20 species of oak and 10 of hickory in the forest, and magnificent stands of beech, yellow poplar, and sugar maple. At Bell Smith Springs on Bay Creek and Indian Kitchen on Lusk Creek (both near Eddyville) you can hike through hardwood forests amid vast formations of eroding sandstone.

Understory wildflowers, including trillium, mayapple, rue anemone, and wild ginger usually

Dogwood blossom (left). The flute-like song of the wood thrush (right) is a distinctive sound in Shawnee.

bloom in late April, which is when songbirds such as wood thrush, Carolina wren, northern parula, and eastern wood-pewee are in full voice. Dogwood and redbud are at their blossoming peak in the middle of May and fragrant native azaleas bloom later in the month.

Looking across the forest (above). The Rimrock Trail leads to some of the forest's most remarkable geological formations (left). The northern parula (below left) favors swampy country.

There is also a considerable amount of hot, exposed rock within the forest. Prickly pear, Illinois agave, flower-of-an-hour, and several rare species of lichen thrive on these rocky outcrops. Miniature prairies, known as barrens, also flourish on south-facing, well-drained slopes.

Hiking at Garden of the Gods, Rimrock–Pounds Hollow (both near Karbers Ridge), and Little Grand Canyon (not far from Carbondale) will show you the forest's sunnier side, with weirdly eroded bluffs and views across the forested hills. Prairie wildflowers, such as purple coneflower, butterfly weed, and black-eyed Susan, are a glorious sight at Simpson Township Barrens during June and July, and the stands of prairie grass turn golden as the weather becomes cooler.

At sundown and well into the night, yipping coyote choruses can be heard throughout the forest, and bats flit against the twilight sky. The most common of these are the eastern pipistrelle and the little brown bat, but the forest also provides sanctuary for three endangered species—the Indiana bat, the gray bat, and Rafinesque's big-eared bat.

TRAVELER'S NOTES

Information *Supervisor, Shawnee National Forest, 901 S. Commercial St, Harrisburg, IL 62946; tel. (618) 253-7114. District offices in Elizabethtown, Vienna, Jonesboro, Murphysboro*

Hours *Always open*

Visitor center *None. National Forest offices will supply information and maps*

Fees *Certain camping areas*

Permits *Hunting, fishing (state licenses)*

Camping *17 campgrounds (400+ sites). Camping limited to 14 days*

Lodging *Carbondale, Marion, Harrisburg*

Supplies *Carbondale, Marion, Harrisburg*

Access for people with disabilities *Green Tree Reservoir Interpretive Trail near Gorham*

When to visit *May–June, Oct*

Backcountry maps *USGS Gorham, Wolfe Lake, Waltersburg, Eddyville, Karbers Ridge, Stonefort, Herod, Rudement, Glendale, Vienna and vicinity*

Indiana Dunes National Lakeshore

Indiana

From places along Indiana Dunes National Lakeshore you can see signs of Gary and even Chicago on the Lake Michigan horizon. This view of urban development provides a poignant reminder of what this national treasure might have become, had not a successful grassroots campaign helped to preserve it. Indiana Dunes is home to more than 1,400 plant species. This constitutes more plant species per acre than in any other area administered by the National Park Service and the third largest number of plant species in any park.

Here, in the 1890s, Dr Henry Chandler Cowles introduced the concept of ecology through his studies of succession—the changes that take place in plant communities as they develop toward maturity. At Indiana Dunes, succession begins with the grasses that anchor the huge, golden dunes that hug Lake Michigan's shores. Among the world's highest freshwater dunes, they form a dramatic backdrop for the park's broad sandy beaches and the immense lake.

During the heat of summer, lolling on the shore is a delightful way to experience the park. The rolling waves and cool waters are a perfect complement to the sun-baked beaches. In fall, the lake changes to match the season, becoming choppy in brisk weather and a maelstrom when storms roll in.

INLAND HABITATS

Moving away from the lake, dune grasses provide footholds for the succession of plants that follow: beach pea and other wildflowers,

In the forests, listen for the distinctive scratching of rufous-sided towhees (left) foraging in the leaf litter for food. Beach pea (above) is among the wildflowers that grow on the sand dunes.

The massive dunes along the shore of Lake Michigan (above). A damsel fly on a sundew (right). Pink lady's-slipper orchid (below).

low shrubs such as juniper and sand cherry, then larger shrubs, and finally trees—mostly cottonwoods and oaks.

The ancient lake bed and eroded dunes of a much earlier and larger predecessor of Lake Michigan comprise the parkland. Beech-maple climax forests shade the flatter areas, oak savannas provide airy cover on the hills, and marshes, ponds, and bogs fill low-lying areas between ancient, forest-covered dunes. The park even includes a piece of prairie, precious because so few areas of America's native grasslands remain.

With such plant diversity, Indiana Dunes is flush with birdlife, ranging from forest dwellers, such as towhees and woodpeckers, to ducks, gulls, and other waterfowl.

At this crossroads of American plant life, perhaps the strangest places are Cowles and Pinhook bogs. A relic of the last ice age, Pinhook contains quaking mats of sphagnum moss and plants usually found much farther north, such as tamarack and white pine. The bog is also rich in rare and unusual plants, including insect-eating sundews and pitcher plants as well as yellow fringed and pink lady's-slipper orchids. MS

TRAVELER'S NOTES

Information *Superintendent, Indiana Dunes National Lakeshore, 1100 N. Mineral Springs Rd, Porter, IN 46304-1299; tel. and fax (219) 926-7561*

Hours *Always open*

Visitor center *US 12 and Kemil Rd. Publications, permits*

Fees *Campgrounds, access to West Beach*

Permits *Fishing*

Camping *1 campground (54 sites), 25 walk-in sites*

Lodging *Michigan City, Chesterton, Porter*

Supplies *Michigan City, Chesterton, Porter*

Access for people with disabilities *All facilities, some campsites*

When to visit *Spring for bird migration; summer for swimming, beaches*

Backcountry maps *USGS Indiana Dunes National Seashore*

Isle Royale National Park

Michigan

The largest island in the world's largest lake, Isle Royale National Park is closer to Canadian shores than to its home state of Michigan. No roads or cars sully this Lake Superior island, and its 100,000 plus acres (over 40,500 ha) are almost all designated wilderness. The fact that visitors can reach Isle Royale only by boat or seaplane also makes it one of the least-visited and most pristine parks in the Midwest.

This 45 mile (70 km) long, 9 mile (14.5 km) wide island is shaped like a long, keeled boat, flanked by

A lone hiker on Minong Ridge.

narrow "outrigger" islands. Extruded more than a billion years ago from the lava flows that formed the Lake Superior basin, Isle Royale's greenstone rock is some of the oldest in North America. The island's most recent sculpting took place 10,000 years ago when glaciers gouged holes that filled with water, creating dozens of lakes.

ISLAND LIFE

Plants gradually colonized Isle Royale and now the lands bordering Lake Superior are rich with northern boreal forest. Spruce, paper birch, and sweet-scented balsam form a shadowed refuge for carpets of wildflowers and ferns. In all, more than 700 species of plant, including 32 types of orchid, are found here. Cloaked with sugar maple and yellow birch, the island's warmer interior ridges are accessible by some of the park's 166 miles (267 km) of trails. The island's rocky coast is ringed by crashing surf, and the cries of loons and a host of other water-fowl can be heard through the fogs that roll in.

Caribou and coyote once inhabited Isle Royale, but the former were probably hunted out by white settlers and the latter out-competed by wolves. The species that replaced them—the wolf and the moose—have been the focus of

Boats and feet are the only modes of transport in this remote island park (above).

North America's longest-running wildlife study, which began in 1958. In the early 1900s, moose reached the island, probably swimming the 15 miles (24 km) from Canada. With no predators, their numbers soared, then crashed as forage ran short. In the winter of 1949, a pack of gray wolves crossed the ice from Canada and became the moose population's predatory control. Now the two species are engaged in a delicately balanced dance of survival.

HUMAN ACTIVITIES

Indigenous peoples mined copper on Isle Royale some 4,500 years ago. More recently, the island was Chippewa territory, claimed in 1671 by the French, then in 1783 by the United States. Modern copper mining spanned the second half of the nineteenth century and, although the island became a national park in 1940, signs of mining, including mines and abandoned equipment, are still to be found. MS

TRAVELER'S NOTES

Information Isle Royale National Park, 800 East Lakeshore Drive, Houghton, MI 49931; tel. (906) 482-0984

Hours Mid-May to mid-Oct, 24 hrs

Visitor center 87 North Ripley St, Houghton, MI: Mon–Sat, 8 am–4.30 pm. Boat tickets, permits, publications

Fees None

Permits Camping, fishing (state license), scuba diving

Camping 36 campgrounds (245 sites)

Lodging Winter Contact: National Park Concessions, Inc., General Offices, P.O. Box 77, Mammoth Cave, KY 42259-0027; Summer Contact: National Park Concessions, Inc., P.O. Box 605, Houghton, MI 49931-0605, May–Sept: (502) 773-2191, Sept–May (270) 773-2191

Supplies Rock Harbor, Windigo

Access for people with disabilities Some lodge rooms, camping shelters

When to visit June–Sept

Backcountry maps USGS Isle Royale National Park

Note Purchase boat, seaplane tickets in advance

Researchers monitor wolf and moose populations, which reflect the delicate balance between predator (below) and prey (above left).

Pictured Rocks National Lakeshore

Michigan

After the monochromatic blue of vast Lake Superior, seventeenth-century French *voyageurs* may well have been dazzled by the riot of color when they reached what is now known as Pictured Rocks National Lakeshore. Running more than 40 miles (65 km) along the Lake Superior shores of Michigan's Upper Peninsula, Pictured Rocks was designated in 1966 as the nation's first national lakeshore. It was selected for its sandstone wonders, but Pictured Rocks has much more to offer than these parti-colored cliffs.

Although only 3 miles (5 km) wide, this long strand shelters streams, rivers, and waterfalls; more than half a dozen lakes; and the majestic Grand Sable Dunes, which are among the country's finest perched dunes. Behind the beaches and cliffs lie hardwood forests that glow red and yellow in fall. Winter brings an average of 17 feet (5 m) of snow, and the dozens of miles of hiking trails become serene cross-country ski trails. In spring, before maple, beech, and birch leaf out, drifts of wildflowers color the forest floors. Munising Falls slips smoothly over a rock ledge, dropping into a fern-hung rock gorge.

Although Lake Superior is generally too cold for swimming even in summer, a hike out to Twelve-mile Beach brings visitors to a stretch of peaceful, uncluttered sands. Farther along the shore lies historic Au Sable Light Station. Another highlight is Sand Point Marsh Trail. This interpretive boardwalk winds past swampy areas filled with leatherleaf and other swamp shrubs; past pink lady's-slipper orchids; past

Surf breaking along Grand Sable Dunes.

The Lake Superior shoreline at Miners Castle (above). Moss covers a fallen tree in a forest of sugar maples (left).

LIGHT ON THE ROCKS

The park's gems—the Pictured Rocks—are best saved for the end of the afternoon, when the light of the setting sun intensifies their colors. Deposited more than 500 million years ago, when plants were just beginning to colonize the Earth's land masses, these soaring walls of multicolored sandstone were most recently exposed and carved by ice-age glaciers.

In boats or sea-kayaks, visitors can float past Miners Castle with its intricate battlements; Indian Head Rock; Broken Flowerpot; and the imposing stone prows of Battleship Row. Viewing these mineral-stained rocks of pale blue and onyx, green and ocher, pink and rusty red, provides a capstone to a trip along this varied stretch of shoreline. MS

The best way to see the sandstone glories of Pictured Rocks is from the water.

beaver lodges and the trails beavers have cleared through the flora-filled waters; past tamarack, black spruce, and other water-loving conifers.

TRAVELER'S NOTES

Information Superintendent, Pictured Rocks National Lakeshore, P.O. Box 40, N8391 Sand Point Rd, Munising, MI 49862-0040; tel: (906) 387-3700

Hours Always open

Visitor centers Munising: Summer, Mon–Sun, 8 am–6 pm. Winter, Mon–Sat, 9 am–4 pm. Publications, permits. Grand Sable (10 am–6 pm), Munising Falls (8.30 am–4 pm), summer only

Fees Camping

Permits Backcountry camping, scuba diving; fishing, hunting (state licenses)

Camping 3 campgrounds (67 sites), 70+ backcountry sites

Lodging Munising, Grand Marais

Supplies Munising, Grand Marais

Access for people with disabilities 2 trails, visitor centers, campsites

When to visit Spring for wildflowers, summer generally, winter for skiing, fall for foliage colors

Backcountry maps USGS Au Sable Point, Grand Marais, Grand Portal Point, Grand Sable Lake, Melstrand, Munising, Trappers Lake, Wood Island SE

Voyageurs National Park

Minnesota

Named after the early French-Canadian fur traders who made their way across much of the continent by canoe, Voyageurs National Park covers 219,000 acres (88,700 ha) of wilderness on the Canadian border. Water covers one-third of the park, in the form of 30 small lakes, large areas of four major ones, and numerous ponds, streams, and bogs. There are no roads—except for an "ice road" that crosses Rainy Lake in winter—and few trails. Most of this forested region is accessible only by boat or canoe, including the largest area of land, the Kabetogama Peninsula. The park is part of an extensive wilderness complex: to the east stretches the Boundary Waters Canoe Area and Ontario's Quetico Provincial Park.

The park's lakes and ponds are products of ice-age glaciers. At least four times in the last million years, vast ice sheets bulldozed across the rocks of the Canadian Shield, on which the park lies. They scraped the rocks flat, leaving scratch-marked depressions which filled with water and around which forests subsequently became established. The forest is the southern-most fringe of the boreal forest that stretches northward toward the tundra. Trees include black spruce, white spruce, white pine, aspens, and the birches from which the *voyageurs* made their canoes. In summer there are blueberries, cranberries, and tiny wild strawberries.

A replica of a voyageur's canoe used for tours of Rainy Lake. The park adjoins a 56 mile (90 km) section of the 3,000 mile (4,830 km) waterway that was used by these hardy fur traders.

Kabetogama Lake (above). Cattails seeding at the water's edge (left). A gray wolf and pup (below).

WOLF COUNTRY

About 200 black bears live in Voyageurs, and moose feed on shrubs and saplings in the park's ponds, streams, and bogs. There are considerable numbers of beavers, coyotes, white-tailed deer, and otters, and the park lies in one of the few areas south of the Canadian border where wolves can be heard at night.

About 1,200 gray, or timber, wolves roam northern Minnesota and a few adjacent areas of northern Wisconsin. Up to 40 of them range through the park, preying on deer and moose. Some people believe that wolves reduce the number of game animals and many farmers are prejudiced against them because they fear losing livestock. Studies have shown, however, that wolves prey on ill or old animals, thus serving a useful purpose by culling the prey population.

TRAVELER'S NOTES

Information *Superintendent, Voyageurs National Park, 3131 Highway 53, International Falls, MN 56649-8904; tel. (218) 283-9821*

Hours *Always open*

Visitor centers *Rainy Lake: May 13–Oct 9, 9 am–5 pm, check for winter hours. Kabetogama Lake: May 14–Sept 30, 9 am–5 pm. Ash River: May 14–Aug 31, 10 am–5 pm. Navigational charts, films, maps, exhibits, activity schedules, parking, boat ramps*

Fees *None*

Permits *Fishing (state license)*

Camping *100 sites with canoe or boat access, pit toilet. 400 primitive sites*

Lodging *Island View, Kabetogama, Ash River, Crane Lake, International Falls*

Supplies *Island View, Kabetogama, Ash River, Crane Lake, International Falls*

Access for people with disabilities *Visitor centers, a few campsites have chair lifts*

When to visit *Summer for boating, wildlife. Winter for cross-country skiing*

Backcountry maps *USGS Voyageurs National Park*

Note *Canadian Customs at Portage Bay, Sand Point Lake, Sand Bay, Rainy Lake. US Customs at Crane Lake Landing, International Falls Bridge*

185

Wolves also keep prey numbers in balance, preventing starvation, destruction of plants, and the spread of disease. Although gray wolves are protected under the Endangered Species Act, people continue to kill them, not always by accident. Others fall victim to diseases such as canine parvo-virus, which is why pets are prohibited on the park's trails and in the backcountry. Wolves are wary, so visitors seldom have the opportunity to see them.

There are some spectacular bird species at Voyageurs, such as the American bald eagle. Ospreys can be seen plunging into the water from great heights and then rising with fish in their talons. About 25 pairs of osprey live in the park, often building their large stick nests on dead trees in beaver ponds. They are often pursued and harassed by eagles into dropping the fish they have just caught, and the eagles then consume the meal themselves.

Great blue herons also nest in trees drowned by beaver dams, and there are three heron nesting colonies within the park. Many other species of aquatic bird spend time at Voyageurs, although most, like the herons, fly south before the winter ice sets in. White pelicans congregate on the small, rocky islands in the lakes, and you have an excellent chance of seeing kingfishers, mergansers, loons, and cormorants.

TRAILS AND CANOE ROUTES

The best time for hiking is late summer and early fall. (In spring, the abundance of biting insects can be a problem.) The two main trails on the peninsula are accessible by crossing Kabetogama Lake. The Locator Lake Nature Trail is a 2 mile (3 km) round trip from the northwest shore, leading to Locator Lake with its steep cliffs. The Cruiser Lake Trail, which is 10 miles (16 km) long, crosses the peninsula from Lost Bay to Anderson Bay on Rainy Lake.

For enthusiastic canoeists, the 68 mile (110 km) Kabetogama Peninsula Loop takes them around the peninsula, usually requiring from five to seven days. Portages are required at the Kettle Falls dam and at Gold Portage.

A maple seedling growing between lichen-covered rocks.

The rich fall colors of the northern woods reflected in the waters of Kabetogama Lake (left). Namakan Lake (above), shared by boaters and loons. Bald eagles (below) build their large, bulky nests high in white pine trees.

At Kettle Falls there is the hotel of the same name, built in 1913 to serve trappers, traders, and lumberjacks. Now restored, it provides a link with the park's logging past.

One fine way to see Rainy Lake and learn more about the region's history and wildlife is to join the North Canoe Voyage, which departs from the Rainy Lake Visitor Center. Costumed guides and naturalists take passengers on a fascinating tour of the lake in a replica of a canoe used by the original *voyageurs*. ER

THE RETURN OF THE BALD EAGLE

As you walk along the lake shores at Voyageurs, scan the sky and the higher branches of white pines for bald eagles. Protected by the Endangered Species Act, these fine birds have made a remarkable comeback in recent years.

Adult eagles return to the park from southern wintering areas in the middle of March, to begin their nesting cycle. At Voyageurs they usually nest within 5 to 15 feet (1.5 to 4.5 m) of the top of tall white pines. Mated for life, a pair will return to the same nest annually, enlarging it year after year.

They lay their eggs—one to three of them—in late March and early April.

Nesting bald eagles are very sensitive to disturbance, so if you see eagles on a nest, stay at least a quarter of a mile away and watch them through binoculars. Picnic areas and campsites near active nests may be temporarily closed and will be clearly marked.

The eggs hatch around the middle of May and the young fledge in late July and August. In October, the adults and young leave the park, beginning their migration south.

Primarily aquatic creatures, river otters are also at ease on land.

187

Ozark National Scenic Riverways

Missouri

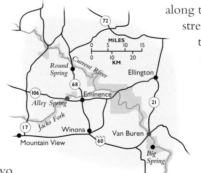

Down in the southeast corner of Missouri lie the Ozarks—a dense cluster of steep but modest mountains clad in hardwood forest. The foundation of this landscape is dolomite, a type of limestone. A network of natural springs bubbles up through fissures and channels in this porous rock to create two small, exquisite rivers—the Current and Jacks Fork. Although there are small settlements

Wild turkey.

along their banks, these are clean streams that flow freely. To preserve their beauty and keep them accessible for recreation, the National Park Service has assembled numerous land parcels along the river channels to form the Scenic Riverways.

FLOAT TRIPS

The best way to experience these riverways is by floating—either using a canoe (the most popular choice), a johnboat (a flat-bottomed craft, usually with an outboard motor), or an inner tube. As the rivers meander 134 miles (216 km) through oak and hickory forest, they change with every turn, sometimes breezing along, then slowing into glassy pools, or churning into riffles. Some stretches are walled by gray dolomite bluffs, rising 100 feet (30 m) or more straight from the water. Just beyond the sycamores lining the banks, groves of dogwood and redbud bloom in spring, and songbird serenades harmonize with the rivers' burbling. The riverways boast the greatest variety of birdlife in the state.

No float trip would be complete without pausing to wonder at some of the many springs that spawn these rivers. Big Spring,

The tranquil Current River (above). The mill at Alley Spring (left).

on the Current just downriver from Van Buren, is one of the largest in the world. It pumps out an average of 276 million gallons (1,213 million l) a day in a colossal dome of water erupting from the base of a dolomite bluff. Blue Spring, near Powder Mill, is a striking indigo color and discharges 90 million gallons (410 million l) a day into the river.

The largest spring on the Jacks Fork is Alley Spring, which churns to the surface from the base of a 100 foot (30 m) bluff, welling up in a large pool. At one time, the nearby mill used power generated by the spring to grind grain. It is now open to visitors.

Round Spring, on the Current, 13 miles (21 km) north of Eminence, is a small, sky-blue jewel. Round Spring Cave, one of the area's many caverns, can be explored on ranger-led tours. Visitors carry flashlights to see the colorful stalactites, stalagmites, and flowstones. EW

TRAVELER'S NOTES

Information Superintendent, Ozark National Scenic Riverways, National Park Service, Box 490, Van Buren, MO 63965; tel. 573-323-4236, fax 573-323-4140

Hours Always open

Visitor centers Park headquarters, Van Buren; daily, 8 am–5 pm, Memorial Day–Labor Day except federal holidays. Publications, audiovisual programs, talks, permits. Alley Spring Mill; daily, 9 am–5 pm, Memorial Day–Labor Day except federal holidays. Publications, talks

Fees Camping, cave tours

Permits Fishing, hunting (state licenses)

Camping 7 campgrounds (531 sites). Also camping on riverbanks

Lodging Cabins at Big Spring. Motels at Alley Spring, Van Buren, Eminence, Mountain View, Winona, Birch Tree

Supplies Stores at Akers, Pulltite, Alley Spring, Round Spring, Two Rivers. Gas at Round Spring. Food and gas at Van Buren, Eminence, Salem, Mountain View, Winona

Access for people with disabilities Park headquarters and Alley Spring Mill. Picnic grounds at Round, Big, and Alley Springs. Campgrounds at Alley and Big Springs. Fishing ramp near Baptist on Current River

When to visit Spring, fall. Water levels higher after spring rains. Mid–late Oct for full colors. Summer busy

Note Exploring caves can be dangerous and should only be attempted by experienced spelunkers

Mink hunt in ponds and streams.

189

Theodore Roosevelt National Park

North Dakota

A monument to a great conservationist, Theodore Roosevelt National Park consists of two units of land together comprising around 70,500 acres (28,550 ha). They are approximately 70 miles (110 km) apart, straddling the remote Little Missouri River, with Roosevelt's Elkhorn Ranch lying between them. The South Unit contains some of the finest parts of the North Dakota badlands—a rugged, surrealistic landscape carved out by wind and water.

Squaw Creek

NORTH UNIT

Grassy Butte

ELKHORN
RANCH SITE

MILES
0   5   10

0   10
KM

SOUTH UNIT   85

94   Painted
Medora   Canyon   Belfield
                              Dickinson

FRONTIER COUNTRY

The park is a superb place in which to see large mammals. Six big game species found in the region in the days when Roosevelt ranched here are in evidence: white-tailed deer, mule deer, elk, bison, bighorn sheep, and pronghorn. Elk, bison, and bighorn sheep, which had vanished from the park, have been reestablished.

Bison roam the North Unit and frequent the area around Ridgeline Trail, a short nature trail in the South Unit. Spotting bighorn sheep is a chancy affair, however, as they have not flourished since they were reintroduced. The South Unit herd is kept in a large enclosure, off the road. A few sheep are allowed to roam freely in the North Unit, but are difficult to find. Elk may be seen in the South Unit.

The park is one of the few remaining places where free-roaming mustangs can be seen easily. The southeastern area of the South Unit supports between 50 and 90 of them, descendants of domesticated animals that escaped years ago. Small groups of mustang can often be seen from Interstate 94, along the park's southern

A bull bison in the Theodore Roosevelt badlands.

boundary and, in summer, from the uplands of the Painted Canyon Overlook or Buck Hill.

Vegetation in the park is surprisingly varied. There are hardwood and juniper draws, sagebrush flats, bottomland forests, and areas of true native prairie. In the Ridgeline Trail area, silver sage, prickly pear cactus, and narrowleaf yuccas grow. The stringy veins and needles of this yucca were once used as needle and thread by Native Americans.

The mixture of habitats in the park enables mule deer and white-tailed deer to live here, as they did in Roosevelt's time. The grasslands are dotted with herds of pronghorn, the fleetest animal on the western plains.

Among the burrowing residents are black-tailed prairie dogs and badgers, and there are several prairie dog towns in the park. One of the easiest to reach is along the Scenic Loop Drive in the South Unit. Abandoned prairie dog burrows are used as nests by burrowing owls, and prairie rattlesnakes also shelter in them.

The park is not a great spot for birding, but Bohemian waxwings visit in winter, mountain

Black-tailed prairie dogs are among the park's smaller residents.

The Little Missouri River (above), seen from Wind Canyon Trail in the early morning. A buck pronghorn (right).

bluebirds can be seen from spring through fall, and sandhill cranes are fairly common in fall along the Little Missouri flats. During spring and summer, the flute-like calls of western meadowlarks can be heard, rising above the prairies.   ER

TRAVELER'S NOTES

Information *Theodore Roosevelt National Park, P.O. Box 7, 315 Second Ave, Medora, ND 58645-0007; tel. (701) 623- 4466*

Hours *Year-round*

Visitor centers *Medora: June–Aug, 8 am–8 pm; May and Sept, 8 am–5 pm; rest of year, 8 am–4.30 pm. Painted Canyon: Apr to mid-Nov, 8.30 am–4.30 pm; rest of year, 8 am–6 pm . Squaw Creek: year-round, 9 am–5.30 pm. All closed Thanksgiving, Dec 25, Jan 1*

Fees *Admission, camping*

Permits *None*

Camping *South Unit: Cottonwood Campground (80 sites). North Unit: Squaw*

Creek Campground (50 sites)

Lodging *Medora, Dickinson, Beach, Belfield*

Supplies *Medora, Dickinson, Beach, Belfield, Watford City*

Access for people with disabilities *Some sites at campgrounds. Squaw Creek Nature Trail in North Unit wheelchair accessible*

When to visit *All year*

Backcountry maps *USGS Medora, Fryburg NW, Long X Divide, Sperati Pt*

Note *Don't touch prairie dogs as they carry diseases. Beware of rattlesnakes*

191

The Tallgrass Prairie Preserve

Oklahoma

The Tallgrass Prairie Preserve, which stretches across 37,000 acres (15,000 ha) of the Osage Hills in northeastern Oklahoma, is the largest protected remnant of native tallgrass in North America. True prairie, as these grasslands are often called, once covered over 142 million acres (57.5 million ha) of the Great Plains.

The heart of the original tallgrass prairie lay in Illinois and Iowa and along the eastern fringes of the Dakotas, Nebraska, Kansas, and Oklahoma. This oceanic landscape, where grasses grew high above a grown man's head, proved to be immensely fertile and most gave way to

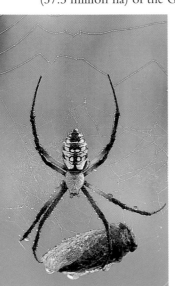

A black-and-yellow argiope spider, feeding on an insect caught in its web.

the plow. Only a few large swaths persist, mainly in the Flint Hills of Kansas and in Oklahoma's Osage Hills. In these regions, people ranched rather than farmed, so the prairie sod was never busted.

The Tallgrass Prairie Preserve is owned by The Nature Conservancy, a private organization that protects and restores threatened ecosystems. At the Tallgrass, the Conservancy is conducting periodic controlled fires designed to mimic the natural fires that once burned in this country and which are necessary for the maintenance of the ecosystem. Fire destroys dead vegetation, returns nutrients to the soil, and increases the vigor and flowering of many plant species. The Conservancy is also reintroducing bison—the largest terrestrial animal in North America and the primary force that shaped the Great Plains grasslands.

Bison are the tillers of the prairie. They literally mow down the grasses as they graze, constantly creating new seedbeds where areas of wild-flowers and other prairie plants can then take hold. An estimated 60 million bison once roamed throughout the Great Plains, but by the end of the nineteenth century they had been hunted almost to extinction. Now they are being

In midsummer, the tallgrass prairie is dotted with purple coneflowers.

returned to their natural habitat. At the preserve, a herd of 300, established in 1993, is expected to eventually increase to around 2,000 animals.

PRAIRIE PATHWAYS

A 50 mile (80 km) road loops through the preserve and signs guide visitors along the route, which crosses a portion of pasture grazed by bison. If you drive slowly, the chances are you will see some of these colossal beasts. The trip will take about three hours: if you travel any faster you are unlikely to fully experience this striking country. There is also

a 2 mile (3 km) self-guided nature trail not far from the preserve headquarters.

The prairie changes dramatically with the seasons. In May, velvety grass shoots grow among the dun-colored stalks of the previous year's growth. The wealth of birds includes chuck-will's-widows, upland sandpipers, and swallows, which are abundant and easy to see, and the smaller and more elusive meadowlarks, dickcissels, and grasshopper sparrows, whose songs are so much part of spring. In summer, as the grasses grow to their full glory, there is a changing show of wildflowers. Then, as October comes around, the grasses begin turning gold and umber. SW

TRAVELER'S NOTES

Information The Nature Conservancy, PO Box 458, Pawhuska, OK 74056; tel. (918) 287-4803

Hours Year-round, daylight hours

Visitor center 17 miles north of Pawhuska on Osage Ave. May 1–Oct 3. Docents on duty Sat, Sun, Wed, and holidays 9.30 am–3.30 pm. Information kiosk

Fees None

Permits None

Camping Not permitted, but campground (35 tent sites, 20 RV sites, 8 cabins) at Osage Hills State Park, 11 miles east of Pawhuska

Lodging Pawhuska, Bartlesville. 8 year-round cabins at Osage Hills State Park

Supplies Pawhuska

Access for people with disabilities Preserve headquarters and restrooms

When to visit May–Nov, peak visitation June–Aug

Big bluestem (above left) is the principal grass of the tallgrass prairie. A male greater prairie chicken (below) inflates air pouches on its neck and performs an intricate dance to attract a mate.

193

Wichita Mountains National Wildlife Refuge

Oklahoma

A trip to Wichita Mountains is like a journey back in time. With bison grazing peacefully on the prairie, it looks much as it did 250 years ago, before ranchers, farmers, and other settlers domesticated the landscape. President Theodore Roosevelt initiated federal wildlife refuges in 1903 and, in 1905, he designated Wichita Mountains as the second in the system. Initially known as the Wichita National Forest Reserve, these 59,000 plus acres (23,900 plus ha) of land were set aside to help save bison from extinction.

About half the refuge is mixed-grass prairie, ranging from species that are less than 2 feet (0.6 m) tall to some, such as switch-grass, that grow to 8 or 9 feet (2.5 or 2.7 m). The other half of the refuge is forested—more scrub than tall timber—with post oak and blackjack oak predominating.

May is one of the prairie's months of glory, with new grasses growing in a variety of subtle greens, touched here and there with blue, yellow, deep red, even purple. Mingling with the grasses are wildflowers such as black-eyed Susans, purple and prairie coneflowers, and blue and yellow indigos, the breezes stirring the vegetation into a rippling sea of color.

Along the Kite Trail (left).
Prairie coneflower (right).

Bison grazing on the prairie (above). A bison breeding sanctuary was established at Wichita in 1904. Lichen-covered granite rocks at Charons Garden Wilderness (left).

During summer the plains bake, with temperatures of 100 degrees Fahrenheit (38° C) and more often persisting for days on end. By September, the delicate grass blossoms will be fading, their leaves will be turning a golden, tawny hue, and the wildflower cast will have changed to the likes of Indian blanket and asters.

The flatness of the prairie is interrupted by the Wichita Mountains, blocky islands of pink- and charcoal-colored rock thrusting up through the sod. These outcroppings are the result of volcanic activity around 500 to 600 million years ago. A paved road leads to the summit of Mount Scott, at 2,464 feet (752 m), and a glorious view of the prairie.

TRAVELER'S NOTES

Information *Refuge Manager, Wichita Mountains National Wildlife Refuge, R.R. 1, Box 448, Indiahoma, OK 73552; tel. (580) 429-3222*

Hours *Year-round, sunrise to sunset*

Visitor centers *Quanah Parker Lake: Fri–Sun, Mar 1– Nov 30, hours variable. Brochures, trail maps, books, exhibits, audio-visual programs. Refuge headquarters: Mon–Fri, 8 am–4.30 pm, year-round except federal holidays. Brochures, trail maps, guidebooks, permits, tour schedules*

Fees *Camping, special tours*

Permits *Backcountry camping, mountain biking; fishing (state license)*

Camping *Campground (83 sites) with drinking water, showers, flush toilets, limited electrical hookups. Backcountry camping limited to 10 people at a time, 3 day limit*

Lodging *Lawton*

Supplies *Lawton, Indiahoma, Cache*

Access for people with disabilities *Visitor center, headquarters, campground picnic areas. Special tour bus. Interpretive trail and fishing pier near visitor center*

When to visit *Spring and fall. Wildlife birthing season: late Mar–Apr. Elk rut, fall colors: Sept–Oct. Summer is very hot*

Backcountry maps *USGS Saddle Mountain, Meers, Odetta, Quanah Mountain, Mount Scott*

The burrowing owl, which can be identified by its long legs, usually nests in prairie dog towns.

Jed Johnson Lake, one of Wichita's many lakes (above). Texas longhorn (left).

The grassy landscape is a perfect setting for the refuge's main attraction, large mammals, especially the bison (more commonly known as buffalo). Mature bulls stand up to 6 feet (2 m) at the shoulder and weigh about a ton. With their heavy, horned heads and humped shoulders, they look as if they could easily demolish a brick building. The refuge supports a herd of about 500, but they tend to roam in groups of about 50—mostly females, calves, and juvenile males. Mature bulls keep to themselves. May is a good time to go bison-watching and see the calves frolicking. All the refuge animals are more active in spring than in the heat of summer.

White-tailed deer are usually found in the forest and at woodland edges, and elk frequent both forest and grasslands. Mature bull elk are an impressive sight, with antlers that can be more than 5 feet (1.5 m) long with 10 to 14 spikes. The annual rut takes place in September, when bulls challenge each other by bugling (a prolonged, unmusical bellow) and dueling for mating rights.

A legacy from earlier days exists in the form of a 300 strong herd of Texas longhorns. (Their horns can reach a width of 5 feet [1.5 m].) Descended from cattle brought by Spanish settlers, these great beasts were once the mainstay of the beef industry and 10 million or more roamed the range. In time, breeds that yielded more meat replaced them.

PRAIRIE DOGS AND OTHER RESIDENTS

A colony of prairie dogs provides one of the liveliest sights on the refuge. These chubby, buff-colored rodents scamper around the surface openings of their town—an underground network of tunnels and rooms. Coyotes are present but, being night prowlers, they generally go unseen, except at dawn. You are more likely to hear them howling after dark. Easier to spot

Collared lizard.

196

A view across the refuge (top) where Mississippi kites (above) can sometimes be seen, soaring gracefully.

are collared lizards, especially on Mount Scott. About a foot (30 cm) long, they have a pale green body, a yellow head, and a black "collar".

The refuge counts 240 bird species, but the one that most people hope to see is the endangered Mississippi kite. The size of a small falcon, these elegant birds of prey nest in the refuge. They streak across the prairie in pursuit of flying insects, banking and wheeling with a level of skill about which human pilots can only fantasize. Occasionally they plunge to the ground to snatch up unsuspecting mice, frogs, lizards, or insects. EW

BRINGING BACK THE BISON

Before Europeans began rearranging the landscape, 60 million bison roamed the grasslands stretching from the Rocky Mountains to western New York State and from southcentral Canada to northeastern Mexico.

Native Americans had always hunted bison but had made no impact on the population. In the nineteenth century, however, a combination of events, not least the arrival of the railroads, led to the near extinction of the species. As routes pushed farther west, bloodthirsty "sportsmen" climbed aboard the trains and fired away at the bison as if they were waging war, leaving thousands of rotting carcasses. By 1895, the estimated bison population was 800.

To help insure the species' survival, the Bronx Zoo in New York City launched a breeding program. In 1904, the zoo's parent organization, the New York Zoological Society, and various conservationists

persuaded the federal government to establish a bison breeding sanctuary in Oklahoma. The zoo shipped 15 of its 32 bison in railroad cars to the preserve that ultimately became the Wichita Mountains National Wildlife Refuge.

The bison in the refuge today are mostly descendants of that original nucleus. Captive breeding programs at zoos, ranches, and in other refuges have made it possible to restore bison at a number of other protected sites, and the population now seems to be out of danger, standing at about 30,000.

Shipping a bison from the Bronx Zoo.

197

0   100   200   miles
0   200   400   km

Washington DC

Shenandoah NP

Chincoteague NWR

W V

Monongahela NF   Richmond

VIRGINIA

Louisville

KENTUCKY

Mammoth Cave NP   *Great Smoky Mountains NP*   NORTH CAROLINA

Nashville

TENNESSEE   SOUTH CAROLINA

ARKANSAS

MISSISSIPPI   ALABAMA   GEORGIA

Atlanta

Cumberland Island NS

Jacksonville

LOUISIANA   FLORIDA

New Orleans

Miami

John Pennekamp Coral Reef SP

Everglades NP

The Southeast

Everglades National Park

Florida

Only a short drive from Miami's glitter is a watery wilderness where the ecology of the tropics overlaps that of the temperate zone, producing an extraordinary mix of plants and animals—more than 700 plant species, nearly 350 kinds of bird, and a multitude of mammals, reptiles, and invertebrates. The park, third largest in the lower 48 states, occupies about one-third of the entire Everglades ecosystem of 4.3 million acres (1.7 million ha).

The system is actually a fresh-water river close to 50 miles (80 ha) wide, slowly flowing south from Lake Okeechobee 100 miles (160 km) to Florida Bay. The water spreads over a bed of porous limestone at depths of a few inches to 6 feet (2 m) at most.

SAW GRASS AND HAMMOCKS

Vast stands of saw grass, a type of sedge, sweep across this aquatic landscape, in some places rising to 15 feet (4.5 m). Scattered throughout are raised "islands", known as hammocks, thick with tropical hardwood trees, notably live oak and mahogany. In drier spots there are groves of slash pines. Damper sites harbor forest islands of baldcypresses up to 60 feet (18 m) tall. Masses of mangrove trees cover most of the park's coastal rim, their prop roots extending like slender flying buttresses into the shallows. Thickets of these leathery leaved trees are havens for wildlife, especially nesting birds.

A fine way to sample the park is to explore the series of short trails along the drive from the main entrance to Flamingo. At the Royal Palm Visitor Center, you'll find these tallest of all palms, which grow nowhere else in North America. You'll also find the Anhinga Trail,

A palmetto palm growing among slash pines (above). The rare Florida panther (left). An alligator hatching (right).

Roseate spoonbills (above). A mangrove, with its stilt-like roots (left). An anhinga (below).

a short excursion around a slough—a relatively deep channel of water. Bromeliads and clusters of Spanish moss dangle from live oak trees, and, during winter, white swamp lily blossoms emerge amid the saw grass. Zebra butterflies—their broad, black wings penciled with yellow stripes—flit around the vegetation.

In the slough's clear water you can see bass, catfish, bluegills, and Florida gars, many of which will be food for the area's most conspicuous inhabitants, the alligators. These toothy beasts cruise open waters and often haul themselves out to lie in the sun alongside the trail. They are best admired from a distance.

Most of the avian action is provided by the anhingas (also called snakebirds or water turkeys). When hungry, an anhinga plunges into the water and spears a fish with its long, dagger-like beak, then tosses the catch in the air and swallows it.

Nearby is the Gumbo-limbo Trail, named for a twisty tree with coppery red, perpetually peeling bark. Other vegetation includes shrubs such as coral bean and wild coffee and a profusion of orchids and ferns. This is a good spot to see seasonal migrants such as warblers and hummingbirds.

TRAVELER'S NOTES

Information Superintendent, Everglades National Park, 40001 State Rd 9336, Homestead, FL 33031-6733; tel. (305) 242-7700, fax (305) 242-7728

Hours Always open

Visitor centers Main: daily, 8 am–5 pm. Royal Palm: daily, 8 am–4.15 pm. Flamingo: Dec 15–Apr 15, 9 am–5 pm. Permits, tour tickets. Shark Valley: daily, 9 am–5 pm. Tram tour tickets. Gulf Coast/Everglades City: Dec 15–Apr 15, 9 am–5 pm. Backcountry permits, boat tour tickets. All offer brochures, maps, nautical charts, ranger-led activities

Fees Admission main entrance, Shark Valley, and Chekika campground. All campgrounds Dec 15–Apr 15

Permits Backcountry camping, fishing (state license)

Camping 3 campgrounds (123 sites). 48 boat-accessible backcountry sites

Lodging Flamingo, Homestead, Everglades City, Chokoloskee

Supplies Everglades City, Homestead

Access for people with disabilities Visitor centers, picnic grounds, boat and tram tours. Anhinga, Gumbo-limbo, Pineland, Pa-hay-okee Overlook, Mahogany Hammock, West Lake, Eco Pond, and Shark Valley trails wheelchair accessible. Taped tour of Anhinga Trail

When to visit Dec 15–Apr 15 (dry season): mild weather; best wildlife viewing. Rest of year (wet season) hot and rainy, many biting insects. Hurricanes May–Oct

201

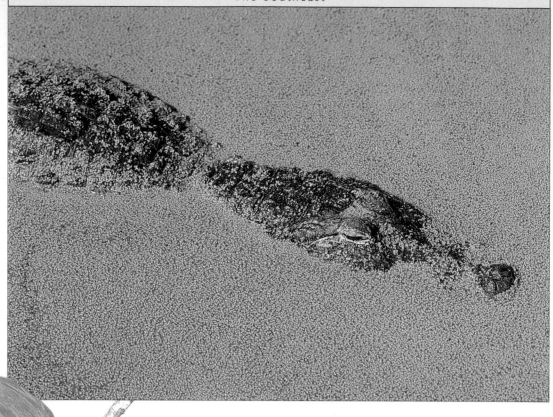

A cruise from Flamingo around Florida Bay will bring you close to alligators and their slender-snouted cousins, American crocodiles, and leaping bottlenose dolphins may escort the boat. Sometimes you can see massive loggerhead sea turtles surfacing. The birdlife is over-whelming. You can't miss roseate spoonbills—tall waders with pale, shell-pink plumage accented by splashes of red, and tangerine tails. To feed, they swish their paddle-shaped bills from side to side in shallow

water and mud. Also impressive are the magnificent frigatebirds soaring overhead, their slender black wings spanning 7 to 8 feet (2 to 2.5 m). Countless thousands of birds nest on the mangrove keys that dot the bay, among them white ibis, brown pelicans, snowy and reddish egrets, bald eagles, ospreys, and herons (great white, little blue, green, and tricolored).

Alligators frequent the fresh and brackish water (above), whereas crocodiles (above right) favor salt water. A green heron poised to dive for fish (top left). A manatee forages on the sea bed (below).

THE WILDERNESS WATERWAY

The Wilderness Waterway, a 99 mile (160 km) aquatic trail, runs along creeks, tidal rivers, and open bays between Flamingo and the park's northwestern corner. A trip along this waterway by canoe or tour boat will bring you close to numerous bird species, including the elegant mangrove cuckoo. This is also the best place in the Everglades to see manatees, enormous (some weigh more than a ton), slow-moving aquatic mammals that feed on marine plants.

Eastward, south of the Tamiami Trail, is Shark Valley. From here you can travel by tram, bicycle, or on foot along a 15 mile (24 km) loop

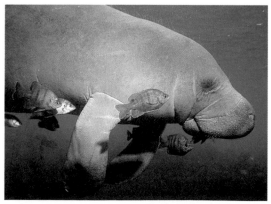

A purple gallinule (above). The wood stork (below) is the only species of stork found in North America. Marjory Stoneman Douglas (below right), who, in 1993, at the age of 103, received a Medal of Freedom for her contribution to conservation.

which leads to two short nature trails and a 65 foot (20 m) observation tower. Many alligators nest in the area, and there are also brown water snakes and water moccasins.

This is also a likely spot for wood storks. These tall, mostly white, bald birds stride through the water sweeping their long, curving bills back and forth prospecting for food. Shark Valley is also a nesting area for the rare snail kite. The beaks of these small birds of prey end in a pronounced hook, an adaptation for feeding on apple snails. EW

PARADISE ALMOST LOST

In 1947, the year Everglades National Park was dedicated, a book entitled The Everglades: River of Grass was published. The author, Marjory Stoneman Douglas, celebrated the glories of the Glades but warned of damage caused by a system of canals, dikes, and dams (created to supply water to homes and farms), real-estate development, and pollution.

Mrs Douglas and her book became rallying points for conservationists, but the ecosystem's hydrology had been so severely compromised that they were unable to markedly improve the situation. Today, half of the Glades are unsuitable for wildlife, wading bird populations have declined 93 percent from natural levels, and Florida's human population is increasing at the rate of 900 a day. To make matters worse, introduced species of plant and fish have wreaked havoc on the ecosystem.

In 1994, serious steps were at last made toward restoration. An agreement was worked out with farmers to curb agricultural pollution (though conservationists fear it is insufficiently strict), and the federal government launched a plan aimed at reversing the effects of a century of drainage and development. Canals and dams have been replaced or eliminated, to help restore the natural waterflow. While these measures do not mean that salvation is assured, they are a step in the right direction.

203

John Pennekamp
Coral Reef State Park

Florida

A visit to Florida is incomplete without seeing the keys and their spectacular coral reefs. Lying just south of the tip of Florida, John Pennekamp Coral Reef State Park was named for a Miami newspaperman who was instrumental in establishing several of Florida's state parks. This is a beach park, where you can camp among tropical hardwoods, canoe in mangroves, swim from beaches, and enjoy the reef by snorkeling, diving,

Miami

MILES
0   5   10   15
0   10   20
KM

Biscayne Bay

Key Largo

or viewing it from a glass–bottom boat. The park preserves 70 square miles (180 sq km) of luxuriant underwater gardens, home to hundreds of species of tropical fish, such as parrotfish, wrasse, and ray.

Corals are tiny animals that live in great colonies. There are two major types of coral: hard and soft. Both incorporate plant cells that help them photosynthesize the energy of the sun, and in the process they excrete limestone from the calcium carbonate in the water. In hard corals, the limestone forms a skeleton inside the coral, and this buildup in turn creates the reef. Soft corals do not have limestone skeletons and grow in myriad forms that resemble plants. You can see many species of coral at John Pennekamp, among them forests of waving sea whips and sea fans.

The park was created to protect the coral, but there are many fascinating species of plant, bird, reptile, and mammal on the keys. Walking trails wind through tropical hardwood

A spider crab on a sea fan.

hammocks of tamarind, iron-
wood, and mahogany, and
canoe trails lace through
mangroves that grow where
land and sea meet.

Many West Indian bird
species occur here. Noddies and
frigatebirds fly overhead; herons
and shorebirds feed on the tidal
flats; and rare mangrove cuckoos
and white-crowned pigeons are
found among the mangroves.
Reptiles include the American crocodile, the
reef gecko, and three endangered sea turtle
species. Mammals include the tiny key deer
and, in the water, the huge, gentle manatee.

A diver and a school of grunts (above).
Sea fan (left); queen angelfish (below).

PROTECTING THE REEF
Degradation of the Florida Reef is a growing
concern. Hurricanes, coral-eating fish, and
diseases that affect the coral are a major problem.

Extensive damage is also
being caused by water
pollution, habitat destruction,
overfishing, and negligent
boating. The flow of fresh
water from the Everglades into
the reef has been reduced and
polluted by dams and canals,
built to serve the burgeoning
human population and irrigate extensive areas
used for farming.

All habitats in this fragile world are inter-
dependent. The reefs protect the seagrass flats
and mangroves from storm waves. The seagrass,
in turn, purifies the water for the reef to grow in
and provides nurseries for tropical fish.

In 1990, the 2,600 square mile (6,700 sq km)
Key Largo National Marine Sanctuary was set up
next to John Pennekamp, as part
of an overall plan to protect the
Florida Reef. SM

TRAVELER'S NOTES

Information *John Pennekamp Coral
Reef State Park, PO Box 487, Key
Largo, FL 33037; tel. (305) 451-1202*

Hours *Year-round, 8 am to sundown*

Visitor center *Year-round,
8 am–5 pm. Information, aquarium*

Fees *Admission, camping*

Permits *Fishing (state license)*

Camping *47 sites*

Lodging *Key Largo, Miami*

Supplies *Key Largo, Miami*

**Access for people with
disabilities** *Visitor center,
beach areas*

When to visit *Year-round.
Tropical storms Jun–Oct*

Note *Boat rentals, dive shop
at marina*

205

Cumberland Island National Seashore

Georgia

Cumberland is the southern-most member of the Golden Isles—a subtropical chain that stretches from Savannah to Brunswick. Spanish moss hanging from the branches of live oaks and a collection of ante-bellum mansions give this 16 mile (26 km) long island an air of the Old South, which is enhanced by the unspoiled landscape. Over three-fourths of the island is protected and preserved by the National Park Service and development of any kind is prohibited.

Access is restricted to boats only. The park service operates a passenger ferry twice a day, seven days a week. Reservations are advisable, especially in summer, during the height of the tourist season. Small boats can be tied up at a floating dock in a channel off the Intracoastal Waterway. Large boats must be moored at offshore anchorages and skiffs used to get to shore.

EXPLORING ON FOOT

No vehicles are allowed on the island, so the only way to explore is on foot. A good tip is to take one of the guided tours led by park service naturalists, as they cover the island's main features. Afterwards you can strike off on your own, following any of the marked trails. The western edge of the island is lined with 40 foot (12 m) sand dunes, salt marshes, and miles of white sand beaches that are perfect for swimming. (Don't forget to leave time to catch the ferry back.) The interior is forested with live

Migrating sand dunes (above). Cumberland Island's sweeping beaches (left) offer visitors excellent walking and swimming.

Between April and August, loggerhead turtles (left) come ashore to lay their eggs in the sand. Shorebirds, such as the ruddy turnstone (below), are common on the beaches and in the dunes.

in the woods. Loggerhead turtles lay their eggs in the sand and numerous shorebirds dance along the water's edge. Cattle egrets, American coots, and Virginia rails inhabit the marshes. Noisy clapper rails signal dawn and dusk each day with their unmusical cries. Red winged blackbirds flit among clumps of reed grass. The marshes are also home to lemon shark, sea trout, and bluefish.

oaks, long-leaf slash pines, palmettos, and camellias, all interspersed with grassy freshwater marshes. You can often see herds of horses and deer grazing.

Other species of wildlife are also plentiful. Raccoons, opossums, squirrels, and skunks live

Cumberland has had an interesting past. Indians once hunted here for sea turtles and waterfowl. Later, Spanish missionaries came, followed by French and English settlers.

Several historical mansions dot the island. Once a month the park service leads trips to Plum Orchard, a restored mansion originally built by the Carnegie family on the banks of the Brick Hill River in 1898, when the island was the family's personal playground. DH

TRAVELER'S NOTES

Information Superintendent, Cumberland Island National Seashore, Box 806, St Marys, GA 31558; tel. 912-882-4702

Hours Always open. Access by boat only; ferry leaves twice a day

Visitor center St Marys: 8.15 am–4.30 pm

Fees Ferry

Permits Backcountry use

Camping Limited to 120 people a night; 7 day maximum stay. Sea Camp developed, other campgrounds primitive

Lodging Greyfield Inn, at edge of Cumberland Sound

Supplies St Marys

Access for people with disabilities Visitor center and ferry. When making reservations, request a "beach chair"— a wheelchair with oversized tires for use on sand

When to visit Summer for beach activities; spring and fall for migrating birds

Backcountry maps USGS Cumberland Island North; Cumberland Island South; Kingsland NE

Mammoth Cave National Park

Kentucky

About 330 miles (530 km) of mapped passages, some running beyond the park boundary, form Mammoth Cave—the longest known cave system in the world. Native Americans mined minerals here 4,000 years ago, and during the early 1800s, calcium nitrate, known as false saltpeter, was mined here for making gunpowder. Not long afterwards, tourists began coming to wonder at this breathtaking network of massive dry halls and smaller dank chambers. Despite being one of the first natural tourist attractions in the country, however, it was not until 1941 that the area was designated a national park.

Spectacular stalactites (left). Blind cavefish (right) are among the creatures that have adapted to the lightless environment.

The movement of water through beds of limestone is what has created Mammoth Cave's spectacular caverns and decorations of stalactites, stalagmites, and columns. Flowstone, formed by water seeping from vertical walls, has shaped itself into rich swirls and mounds, the most famous of which is known as Frozen Niagara.

Another phenomenon which creates "sculpture" of surpassing beauty is the gradual build-up of crystals formed from seeping gypsum, creating delicate white and golden-brown shapes that resemble feathers, flowers, and needles.

TROGLODITES

While most of the cave-dwelling species (known as troglodites) keep themselves hidden much of the time, their existence is part of the fascination of the caves. Troglodites trapped eons ago and still winning the struggle for survival include cavefish, crayfish, shrimp, spiders, cave snails, and beetles. So adapted are these creatures to this world of darkness that they are eyeless and colorless.

Some of the underworld wonders at Mammoth Cave (above).
A fall morning in the forest (left).

The park also consists of some 50,000 heavily forested acres (20,235 ha) and a total of 60 miles (100 km) of hiking trails winds through the trees. A part of the forest known as Big Woods, which covers 300 acres (120 hectares), is one of the largest surviving sections of Kentucky's ancient forest, which once spread over vast areas of the state. The yellow poplar, also known as the tulip tree because of its beautiful blossom, is among the species that thrive in the forest's moist soil.

The cave salamander, a little orange amphibian with black spots, lives near the cave entrance. Bats and cave crickets divide their time between the caves and the outside world.

To see Mammoth Cave you will need to take one of the National Park Service tours, all of which require a certain amount of walking. Experienced spelunkers can arrange to explore Ganter Cave with a guide.

In spring and summer, hikers are treated to a glorious display of wildflowers, such as trout lily, columbine, and hepatica. White-tailed deer can be seen in among the trees, and the American kestrel and the pileated woodpecker can be spotted from time to time.

Keep an eye out for copperhead snakes, and also for the tick associated with Lyme disease. EB

TRAVELER'S NOTES

Information Mammoth Cave National Park, P.O. Box 7, Mammoth Cave KY 42259-0007; tel. (270) 758-2238

Hours Year round, 8 am–5 pm

Visitor center Mammoth Cave: daily, 8 am–5 pm Orientation programs, book sales, exhibits

Fees Cave visits, camping

Permits Spelunking

Camping 127 campsites, closed in winter

Lodging Hotel at visitor center

Supplies Adjacent to visitor center

Access for people with disabilities Ranger-led tour of caves; 2 campgrounds, 1 surface trail

When to visit Fall. Most visitors mid June–Labor Day

Backcountry maps USGS Mammoth Cave National Park

White-tailed deer doe.

Great Smoky Mountains National Park

North Carolina and Tennessee

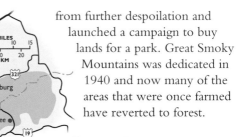

The ethereal haze given off by the trees in this part of the Appalachians prompted the Cherokees to describe the region as "the place of blue smoke". Great Smoky Mountains National Park is a 500,000 acre (200,000 ha) treasure-trove of rugged, forested ridges with occasional grassy open areas known as balds, tumbling streams and waterfalls, and abundant wildlife.

Until the beginning of the nineteenth century, this region was Cherokee land, which was then taken over by white settlers. By the 1920s, over 7,000 farming people lived in what is now the park and lumbermen were busy tearing down vast areas of forest. Conservationists saw a great need to save the area

The red wolf (left), recently reintroduced to Great Smoky. American beech and rosebay rhododendron (right).

from further despoilation and launched a campaign to buy lands for a park. Great Smoky Mountains was dedicated in 1940 and now many of the areas that were once farmed have reverted to forest.

DENSE FORESTS

Blessed with abundant rainfall, the forests here are as diverse as any found on the continent,

consisting of several overlapping but distinct types. Trees such as red spruce and Fraser fir grow on the exposed upper slopes— remnants of northern forest that covered the East during the ice age. Down-slope grow mixed oaks and cove hardwood forest, while lower still are the familiar deciduous trees of the region—maple and tulip trees— providing a blazing display of color in fall.

A mere 45 minute auto trip can take one through such a range of vegetation that the journey resembles a drive from Georgia to Canada. With altitudes varying from 850 to 6,650 feet (260 to 2,025 m), some of the plant species that bloom in the lower regions at the beginning of spring do not flower until late June on nearby heights.

Fall colors on the slopes above Deep Creek Canyon (above). The black-chinned red salamander (left) is unique to this region.

Great thickets of evergreen shrubs such as rhododendron and laurel grow throughout the park, blossoming in clouds of pink and white in spring and summer. And on the floor of the forest, when the weather starts to warm, wildflowers bloom in among the varied greens of ferns and mosses.

The dense regions of forest provide an ideal environment for a large variety of animals and birds, but they are not always easy for visitors to see. Black bears are a great attraction, and their numbers have increased considerably since the days when the forest was heavily logged.

The red wolf and the river otter are back in the region once more, having been reintroduced, and opossums, skunks, raccoons, and wood-chucks are plentiful. There are also some two dozen species of salamander in Great Smoky, including the black-chinned red, which is known nowhere else.

Woodchucks hibernate in winter, emerging from their burrows in spring to feed on green vegetation.

TRAVELER'S NOTES

Information *Great Smoky Mountains National Park, 107 Park Headquarters Rd, Gatlinburg TN 37738; tel. 865-436-1200*

Hours *Always open*

Visitor centers *Sugarlands: 8.30 am–4.30 pm, closed Dec 25. Also Oconaluftee (year-round) and Cades Cove (Apr 15–Oct 3 only)*

Fees *Admission, camping*

Permits *Backcountry travel, fishing (state license)*

Camping *10 campgrounds (1,000 sites)*

Lodging *Gatlinburg, Cherokee*

Supplies *Gatlinburg, Cherokee*

Access for people with disabilities *Wheelchair access to all visitor centers, campgrounds at Sugarlands, Valley Trail*

When to visit *Spring and fall. Busy Easter through fall*

Backcountry maps *USGS Great Smoky Mountains National Park*

THE BLACK BEAR

Of all the animals roaming Great Smoky, the black bear is probably the one that visitors most hope to see, and there is a fair chance of spotting one, for there are at least 400 in the park.

Black bears are a striking sight. Averaging 200 pounds (90 kg), when standing erect they are about 6 feet (180 cm) tall. Grasses and herbaceous plants form a major part of their diet, and in fall they gorge themselves on berries and acorns. They spend part or all of the winter dormant, generally in cavities high in mature trees, although they may use thickets or rock crevices.

Black bears are intelligent creatures. They are solitary (except for a short time during the breeding season) but tolerant of other bears and people. They are immensely curious, but if you meet one it will usually run away. If you find one at a campsite, the chances are it will be foraging. Always make sure your food supplies are bearproof and never feed a bear as it will encourage it to become a nuisance, putting both the bear and humans at risk.

An adult black bear feeding on mountain ash berries.

TOURING ROUTES

The Newfound Gap Road provides access to the park's interior, running between Gatlinburg, Tennessee, and Oconaluftee, North Carolina. Traveling southward, it ascends steeply, providing views of a rapidly changing tapestry of vegetation. To the west is Clingmans Dome, the highest point in the park. This can be reached by road, a spiral ramp carrying visitors to a lookout tower above the fir-clad slopes. Andrews Bald nearby, is soaked by 85 inches (205 cm) of rain annually and some days standing in this part of the park you feel as if you're in the clouds.

An interesting drive is along the Cades Cove Loop Road which tours Cades Cove, a broad valley several miles long that is being kept the way it looked in the last century, with cabins, pastures, churches, and a mill. Here, white-tailed deer, another abundant species in the park, wander down from the deciduous forests that surround the valley to graze peacefully in full view of visitors.

There are more than 800 miles (1,280 km) of hiking trails in the park, of varying levels of difficulty, and the Appalachian Trail passes through the region (see p. 80). In the eastern part of the park stands Mount LeConte, rising to a height of 6,593 feet (2,010 m)—a popular destination for hikers, offering glorious views and the tranquility of the wild.

The fact that more than half the population of the United States lives within a day's drive of the park presents management with the dilemma of balancing use of the park with its preservation, but greater problems exist in the form of air pollution from nearby power plants, and pests of various kinds that are killing the trees.

The haze that gives the park its name (far left), and the golden glow of a hardwood forest in winter (above). The John Oliver Cabin at Cades Cove (left) is one of a number of buildings constructed in the second half of the nineteenth century by local farmers.

Also doing considerable damage are wild boars, descendants of ones that escaped from a nearby game preserve several decades ago. As is the case with all ecosystems, Great Smoky is a place of complex natural interactions. These difficulties remind us that even within parks and preserves, habitat and wildlife can be vulnerable. EB

The crest of Mount LeConte (left). Hikers on the Appalachian Trail (below).

Chincoteague
National Wildlife Refuge

Virginia

Assateague is one of countless barrier islands trailing down America's Atlantic coast—skinny strips of sand beaten by ocean surf, eternally changing shape and size. The Maryland–Virginia border bisects the 37 mile (60 km) long island, and the Virginia side is the Chincoteague National Wildlife Refuge. North of the line is Assateague National Seashore. The island is a favorite haven for thousands of birds during spring and fall migration; 316 species have been identified.

Most anywhere along the refuge's 12 miles (20 km) of wild beach in April and May, for instance, flocks of sanderlings alight on the wet sand as the surf recedes. These speckled, rusty brown birds skitter about, poking their bills into the sand to dine on marine creatures deposited by the surging sea. Another wave charges in and the birds explode into the air, sweeping out over the ocean and then back to continue feeding. Sanderlings are one of more than 20 species of sandpiper and close relatives that come to Chincoteague.

At the southern tip of the island, where a sand spit hooks around to shelter Toms Cove, a great variety of shorebirds congregate in large numbers on the mud flats to poke and dig for dinner. The cove is also a good spot for looking at seashells.

A substantial portion of Assateague's 9,450 acres (3,830 ha) is forested. The dominant vegetation is loblolly pine, a southern species whose needle-covered branches are more spaced apart than the limbs of, say, white or red pine. In the forest it grows to its normal height of 80 to 100 feet (25 to 30 m), but nearer the shore the wind and salt spray stunt the loblollies and twist

Chincoteague's ponies are wild descendants of horses brought to the island in the seventeenth century by English plantation owners.

Egrets, herons, and waterfowl gather on a tidal marsh (above). The Delmarva fox squirrel (left) is twice the size of a common gray squirrel and has a bushier tail.

them into gnarled shapes. The island also has a freshwater marsh—a cattail-cloaked wetland favored by herons and egrets.

THE WILDLIFE LOOP

One of the most rewarding routes to take is the Wildlife Loop. This 3¹/₂ mile (5.5 km) paved trail is restricted to pedestrians, wheelchair users, and cyclists until 3 pm, when cars are permitted. The loop passes woodland of loblolly pines, blueberry bushes, sweetgums, and holly, and at its center lies a large pond known as Snow Goose Pool. During fall and winter, the pond does, indeed, attract snow geese, plus Canada geese, tundra swans, and other waterfowl. This is a likely spot to see rare Delmarva fox squirrels. If you surprise these pale gray rodents, they usually bound along the forest floor rather than scoot up a tree the way their gray cousins do.

The best known animals at Chincoteague are the shaggy-coated ponies. Despite their benign appearance, they are likely to kick and bite if approached closely. EW

TRAVELER'S NOTES

Information *Refuge Manager, Chincoteague National Wildlife Refuge, PO. Box 62, Chincoteague, VA 23336; tel. 757-336-6122, fax 757-336-5273*

Hours *May–Sept, 5 am–10 pm; Apr and Oct, 6 am–8 pm; Nov–Mar, 6 am–6 pm*

Visitor centers *Refuge Center, Beach Rd: daily, 9 am–4 pm, except federal hols. Toms Cove, end of Beach Rd: daily, 9 am–5 pm, except federal hols; tel. 757-336-6122. Publications, permits, interpretive programs. Guided walks, children's programs, bookings for safari tours at Refuge Center only*

Fees *Admission for cars*

Permits *Off-road vehicles, hunting (state license)*

Camping *Not permitted on refuge.*

Public campgrounds and backcountry camping in adjacent National Seashore. Contact Assateague Island National Seashore, tel. (410) 641-3030 or 641-1441

Lodging *Chincoteague Island. Contact Chincoteague Chamber of Commerce, PO Box 258, Chincoteague, VA 23336, tel. (757) 336-6161*

Supplies *Chincoteague Island*

Access for people with disabilities *Visitor centers, Wildlife Loop Trail, boardwalk portion of Marsh Trail; wheelchair ramp at beach*

When to visit *Spring and fall. Apr–June for shorebirds, wading birds, songbirds, waterfowl; Sept–Nov primarily waterfowl. Busy in summer*

Shenandoah National Park

Virginia

Among the oldest mountains on Earth, the Appalachians originally stood as high as today's Rocky Mountains. These once-towering giants have been eroded over the ages to the low, rounded ranges that are now the center of Shenandoah National Park. From Skyline Drive, which runs the length of the park, the view to the east is of Virginia's Piedmont Plateau, which rolls out toward the coastal plain and Chesapeake Bay. To the west lies the valley of the Shenandoah River.

Shenandoah National Park is about 100 miles (160 km) long and 1 to 13 miles (1.6 to 21 km) wide, but lush vegetation makes it seem more extensive. The park's complex ecosystems are ancient and contain more plant species than are found in all Europe. Basswood, pines, ash, hemlock, hickories, and a wide variety of oaks form Shenandoah's tree community, along with firs that grow on the highest peaks. These ancient hardwood forests once covered much of the mideastern United States.

In spring, redbuds, with their dark bark and vibrant purple-pink flowers, dot the lower slopes, interspersed with billows of white serviceberry blooms. Deeper in the woods, pink azaleas and the pink-and-white cups of mountain laurel color the forest glades.

Jack-in-the-pulpit and trillium are among the park's spring wildflowers. In the summer, goldenrod

The opening of Skyline Drive in 1934. It was said that the air was so clean in those early years that, on clear days, park visitors could see the Washington Monument about 75 miles (120 km) away.

The view over the Shenandoah ridges from Hazel Mountain Overlook on Skyline Drive (above). In spring, clumps of mountain laurel (below) bloom in glades.

TRAVELER'S NOTES

Information Superintendent, Shenandoah National Park, 3655 U.S. Highway 211 E, Luray, Virginia 22835-9036; tel. 540-999-3500

Hours Always open

Visitor centers Dickey Ridge: Apr–Oct. Byrd: Apr–Nov. Both 9 am–5 pm. Publications, permits

Fees Admission, camping

Permits Backcountry camping, fishing (state license)

Camping 3 campgrounds (470 sites), reservations advised. Lewis Mountain, Loft Mountain have showers, laundry facilities. Loft Mountain has sewage disposal

Lodging Park cabins and rooms: ARAMARK Virginia

Sky-Line Company, Box 7727NP, Luray, VA 22835; tel. (800) 999-4714. Other accommodation in nearby towns

Supplies Gas and food at Elkwallow, Big Meadows, Loft Mountain; food at Lewis Mountain

Access for people with disabilities Visitor centers, lodges, campsites

When to visit Spring for flowers; Sept–Oct for fall colors

Backcountry maps USGS Shenandoah National Park

and other sun-loving flowers brighten the park's meadows and roadsides. Fall brings a wonderful show, but be forewarned: Shenandoah is little more than an hour's drive from the Washington DC metropolitan area, so the park is often crowded on weekends. When fall colors are at their peak, so is Skyline Drive traffic. The best plan is to park the car and hike.

White-tailed deer are common in Shenandoah and can be seen near the forest fringes.

One of the longest, most satisfying hikes starts at the base of the mountains and switchbacks up to the summit of Old Rag Mountain. Viewed from that hilltop in fall, the Virginia country-side glows with color. In spring, when runoff is at its height, Whiteoak Canyon, with its six waterfalls, is the place to visit.

217

Cascades spill down narrow rock gorges, and the trail provides numerous places to sit while watching and listening to the falling water. The Whiteoak Trail leads to the Limberlost, one of the last old-growth areas in this part of the Appalachians. The longest of

ALIEN INVADERS

Shenandoah's forests were once thick with American chestnut. Used for furniture, railroad ties, and tannin, chestnut was as durable as it was handsome. Sadly, a fungus, inadvertently introduced in the early 1900s, has killed almost all American chestnuts. Some stumps still manage to produce sprouts, but they live only a few years before the fungus kills the trees back to their roots.

Scientists are working on viruses to attack the fungus. But no niche remains empty: oaks and hickories have replaced the chestnuts, and black bears, whose ancestors gorged on chestnuts, now feast on acorns.

Other park aliens include wild mustard, vinca, and coltsfoot. The latter arrived in crushed rock used to surface the Byrd Visitor Center parking lot.

The woolly adelgid, an insect from the Orient, has attacked most park hemlocks, sucking nutrients from the needles and injecting toxins. Trees thus weakened often die. At present, no effective means of combating adelgids exists.

With so much at stake, the Park Service now informs visitors why protections are needed to maintain healthy ecosystems.

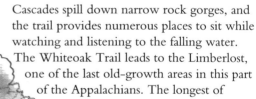

The American chestnut tree and a close-up of seeds (right) inside the spiny green fruit.

Fall colors along Skyline Drive (left). A young hiker takes in the panorama from high in the Blue Ridge Mountains (above). Picturesque Dark Hollow Falls (below) lies along a short trail not far from the Byrd Visitor Center.

Shenandoah's more than 500 miles (800 km) of hiking trails is a 95 mile (150 km) segment of the Appalachian Trail, which runs the entire length of the mountains—2,100 miles (3,400 km)—all the way from Maine to Georgia.

From lodge room or campsite, the visitor can roll out of bed to the morning mists that fill the valleys and hollows, with the hills shimmering in ranks to the horizon. In fall, when the fiery colors of the hills are heightened by the setting sun, black bears can often be seen browsing for blueberries in Big Meadows.

Woodpeckers and owls live deep in the woods. Goldfinches flit from tree to tree and catbirds feed on berries. More than 200 bird species are either residents or migrate through Shenandoah. Exciting bird news is the return of the peregrine falcon, which disappeared from Virginia in the 1950s as a result of DDT usage.

The peregrine is not the only species to have returned to the park. In the nineteenth century, pioneers attempted to farm these mountains, but once the thin soils gave out the farmers left. After the park was established in 1926, cleared land was allowed to revert. As it did so, deer, bobcat, wild turkey, and other animals that had been driven out by agriculture came back. Now, with 40 percent of the park designated as wilderness, Shenandoah is in the process of coming full circle. MS

Peregrine falcons have returned to the park after being all but wiped out by pesticides.

Monongahela National Forest

West Virginia

Monongahela is a vast, forested tract of towering rock formations, windswept flats, plunging river gorges, deep caverns, and murky bogs. Comprised of 900,000 acres (364,500 ha) along the West Virginia section of the Allegheny Plateau, the forest has 32 recreation sites and over 700 miles (1,130 km) of hiking trails. Monongahela is also home to the headwaters of five major river systems and five federally designated wildernesses lie within its boundaries.

One of the most popular recreation areas is Spruce Knob–Seneca Rocks, which offers thousands of acres to explore. Spruce Knob, at 4,861 feet (1,483 m), is West Virginia's highest peak, and from the observation tower at its

summit you can enjoy views for miles around. The vegetation has adapted to the harsh conditions, spruce trees growing only to leeward and berry plants hugging the ground. The lower elevations are covered with hardwood forest—mainly beech, birch, maple, and cherry.

Seneca Rocks is a rugged quartzite formation rising nearly 900 feet (275 m) above North Fork Valley and a great attraction for climbers. The West Side Trail is for those who wish to reach the top without scaling the sheer rock wall.

THE SMOKE HOLE AND DOLLY SODS

Also within this area of the forest is the Smoke Hole Canyon—a gorge over 20 miles (32 km) long where the South Branch River squeezes between North Fork and Cave mountains, providing a challenge for whitewater enthusiasts.

The windswept heights of Dolly Sods Wilderness are among the most popular areas in the forest. Hiking here is quite strenuous and involves fording Red Creek and its tributaries, so be prepared for wet feet. This rock-strewn region is dotted with spruce, dwarfed and

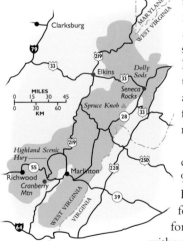

Seneca Rocks.

Fall foliage in Monongahela (above). Stacked boulders on the exposed heights of Dolly Sods (left).

misshapen by the harsh habitat, and at lower elevations there are hardwood forests and laurel thickets, where azaleas and rhododendrons bloom in summer. Fewer people visit the Flatrock and Roaring Plains backcountry nearby.

In the southern part of the forest, the Highland Scenic Highway runs from Richwood to Marlinton, providing spectacular views of the Allegheny Highlands and access to numerous trails, many of which are suitable for cross-country skiing in winter.

The Cranberry Glades Botanical Area protects the largest area of bogs in West Virginia and a boardwalk gives visitors the chance to see the vegetation without harming the fragile habitat. Here you can see fluffy cotton grass, sphagnum moss, jewelweed, marsh marigold, and insect-eating plants such as sundew and pitcher plant.

Animal species in the forest include beaver, snowshoe hare, white-tailed deer, Northern Virginia flying squirrel, Virginia big-eared bat, black bear, a variety of reptiles and amphibians, and more than 100 bird species, notably wild turkey and songbirds. EB

TRAVELER'S NOTES

Information Supervisor's Office, Monongahela National Forest Headquarters, 200 Sycamore St, Elkins, WV 26241; tel. (304) 636-1800

Hours Always open, except for highlands in winter

Visitor centers Cranberry Mountain: Memorial Day–Labor Day, daily, 9 am– 5 pm; Jan through Apr and Nov, Sat–Sun, 10 am–4 pm; May, Sept, Oct, Fri–Sun, 9 am–5 pm; closed Dec. Seneca Rocks: tel. (304) 567-2827

Fees Most sites free

Permits Hunting and fishing; state licenses plus National Forest stamp

Camping 26 campgrounds (442 sites)

Lodging Cabins or lodges in 17 centers. Contact visitor centers for information

Supplies Communities in forest

Access for people with disabilities Picnic areas and overviews at various points along Highland Scenic Highway. Restrooms, fishing pier at Hill Creek Falls

When to visit Spring and Oct

Backcountry maps 70 USGS maps—refer to West Virginia Index Map

The polyphemus moth, with its striking "eyes". 221

0   100   200 miles
0   100   200   300 km

Baxter SP

MAINE

Acadia
NP

White Mountain NF

VT   NH

Boston

Adirondack Park

MA
RI

Monomoy
NWR

NEW YORK   CT

Iroquois
NWR

Presque Isle SP

New York

Erie
NWR

PENNSYLVANIA

NJ

Philadelphia   Edwin B Forsythe NWR

Baltimore   Cape May Point SP

MD   DE   Bombay Hook NWR

Washington DC

The Northeast

Bombay Hook
National Wildlife Refuge

Delaware

Dutch settlers in the seventeenth century used to call this region Bompies Hoeck, meaning "little-tree point", a name later corrupted by English colonists. Today, in an area of nearly 16,000 acres (6,480 ha), Bombay Hook plays host to thousands of birds that pause to rest and feed as they migrate along the Atlantic coast twice a year.

About three-fourths of the refuge is salt marsh—a mosaic of tall grasses and tidal creeks. The rest is woodland (both dry and swampy), meadows, and impoundments—artificial freshwater ponds. A 12 mile (20 km) auto route winds around the ponds, bringing visitors within easy viewing distance. At three spots you can climb observation towers for a more sweeping view, and there are three short nature trails leading through the forested and wetland areas.

Each season has its glories. On April and May mornings, the woodlands are filled with the songs of wood warblers, vireos, tanagers, thrushes, and other songbirds. And at twilight during spring, a chorus of ten frog species serenades the refuge. Bald eagles nest here at this time of year, and may occasionally be seen soaring overhead.

HORSESHOE CRABS

One of America's greatest wildlife spectacles occurs in May—peaking in the second half of the month—when hundreds of

Remaining virtually unchanged for 200 million years, horseshoe crabs are, in fact, arachnids and are therefore related to spiders and scorpions. Despite appearances, they are harmless.

thousands of horseshoe crabs emerge from Delaware Bay to spawn, the females laying billions of eggs along the beaches. At the same time, clouds of migratory shorebirds arrive after nonstop flights of 2,000 to 4,000 miles (3,000 to 6,000 km) from South America. For several days, each bird feasts on thousands of these tiny eggs, then sets off on the final leg of 3,000 miles (5,000 km) to breeding grounds

Clouds of snow geese over Bombay Hook (above). The ruff (right), an Eurasian shorebird species seldom seen in America, stops at Bombay Hook in small but growing numbers in spring.

on Canada's arctic tundra. Between 1 and 1.5 million shorebirds stop in Delaware Bay, tens of thousands at Bombay Hook alone. Of some 20 species, the most numerous at the refuge are red knots, ruddy turnstones, and semipalmated sandpipers.

Despite an abundance of biting bugs, summer shouldn't be missed. New broods of ducklings appear, and wader numbers peak. Herons, egrets, and glossy ibises prowl the waterways in slow motion. In June and July, diamondback terrapins and snapping turtles, usually hard to see, emerge from the water to lay their eggs, often alongside the dikes.

The most popular time to visit Bombay Hook is in October and November, when countless thousands of geese and ducks glide down from the sky to refresh themselves before the next leg of their southbound journey. About 75,000 of the transients are snow geese and, on any given day, there may be up to 20,000 of them parked almost wing to wing on the water. An abundance of Canada geese and 14 duck species also crowd in. Large populations of birds, especially waterfowl, overwinter here. EW

TRAVELER'S NOTES

Information Refuge Manager, Bombay Hook National Wildlife Refuge, 2591 Whitehall Neck Rd, Smyrna, DE 19977; tel. (302) 653-9345, fax (302) 653-0684

Hours Year-round, daylight hours

Visitor center Whitehall Neck Rd (Route 85) entrance; open Mon–Fri, 8 am–4 pm, Sat–Sun, 9 am–5 pm; closed Sat–Sun, June–Aug, Dec–Feb and federal holidays. Brochures, maps, free auto tape tour, books, guides, nature gifts, permits

Fees Admission

Permits Hunting (state license)

Camping None in refuge, but campgrounds at Killens Pond in Felton, south of Dover, and at Lums Pond, at Bear on Route 13, north of refuge

Lodging Dover

Supplies Dover, Smyrna

Access for people with disabilities Visitor center, Bear Swamp Nature Trail

When to visit Mar, Oct, Nov for peak waterfowl migration; Apr–June, late Aug–Sept for shorebirds; June–Aug for wading birds; Apr–May for songbirds. Biting insects a problem June–Sept; ticks common spring through fall

225

Acadia National Park

Maine

Acadia is where the mountains meet the sea—among them pink granite Cadillac Mountain, highest point on the United States Atlantic coast—and is one of the few areas along the rockbound coast of northern New England that has not been developed nor is privately owned. Forests of conifers and deciduous trees grow to the rocky rim of a shoreline swept by crashing waves. Here you can see creatures of both land and ocean, ranging from porcupines and spruce grouse to harbor seals and finback whales.

Most of the 42,000 acre (17,000 ha) park is located on Mount Desert Island, with its cliffs, coves, and inlets. A 20 mile (30 km) loop road with various branches takes visitors to sights ranging from Thunder Hole, a cavern where air compressed by the pounding surf explodes dramatically, to Jordan Pond, a tranquil glacier-gouged lake.

Another part of the park is on the mainland, at the tip of Schoodic Peninsula, and a further portion takes up more than half Isle au Haut, lying in Penobscot Bay, about 15 miles (24 km) southwest of Mount Desert Island. Isle au Haut is linked to the mainland by ferry.

A DROWNED COASTLINE

Like most of the Maine coast, Acadia was shaped by the last ice age. When the ice expanded from the north, it surged over the granite rock of Mount Desert Island to a point further south on the continental shelf, which then lay above sea level. The enormous weight of this ice sheet compressed the land, gouged out valleys, and

The lighthouse at Bass Harbor lies at the southernmost tip of Mount Desert Island. The building dates from 1858.

Waves constantly pound the rocky shores and headlands of Acadia (above). The park's many carriage roads make excellent cross-country ski trails in winter (left).

tilted the Earth's surface seaward. As the ice melted, so the sea level rose, drowning the coastline. Maine's islands, headlands, and cliffs are land that remained above the advancing sea.

Despite its look of permanence, the coast of Acadia continues to change. The surging tides and battering surf hammer at the rock, slowly carving and breaking it. But while the sea destroys the land in one way, it restores it in another. Currents and waves smooth the rock fragments into pebbles, and deposit them to form new shoals and gravel bars.

During summer, the forests and meadows of Acadia are patterned with wildflowers, including pitcher plants, purple-fringed orchids, and rare sundews. In fall, the maples, birches, and other deciduous trees blaze with yellow, orange, and red, set against the dark green of the coniferous woods.

Atlantic puffin.

TRAVELER'S NOTES

Information *Superintendent, Acadia National Park, PO Box 177 Bar Harbor, ME 04609-0177; tel. (207) 288-3338*

Hours *Year-round, 24 hours. Closed federal holidays*

Visitor center *Route 3 south of Hulls Cove. May 1–Oct 31, 8 am–4.30 pm. Cassette-tape tour, publications*

Fees *Admission, camping*

Permits *None*

Camping *2 campgrounds on Mount Desert (374 tent, 127 trailer sites): Blackwoods open all year, reservations June 15–Sept 15; Seawall open late May to late Sept. 1 campground on Isle au Haut*

Lodging *Bar Harbor and other nearby communities*

Supplies *Bar Harbor, Southwest Harbor*

Access for people with disabilities *Access information for campgrounds and some trails available at visitor center and campgrounds*

When to visit *Summer for most activities but crowded. Fall for foliage. Winter can be very cold. May for birding but black flies can be a problem. 2 miles of loop open to vehicles in winter; remainder open to snowmobiles*

Backcountry maps *USGS Acadia National Park*

Note *Pets allowed if kept on leash. Removal of rocks, flowers, and marine life prohibited*

A HISTORY OF ACADIA

Acadia National Park is named after the old French colony in nearby Nova Scotia. For about a century before the British drove them from Canada in 1759, the area where the park now lies was occupied, more or less permanently, by the French. With their departure, English settlers began arriving and, by 1850, Mount Desert had become a farming and seafaring center. At around that time, painters of the Hudson River School introduced the island to a wider public through their paintings. Tourists began to arrive, a hotel was built at Bar Harbor, and millionaires such as the Rockefellers, Fords, Vanderbilts, and Astors built themselves elegant summer mansions, known as "cottages".

At the beginning of this century, it became clear that development of the area threatened to mar its natural beauty. A number of the wealthy residents donated large slices of land, and before long 6,000 acres (2,340 ha) had been obtained for public use. By 1919, it was designated a national park—the first east of the Mississippi.

John D. Rockefeller, Jr was the main donor of land, altogether giving more than 11,000 acres (4,455 ha) to the park over the years. Between 1915 and 1933 he also had an extensive system of carriage roads built within the park. Today, these roads are widely used by hikers, cyclists, and cross-country skiers.

One of Acadia's "cottages".

The view from Cadillac Mountain on a fine summer's day. A male king eider (below).

With a diversity of land and aquatic habitats, including fresh-water lakes and bogs, Acadia attracts more than 300 species of bird, including 122 that breed there. During spring and summer, colonies of Atlantic puffins and guillemots nest on the cliffs. Once rare, bald eagles and ospreys are now a common sight. Black-backed and herring gulls wheel overhead and black-legged kittiwakes skim the waves. Scoter and common eider ducks frequent Acadia's waters all year. In winter, the goose-sized king eider arrives from the north, the male a striking sight with its yellow bill shield and bluish head.

FOREST AND MARINE LIFE

Acadia's forests are filled with songbirds, including veeries, ruby-crowned kinglets, hermit thrushes, goldfinches, red crossbills, and warblers. Woodlands also host a large variety of mammals, although they generally stay well hidden. Coyotes hunt white-tailed deer among the trees, and moose and black bear may occasionally visit. Otters can sometimes be seen in the ponds and streams and there is a healthy beaver population.

Several marine mammals inhabit the waters off Acadia, including finback, humpback, right, and minke whales. Harbor porpoises can be spotted from time to time, and the park offers cruises to see the harbor seals on Baker Island, one of several islets off Mount Desert.

The tide pools contain some of the park's most fascinating communities. At low tide, many of the pools are easy to reach—a plus for visitors with youngsters, though care should be taken as boulders are often slippery and heavy surf is common. Amid the bladdered fronds of rockweed, sea anemones lend splashes of color to the granite

Jordan Pond (above) was originally gouged out of the surrounding rock by glaciers. A humpback whale (left).

and, like living pincushions, sea urchins cling to the rock. There are barnacles everywhere and sea stars slowly creep about on their tube-like feet. Isolated by surrounding rock when the tide ebbs, the pools become ocean when the sea edges in once more. ER

Tide pools are home to fascinating marine communities.

Baxter State Park

Maine

Crowned by the granite peak of 5,267 foot (1,606 m) Mount Katahdin—Maine's highest mountain and the northern terminus of the Appalachian Trail—Baxter is a pristine wilderness. The Baxter State Park Authority, which manages the park's 202,064 acres (81,836 ha), strives to keep it that way. For example, there are no paved roads, and you are not allowed to operate a cellular telephone, a radio, or a chainsaw within its boundaries.

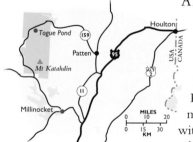

ALPINE TUNDRA

Baxter offers a wealth of natural grandeur and there are nearly 180 miles (290 km) of hiking trails to explore. The windswept heights of Katahdin and other smaller mountains nearby are covered with alpine tundra, offering a wonderful display of wildflowers in summer, such as alpine bistort, with its white or pinkish flowers, and the white blossoms of star saxifrage.

Bearberry willows grow in the alpine regions of Katahdin and in one ravine you can see arctic willows—trees that are rare in New England but quite common in the Arctic. Also keep an eye out for the translucent, gray-brown Katahdin arctic butterfly. This is a variation of a species that is found a good deal farther north. Presumably it was stranded in this stony, exposed habitat toward the end of the last ice age.

230 Baxter's many ponds are visited by waterfowl and moose.

Cedar waxwings nest in the north, flying south in winter.

Moose can often be seen at Sandy Stream Pond and the area nearby. From the trail that loops around the pond you are quite likely to see about a dozen of these animals, some relatively close up. Beavers are common here too, but even if you don't see them, you can spot their lodges and dams. Other mammals that live in the park include eastern coyotes, snowshoe rabbits, black bears, white-tailed deer, pine martens, fishers (related to martens but larger), and porcupines.

Mount Katahdin and Sandy Stream Pond (above). Pitcher plant (left).

The myriad streams, lakes, and ponds in Baxter are home to several species of waterbird, including the great blue heron and the loon, whose haunting call is the cry of the great north woods. Ruffed grouse and spruce grouse are found here and the water pipit, which breeds mostly in the Arctic and high in the Rocky Mountains, also nests on Katahdin. Bald eagles, which have recovered from near extinction, are now common throughout much of Maine, and you may see them in Baxter. Other birds include ravens, vireos, thrushes, and woodpeckers.

ER

TRAVELER'S NOTES

Information *Baxter State Park, Reservation Clerk, 64 Balsam Dr., Millinocket, ME 04462; tel. (207) 723-5140*

Hours *Always open, but impassable to vehicles in winter. Gates open May 15–Oct 15; Togue Pond, 6 am–1 pm, Matagamon, 6 am–9 pm*

Visitor centers *Headquarters: Memorial Day–Labor Day, 8 am–4 pm; Mon–Fri in winter. Slide show, informational materials. Togue Pond: Memorial Day–Labor Day, 7 am–3 pm*

Fees *Admission (non-residents of Maine), camping*

Permits *Camping, research studies, fishing (state license)*

Camping *10 campgrounds, some primitive sites. Campgrounds open from mid-May to Oct 15*

Lodging *Millinocket, Patten*

Supplies *Millinocket, Patten*

Access for people with disabilities *Visitor centers, some cabins*

When to visit *Summer for most activities. Winter weather can be extremely severe*

Adult bull moose can be very aggressive during the mating season.

231

Monomoy
National Wildlife Refuge
Massachusetts

Monomoy constantly changes shape and size. For the first half of the twentieth century, this sliver of sand formed a peninsula dangling from the "elbow" of Cape Cod. In 1958, a hurricane severed the connection and Monomoy became an island, later separating into two. The reserve consists of North and South Monomoy and a portion of Morris Island.

Ninety-four percent of Monomoy is a federally designated wilderness—one of few such areas in the eastern United States. Its 2,700 acres (1,115 ha) incoporate sand dunes, marshes, tidal mud flats,

moors, ponds, and dense thickets of shrubs. Botanists have identified 160 plant species in the refuge.

BEACH BLOSSOMS

On South Monomoy, the back dunes are carpeted with beach heather. During June, its tiny blossoms cast a golden glow over vast stretches of sand. From late June, the marshland fringes are brightened by big, gaudy pink blooms of rose mallow. Much of the inner dune area is covered by thickets of bayberry draped with poison ivy (see p. 48). Indeed, the island crawls with this noxious vine. As you can't avoid it, dress appropriately.

The location and habitat of the islands make them most inviting to thousands of birds: 285 species have been spotted here. In spring, Monomoy is second only to Cape May, New Jersey (p. 236), in numbers of shorebirds, among them willets, greater yellowlegs, dunlins, oyster-catchers, and black-bellied plovers. By summer, hundreds of birds are nesting on the islands.

The reserve is a favorite spot for birders.

A flock of sanderlings, ruddy turnstones, and red knots (above). Gray seal (below).

Monomoy is particularly notable for nesting terns—common, least, arctic, and the endangered roseate tern. Ten duck species also nest here in great numbers, as do a couple of winged predators. Northern harriers (marsh hawks) and short-eared owls (which hunt by day) swoop about the marshy areas, searching for voles to feed to their chicks. To protect rare birds, some areas are closed during the nesting season. The fall spectacle begins with the arrival of numerous shorebirds and scores of songbirds in August. Waterfowl come through later in great numbers. Also in fall, harbor seals begin arriving from Maine, some 2,000 of them staying for winter. Up to 200 gray seals also winter here, and about 60 remain all summer, when pups are born. Geologically, biologically, and botanically, Monomoy is in a constant state of flux. EW

TRAVELER'S NOTES

Information Refuge Manager, Monomoy National Wildlife Refuge, Wikis Way, Morris Island, Chatham, MA 02633; tel. (508) 945-0594, fax (508) 945 9559.

Hours Year-round, daylight hours

Visitor center Morris Island Rd, just past Chatham Lighthouse: irregular hours, call in advance. Brochures, maps, exhibits

Fees None

Permits None

Camping Not permitted on refuge. Public campground at Nickerson State Park in Brewster; private campgrounds in Wellfleet and Brewster

Lodging Chatham, Harwich, Harwichport

Supplies Chatham

Access for people with disabilities Visitor facilities on mainland only

When to visit Spring (Apr to mid-June best for shorebirds) and fall (mid-Aug to mid-Sept best for overall variety; Oct–Nov for waterfowl)

Note Reached only by boat. Rough waters make this a risky trip in one's own boat. Refuge best explored on tours run by Massachusetts Audubon Society's Wellfleet Bay Wildlife Sanctuary (PO Box 236, West Road, South Wellfleet, MA 02663; tel. (508) 349-2615) and Cape Cod Museum of Natural History (Rt. 6A, Box 1710, Brewster, MA 02631; tel. (508) 896-3867). Non-tour boat services available from Chatham; inquire at visitor center

Roseate tern.

233

White Mountain National Forest

New Hampshire and Maine

Mount Washington, tallest mountain in the Northeast, rises gently from the broad flanks of the White Mountains, but its climatic conditions are anything but gentle. Snow falls on this 6,288 foot (1,917 m) peak throughout the year and often the summit is shrouded in cloud. In winter, the mountain resembles an enormous ice cube and winds on its upper slopes

have been clocked at over 200 miles (320 km) per hour. Still, for all its harshness, Mount Washington remains the star attraction of a superb 769,000 acre (310,000 ha) forested wonderland.

White Mountain National Forest boasts

Howling winds ridge the snow and ice on the summit of Mount Washington.

thick stands of virgin red spruce, balsam fir, and yellow and paper birches; hundreds of miles of hiking trails, including a challenging stretch of the Appalachian Trail; several wilderness areas; gem-like lakes; babbling brooks; abundant wildlife, including deer, beavers, black bears, and bobcats; and a remarkable number of rare plants.

Not-to-be-missed spots include the Pinkham Notch Scenic Area, off State Highway 16. Try the trail to Crystal Cascade, an amazing waterfall that lives up to its name. Alpine Garden, off Highway 16 on the way to Mount Washington, is another delight. More than 110 different kinds of plant grow here, 75 of which are true alpine species, in that they live only above the timberline. The rarest is the dwarf yellow cinquefoil. Other rarities include the blackberry-like cloudberry and two kinds of eyebright—distant cousins of the better-known paintbrushes.

Rare plants can also be found in the Lincoln Woods Scenic Area, reached by a trail from Wiley House along US Highway 302. A high elevation bog between Ethan and Shoal ponds

Snow covers the peaks in White Mountain for much of the year (above). Vivid fall colors reflected in the waters of the Ammonoosuc River (right).

is home to species such as Pursh's goldenrod and turtlehead. Unusual birds also alight here, including boreal chickadees and Lincoln sparrows.

THE BACKCOUNTRY

For isolation, visit the Great Gulf Wilderness Area north of Pinkham Notch. This large glacial valley connects Mount Washington with the northern peaks of the Presidential Range. Trails lead to the summits of mounts Madison, Adams,

and Clay, providing glorious views of alpine lakes. The Presidential Range–Dry River Wilderness Area, just south of Mount Washington, is the southern access to the forest's highest point.

The Kancamagus Highway (112) bisects the forest from east to west and has scores of overlooks. From the Rocky Gorge Scenic Area in the southeastern corner of the park, you can see the Swift River tumbling over a two-story drop.

The Patte Brook Auto Tour, on the Maine side of the forest, is designed to show what goes on in a national forest: logging, recreational activities, land management, and preservation. One of the best stops is Patte Brook Marsh, a wetlands home for waterfowl and moose. You can pick up a detailed route map at the Bethel Ranger Station on US Highway 2, at the tour's start. DH

Bobcat.

TRAVELER'S NOTES

Information Superintendent, White Mountain National Forest, 719 Main St, Laconia, NH 03246; tel. (603) 528-8721

Hours Always open

Visitor centers Saco, Conway; Ammonoosuc, Bethlehem; Androscoggin, Gorham; Pemigewasset, Plymouth. All Mon-Fri, 9 am–4.30 pm. Maps, exhibits

Fees Developed campsites

Permits Hunting, fishing (state licenses)

Camping 22 developed campgrounds at such areas as Moose Brook State Park, Oliverian, Wildwood, Franconian

Notch State Park, and Crawford Notch State Park; also backcountry sites

Lodging Laconia, Bethlehem, North Conway, Woodstock, Gorham

Supplies Laconia, Bethlehem, North Conway, Woodstock, Gorham

Access for people with disabilities Developed campsites, picnic areas

When to visit Summer for camping, fall for foliage colors, winter for skiing

Backcountry maps USGS Mount Washington

Cape May Point State Park

New Jersey

The region around the town of Cape May is North America's principal birding hot spot. Although there are abundant resident birds, the majority are transient, and they come by the million: warblers, grosbeaks, finches, vireos, flycatchers, thrushes, kinglets, hawks, falcons, eagles, owls, woodpeckers, cuckoos, swallows, geese, ducks, swans, pelicans, woodcocks, plovers, sandpipers, herons, egrets. A total of 402 species has been logged at Cape May, at least 350 of which are regulars. The heaviest concentration occurs during fall, or southbound, migration— from June 23 to January 10. Spring migration runs from January 10 through June 10, so birds are passing through all year-round.

The cape lies between the Atlantic Coast and the Delaware River Valley flyways. There is also a raptor route, shaped by mountain ridges, to the north.

Fall's north-westerly winds push birds south along the coast and they follow the peninsula down to the cape, at the mouth of Delaware Bay. The birds then rest and feed here, while waiting for winds that will help carry them across the 12 miles (19 km) of open water. When traveling northward, they pause here after the water crossing, gathering their strength for the next leg of their trip.

The American kestrel (left).
Cape May lighthouse (right).

HAWK WATCHING

Cape May Point State Park lies at the tip of the peninsula and is the top spot for observing migrating birds of prey. From late August through November, around 50,000 pass through the park (up to 200,000 fly through the Cape May region). An elevated platform allows visitors to view wave after wave of hawks sweeping past. Of the 15 species coming through, the most common are American kestrels, and sharp-shinned, Cooper's, and red-tailed hawks. Bald and golden eagles appear in late fall, and there are

Cape May Meadows from the East Walk (above). Red-throated loons (left) arrive at the peninsula in March and October.

large flights of barn, long-eared, and northern saw-whet owls.

A 3 mile (5 km) network of trails and boardwalks winds through woodlands that harbor mobs of songbirds in spring and fall and past ponds and marshes that attract gulls, egrets, herons, ducks, and numerous shorebirds. In March, thousands of ducks and geese are joined in the waters off the point by common and red-throated loons, and in May you can see sooty and greater shearwaters and other oceanic species as they come close to shore. The first week of November is when strays from farther afield—such as cave swallows and Bell's vireos—usually show up.

TRAVELER'S NOTES

Information *Superintendent, Cape May Point State Park, PO Box 107, Cape May Point, NJ 08212; tel. (609) 884-2159, fax (609) 884-0352. Cape May Bird Observatory, 701 East Lake Dr.; tel. (609) 884-2736;*

Hours *Year-round, daylight hours*

Visitor centers *State Park: Memorial Day–Labor Day, daily, 8 am–8 pm; Apr 1–May 30, Labor Day–Oct 30, Mon–Fri, 8 am–3.30 pm, Sat–Sun, 8 am–6 pm; Nov 1–Mar 31, Wed–Sun, 8 am–3 pm, closed state holidays. Publications, exhibits. Cape May Bird Observatory: Tues–Sat, 9 am–5 pm; Sun 9 am–2 pm. Maps, checklists, books, various programs*

Fees *None*

Permits *None*

Camping *50 private campgrounds in county. Contact NJ Campground Owners Assn, tel. (609) 465-8444*

Lodging *Cape May and neighboring towns. For information, contact Chamber of Commerce of Greater Cape May, tel. (609) 884 5508*

Supplies *Cape May and neighboring towns*

Access for people with disabilities *Visitor centers, boardwalk trail, hawk platform, picnic facilities*

When to visit *Year-round. Hawks mid-Sept to mid-Oct; shorebirds mid to end May; songbirds April to early May, mid-Aug to end Sept; waterfowl Nov–Dec; seabirds Oct 1–Dec 31; waders Apr–Sept*

The least bittern builds its nest in marshes or shallow ponds.

Bordering the park is the Cape May Migratory Bird Refuge—a sweeping seaside meadow dotted with ponds and patches of marsh. During spring and fall, countless sandpipers, plovers, and other shorebirds stop here. In summer, this is an excellent spot for herons, egrets, and gulls. The meadow also attracts numerous species of dragonfly and damselfly.

HIGBEE AND REEDS BEACHES

At Higbee Beach, a few miles north on Delaware Bay, vine-draped woodlands draw most of the more than 200 songbird species that frequent the area. Some days in September and October—after the arrival of a cold front and strong north-

In late May, horseshoe crabs come ashore to spawn (above), and around 1 million shorebirds (right) arrive to feed on the eggs.

westerly winds—the sky seems to rain warblers, vireos, sparrows, and finches. At times, many of them cannot even find places to perch.

Many woodcocks pass through Cape May, and the open fields at Higbee are packed with them in spring and fall. In the dim light of dusk in early March, you can see them performing their high-flying, acrobatic courtship rituals. In June and July, these fields are alive with butterflies, such as monarchs, buckeyes, mourning cloaks, tiger swallowtails, and red admirals. There are 104 species in the area.

Reeds Beach is the most accessible of a bevy of beaches bordering the bay where a shorebird spectacle occurs like clockwork in the second half of May. Between 1 and 1.5 million birds make their only stop between South America and the Arctic to feed on eggs laid by spawning horseshoe crabs. More than 20 species stop—the majority of them ruddy turnstones, semipalmated sandpipers, sanderlings, and red knots. EW

Sand dunes and sea grasses at the point (left). Green darner dragonfly (above). Buckeye butterfly (above left).

THE MIRACLE OF BIRD MIGRATION

Birds migrate primarily to find food. In spring, as billions of insects hatch, northern latitudes offer quantities of food and long periods of daylight in which to collect it. Many birds therefore migrate north to take advantage of these conditions and raise their young. Come fall, when the food runs out, parents and fledglings fly south.

How do these creatures accomplish such a prodigious feat? Not only must they travel to the "right" place, their timing must be right. If they leave too early, there will not be enough food waiting for them. Too late, and their youngsters won't be ready to fly by the onset of fall.

Birds rely on a variety of cues for orientation and navigation. These include movements of the Sun and the stars; the stirrings of their own physiological "clocks"; polarized and ultraviolet light; barometric pressure; wind direction and turbulence; wave patterns and tides; the pull of the Earth's magnetic field; and probably landmarks such as valleys, lakes, and ponds.

The timing of the trip depends on avian hormones, which respond to a number of the above cues. Hormones also trigger the production of body fat, to build strength for the trip. Many birds, such as the shorebirds that come to Delaware Bay, travel up to 3,000 miles (4,800 km) nonstop, then fly another 2,500 miles (4,000 km) to tundra nesting grounds.

Most songbirds fly by night to avoid hawks and other predators. Larger birds, such as cranes and eagles, tend to be daytime travelers. Small birds that are strong flyers—swallows, for instance—also favor daylight. Waterfowl migrate both day and night.

Not all birds migrate vast distances. Partial migrants move only a few hundred miles, say, from the northeast to the southeast. Some species just shift elevation, nesting at high altitudes in summer, then moving to the valleys. Nor do all birds migrate. Chickadees, for example, simply switch from an insect diet to seeds.

In North America, most migrations are north–south. Millions of birds, primarily waterfowl, follow the four major flyways: Pacific Coast, Central, Mississippi, and Atlantic Coast. There are also many secondary flyways. Birds tend to favor the same paths every year, but they do not necessarily take identical routes in fall and spring. For example, there are thousands of hawks at Cape May in fall but relatively few in spring because they are dispersed by differences in air currents.

The main migration routes: Pacific Coast (A), Central (B), Mississippi (C), Atlantic Coast (D).

239

Edwin B. Forsythe
National Wildlife Refuge

New Jersey

The reserve's proper name is Forsythe, but most people speak of going to Brigantine. The latter, created in 1937, was initially a separate refuge. In 1984 it was joined with the nearby Barnegat Refuge, farther north, and a couple of smaller parcels, to form the Forsythe complex, which now stands at approximately 40,000 acres (16,200 ha), of which Brigantine comprises a little more than half.

Most of Forsythe is tidal salt meadow and marshland, with scattered shallow bays and coves. Dense stands of cordgrass and reeds, plus quantities of fish and molluscs in the tidal waters, act as a magnet to aquatic birds. Food, cover, and nest sites—all are plentiful here.

Dikes have been built to create two huge pools at Brigantine—one filled with fresh water, the other with brackish (a mixture of fresh and salt). These pools attract an even greater diversity of species (289 have been recorded) than would marsh alone. At the western edge of the pools are grasslands, wet woodlands, and forests that attract songbirds, especially during spring and fall migration.

Except for short woodland footpaths, Brigantine is a drive-through refuge. An 8 mile (13 km) road loops around the pools, enabling visitors to see habitats that are partly artificial on one side and natural salt marsh or sea coves on the other. The ponds are broken into winding channels and smaller pools by clumps of tall reeds and grasses. In early fall, in the watery ditches

The black skimmer's unique bill, with its lower part one-third longer than the upper, enables the bird to deftly scoop up fish as it flies over the surface of the water.

Great egrets making their way through the shallows (above). The black duck (right) is more murky brown than black.

alongside the road, you may see great and snowy egrets—the former about a foot taller than the latter. The great egret moves with deliberation, leaning forward then abruptly darting its long yellow beak into the water to grab a fish. The snowy egret has a more frantic style, scurrying about to stir up choice morsels.

DUCKS AND GEESE

The same aquatic alleys are cruised by mallards, green-winged teals, northern shovelers, and black ducks. Periodically, these puddle ducks upend themselves to feed underwater, leaving only their tails above the surface. The black duck is one of the reasons for the refuge's existence. About 70,000 black ducks—much of the species' entire Atlantic flyway population—depend on this place for survival.

Along the east pool, when the tide is out, areas of salt marsh are busy with mobs of greater and lesser yellowlegs, semipalmated sandpipers, shortbilled dowitchers, dunlins, and other shorebirds. The muddy channel bottoms are loaded with tiny organisms that are relished by these birds.

During fall, huge flocks of brant—small geese with black necks and heads—descend on the refuge. As much as 90 percent of the Atlantic population of brant migrates here. Tens of thousands of snow geese also arrive, as do thousands of Canada geese. In November, the waters here are carpeted with up to 150,000 waterfowl.

EW

A flock of brant.

TRAVELER'S NOTES

Information *Refuge Manager, Edwin B. Forsythe National Wildlife Refuge, PO Box 544, 70 Collinstown Road, Barnegat, NJ 08005 U.S.A.; tel. 609-698-1387, fax 609-698-0109*

Hours *Year-round, sunrise to sunset*

Visitor center *Self-service information booth opposite headquarters on Great Creek Rd east of Route 9. Brochures, maps. Headquarters: bird exhibits*

Fees *Admission*

Permits *Hunting, fishing, crabbing (state licenses)*

Camping *Public campgrounds in*

Wharton and Bass River state forests. Private campgrounds in Absecon

Lodging *Absecon, Pleasantville, Atlantic City*

Supplies *Smithville, Absecon*

Access for people with disabilities *Headquarters, auto tour, boardwalk portion of Leeds Echo Trail. Brochure available in braille and large type*

When to visit *Spring and fall. Migration peaks: waterfowl, Mar 20–Apr 15, Sept–Nov; wading birds, shorebirds, songbirds, Apr 20–May 30 (warblers early May) and Aug. Biting bugs plentiful mid-May to Sept*

241

Adirondack Park

New York

The wild northern third of New York remained virtually unexplored until the 1850s. Then timber companies and miners began to exploit the area, leading to erosion, wildfires, and damage to the state's water supply. Fisheries were destroyed and wildlife was overhunted, resulting in the disappearance of several large mammal species.

Seeking to protect the region, the state legislature created a regional forest preserve in 1885 and the Adirondack Park in 1892. Neither halted the loggers. Then, in 1894, all public lands within the park were designated "forever wild". These are not to be leased, sold, or logged. In fact, not a tree upon them can be cut down.

Adirondack Park now covers 6.1 million acres (2.5 million ha). (Yellowstone, Yosemite, Grand Canyon, Glacier, and Great Smoky Mountains national parks, combined, could all fit inside it.) More than 50 percent of it is privately owned, and there are 105 small towns and villages within its borders.

Just under half of the park is "forever wild" forest preserve. Most of this is second-growth timber from 50 to 100 years old, but a significant portion is old-growth forest—the only true wilderness east of the Mississippi.

THE HIGH PEAKS

In the High Peaks region of the park, 42 mountains rise 4,000 feet (1,220 m) or more. Among them is Mount Marcy, the highest peak in the state of New York. The climb up Marcy is long and arduous, but many other peaks are more accessible. One easy way to scale the heights is to drive the toll road up Whiteface.

As well as the vast areas of forest, there are barrens, marshes, bogs, alpine meadows,

River otters (left). The Hudson River viewed from the Blue Ledge Trail (right).

The summit of Algonquin Mountain (above) in the High Peaks region. The shoreline of Lake George and, just offshore, Rogers Rock (left).

The forests are a blend of deciduous hardwoods and conifers. The largest segment of old-growth forest is in the Five Ponds Wilderness, where you'll find white pines, hemlocks, and red spruce up to 300 years old shadowing the trails.

The Hudson River, New York City's polluted waterway, originates on Mount Marcy. In the Adirondacks it's a pristine, wild river. The rapids on the upper Hudson are for the adventurous only, but peaceful boating is also available. A popular canoe route follows the Fulton Chain of Lakes and Raquette River from Old Forge to Saranac Lake, providing an eight to ten day wilderness experience. EW

and about 3,000 lakes and ponds linked by 31,000 miles (50,000 km) of rivers and creeks. Hundreds of plant species grow here, many of them rare. This is the most wildlife-rich area in the East, but the animals—even bear and moose—are not easy to see. Birds are abundant, including the common loon, known for its yodeling, laughing calls.

TRAVELER'S NOTES

Information Contact county or town tourist bureaus. For information on hiking and canoeing, call Bureau of Preservation and Protection Management at the Dept of Environmental Conservation, 50 Wolf Rd, Albany, NY 12233-4750; tel. 518-457-5690

Hours Always open

Visitor centers Paul Smiths: north of town on Route 30, tel. (518) 327-3000. Newcomb: tel. (518) 582-2000. Both centers May–Sept, daily, 9 am–7 pm; Oct–Apr, daily 9 am–5 pm; closed Thanksgiving, Dec 25. Brochures, trail guides, maps, exhibits, audio-visual programs, gift shop (May–Sept only)

Fees Camping

Permits Backcountry camping, fishing (state license)

Camping 42 campgrounds (5,534 sites). Primitive sites in backcountry

Lodging Communities throughout park

Supplies Communities throughout park

Access for people with disabilities Visitor centers, nature trails at visitor centers, most campgrounds

When to visit Spring and fall. Apr–May for wildflowers, late Sept for foliage colors. Black flies a problem late May–July

Backcountry maps Over 300 USGS maps—refer to New York Index Map

The Ausable River in fall.

Iroquois National Wildlife Refuge

New York

Much of northeastern America's topography was shaped during the last ice age. When the ice withdrew from what is now the far western corner of New York, it left behind a great body of water. Gradually, this lake dwindled to swampy remnants. When European settlers arrived early in the nineteenth century, they began logging and draining these areas to turn them into farms. Fortunately for the wildlife, however, this proved expensive and the farmers departed for more promising sites, leaving much of the swamp intact.

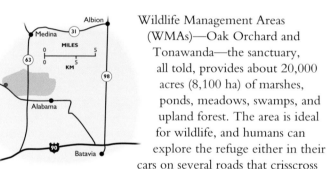

GEESE AND DUCKS

About a century later, the federal government turned nearly 11,000 acres (4,450 ha) of this into the Iroquois National Wildlife Refuge, primarily for the welfare of the thousands of geese and ducks that travel through the area on spring and fall migrations. Lying between two state

Wildlife Management Areas (WMAs)—Oak Orchard and Tonawanda—the sanctuary, all told, provides about 20,000 acres (8,100 ha) of marshes, ponds, meadows, swamps, and upland forest. The area is ideal for wildlife, and humans can explore the refuge either in their cars on several roads that crisscross the area, or on foot, via several trails. There are also a number of hiking trails in the WMAs.

In an average year, during spring migration, 40,000 Canada geese stop at Iroquois. Sometimes there are as many as 65,000, with the record so far standing at 88,000. Large numbers of snow geese also visit. Twenty-four duck species pause

Prothonotary warbler (left). Muskrat (right).

at Iroquois and ten species stay to nest. Tundra swans also call in briefly in spring, although their numbers are small. The springtime waterfowl census is usually about 80,000 birds. In fall, most of the geese travel east of Iroquois, but the duck population doubles.

Refuge records list 266 bird species, many of them aquatic. At present, great blue herons maintain a rookery of some 300 nests, although there have been as many as 700 in the past. In spring and summer, these lanky birds are everywhere, stalking the shallows, freezing in place like feathered statues, then thrusting dagger-like beaks downward to snatch a fish from the water.

Woodland trails tend to be prime spots for warblers in mid-May. The refuge's Onondaga

Trail begins along an open swamp that is a favorite haunt of muskrats and where painted turtles line up on logs to bask in the sun. In the woods beyond the swamp you are likely to come across American redstarts, ovenbirds, red-eyed vireos, and yellow-rumped warblers. More difficult to find, but by no means impossible, is the prothonotary warbler—a golden treasure high on birders' wish lists. The species nests in tree cavities along Oak Orchard Creek, which winds through the refuge.

While spring may be prime time, winter has its rewards, for about 60 bird species spend the cold months in the refuge. EW

TRAVELER'S NOTES

Information Refuge Manager, Iroquois National Wildlife Refuge, PO Box 517, Alabama, NY 14003; tel. (716) 948-5445, fax (716) 948-9538

Hours Year-round, sunrise to sunset

Visitor center Mon–Fri, 7.30 am–4.00 pm, except federal holidays. Brochures, maps, exhibits, permits

Fees None

Permits Use of photo blinds. Hunting (state license)

Camping Not permitted on refuge. Public campgrounds in Indian Falls and Darien Lake State Park

Lodging Medina, Lockport, Pembroke, Clarence, Batavia

Supplies Alabama, Lockport, Batavia, Medina, and Oakville

Access for people with disabilities Visitor center, Cayuga Overlook and deck, Kanyoo Trail. Auditorium listening system for people with hearing disabilities

When to visit Mar–Nov. First two weeks Apr and early Nov for waterfowl migration. Mid-May for warblers. July-Aug for herons. Mar–May and July-Aug for shorebirds. Biting bugs worst May–Aug

Wetlands in the refuge (top).
Nesting great blue herons (above). 245

Erie National Wildlife Refuge

Pennsylvania

Nothing in the animal kingdom is more majestic than a bald eagle soaring overhead, snow-white head and tail shimmering in the sunlight, broad wings spreading 7 feet (2 m) or more. Such a sight is uncommon, as eagles usually keep their distance from people, but you might be lucky enough to see one at Erie National Wildlife Refuge. Erie's wetlands are the kind that appeals to eagles— a mixture of swamp, marshland, creeks, wet meadows, and ponds.

The refuge consists of two units: Sugar Lake, an easily accessible area of 5,127 acres (2,076 ha) and, 10 miles (16 km) to the north, Seneca,

Painted turtles sunbathe on a fallen log (above). Erie is a top spot for observing the United States' national bird, the bald eagle (left).

a swampy, forested region of 3,227 acres (1,307 ha) with only one trail. At both units, eagles can be seen gliding overhead, or perched silently on dead trees. Sometimes they are sufficiently tolerant of people to perch near the fishing pier at Sugar Lake.

Two hundred and thirty-six bird species frequent the refuge, and 33 mammal species have been recorded. Beavers, which are numerous, are particularly popular with visitors. You can't miss their lodges—large, dome-shaped constructions of gnawed tree limbs cemented together with mud, rising above the water—but you need to be in the refuge around sunrise or sunset to see the beavers themselves as they are nocturnal.

WOOD DUCKS

Ducks are a specialty at Erie: 20 species are regulars. Of the five species nesting in the refuge, wood ducks are the most prolific. In the early 1900s, this beautiful bird was threatened with extinction because of excessive hunting and habitat destruction, and it was the creation of refuges like Erie and a widespread program to erect nestboxes that restored its numbers.

Around late May, you can see wood duck parents with their newly hatched bundles of golden fluff.

The Tsuga Trail winds among several habitats, including extensive fields of native grasses that provide nesting cover for ducks. The grasslands are also home to many of the dozen kinds of sparrow found here, the rarest of which is the Henslow's. The woodlands come alive with warblers and vireos in April and May, and wildflowers such as trout lilies, spring beauties, violets, and marsh marigolds bloom along the path in colorful profusion.

From the edge of the woodland the path leads to a boardwalk across a murky pond produced by beaver labor—a great spot for bird-watching. If you see flashes of brilliant blue zipping in and out of cavities in snags poking from the water, they'll be tree swallows. Their activity contrasts markedly with the slow-moving painted turtles soaking up the sun on fallen logs. Habitat diversity fosters wildlife diversity. EW

The male wood duck (below) is one of America's most handsome ducks. Beavers (below left) are most active after dark so look for them early or late in the day.

TRAVELER'S NOTES

Information Refuge Manager, Erie National Wildlife Refuge, 11296 Wood Duck Lane, Guys Mills, PA 16327; tel. (814) 789-3585, fax (814) 789-2909. TDD: Pennsylvania relay service, (800) 654-5984

Hours Year-round, sunrise to sunset

Visitor center Near Guys Mills. Mon–Fri, 8.00 am–4.30 pm, except federal holidays. Brochures, maps, exhibits

Fees None

Permits None

Camping Not permitted in refuge

Commercial campgrounds in Guys Mills

Lodging Meadville, Cochranton

Supplies Food and gas at Meadville and Frenchtown; food at Guys Mills

Access for people with disabilities Visitor center, parking, nature trail in Seneca division

When to visit Spring and fall. Mar–early Apr, Sept–Nov for waterfowl; May for warblers; summer for shorebirds, wading birds; fall for deer fawns

247

Presque Isle State Park

Pennsylvania

First come the hawks, starting in late February, and by April hundreds of birds of prey are soaring past. Waterfowl and gulls begin arriving in March, shore-birds in April. Come May, the woodlands are pulsating with songbirds, and this is when the birder population, binoculars fixed to their faces, reaches its peak. It's springtime at Presque Isle.

One of America's top ten birding hot spots, the peninsula (the name of which is French for "almost an island") pokes into the vastness of Lake Erie, only a short distance from the city of Erie. It is actually a sandspit, created by the combined forces of wind, waves, and water currents about 600 years ago. From above, it looks like a giant lamb chop, a few hundred yards wide at its neck and more than a mile wide in the center. Jutting northward, it's a magnet for spring migrants—the last land from which to launch themselves over the water. And in fall it's their first landfall after crossing the lake.

In mid-May, Presque Isle's sandy beaches and lagoon shores are swamped by scurrying shorebirds, including a veritable catalog of the sandpiper and plover families. The woods are filled with mating melodies and colors—the signatures of male warblers. Fiery oranges, electric yellows, pale greens, deep blues, and rich chestnut flash among the new leaves. Thirty-three warbler species are regulars here, along with an abundance of tanagers, flycatchers, thrushes, vireos, sparrows, and orioles. The park has recorded 318 bird species, and most appear every year.

Fall migration is almost as intense. This is also the time when mobs of monarch butterflies pause to rest at Presque Isle on their way to overwinter in the south.

FROM NEW SOIL TO CLIMAX FOREST

Migrants are also drawn here by the exceptionally diverse habitat. Indeed, the park illustrates the entire ecological phenomenon of succession—

Greater yellowlegs spend much of the year along the coasts, migrating to the far north to nest.

Presque Isle

Lake Erie

Erie

MILES

KM

20

832

79

90

McKean

248

from newly formed soil to climax forest. Within a space of about 3 miles (5 km), you can trace a series of land forms—from sand bars, to beach, to plains, to dunes and ridges—each with its own brand of vegetation: grasses, vines, scrubby thickets, mixed subclimax forest, and the botanical finale of oak–maple forest. Lagoons, ponds, and marshes separate the various stages. Presque Isle is the only place in North America where you can see the full progression of plant associations in a single, relatively small, area.

WILDFLOWERS

More than 500 plant species grow in the park, 65 of which Pennsylvania has classified as species of special concern. These include the endangered Kalm or brook lobelia. Its delicate, white-throated blue blossoms appear in damp places in late July and August. Rose gentian, yellow flax, and purple gerardia also bloom at this time of year,

Dunlins and least sandpipers (above). A male Blackburnian warbler (below), one of the peninsula's many songbirds.

but there are plants of all sorts flowering in the park from early spring well into fall.

When a day of warbler or wildflower viewing begins to wind down, visitors often head for a point near Budney Beach on the park's northern coast to witness further pyrotechnics—one of Presque Isle's well-known sunsets, which are among the best in the world. EW

A male scarlet tanager, one of the continent's most colorful birds.

TRAVELER'S NOTES

Information *Superintendent, Presque Isle State Park, Department of Environmental Resources, PO Box 8510, Erie, PA 16505-0510; tel. 814-833-7424, or 888-727-2757, fax (814) 833-0266*

Hours *Memorial Day–Labor Day, 5 am–11 pm; off-season, 5 am–9 pm*

Visitor center *Memorial Day–Labor Day, 10 am–6 pm; irregular hours off-season. Brochures, maps, exhibits. Free interpretive pontoon-boat rides in summer*

Fees *None*

Permits *Hunting (state license)*

Camping *None in park. Public campgrounds nearby in Erie, Lake City, Fairview, McKean*

Lodging *Erie*

Supplies *Food stalls in park in summer; Erie*

Access for people with disabilities *Visitor center, special picnic tables throughout park; multi-use trail. Wheelchair access ramp, Beach 7. Fishing area at East Pier*

When to visit *Spring and fall. May, Sept for songbird and shorebird peaks; Apr for birds of prey; Mar, Oct for waterfowl. Summer crowded. Many birds to see even in winter, but the peninsula is windy and cold*

249

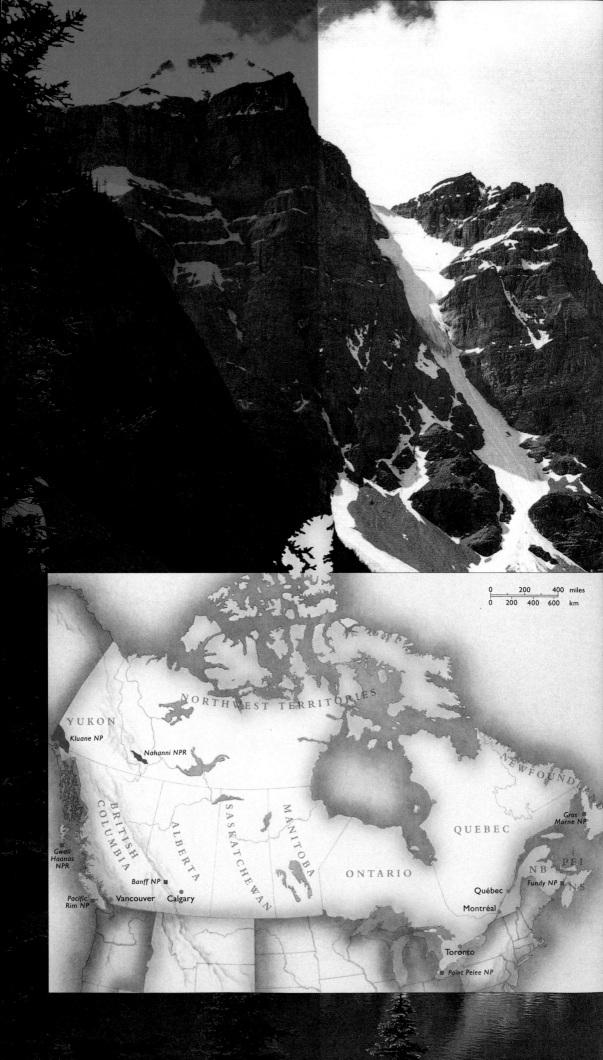

0   200   400   miles
0   200   400   600   km

YUKON

Kluane NP

Nahanni NPR

NORTHWEST TERRITORIES

NEWFOUNDLAND

BRITISH COLUMBIA

ALBERTA

SASKATCHEWAN

MANITOBA

QUEBEC

Gros Morne NP

Gwaii Haanas NPR

Banff NP

ONTARIO

NB   PEI

NS

Fundy NP

Pacific Rim NP

Vancouver

Calgary

Québec

Montréal

Toronto

Point Pelee NP

Canada

Banff National Park

Alberta

The history of Banff and Canada's national parks began in the Rocky Mountains with the building of a railroad linking the Pacific Ocean with what is now Ontario and Quebec. In 1883, railway workers were drawn by the smell of sulfur to several hot springs on the side of Terrace (now called Sulphur) Mountain. Mineral baths had long been popular in Europe for their curative and medicinal powers, and when the head of the Canadian Pacific Railroad visited these springs he declared them to be "worth a million dollars!"

In a rare moment of foresight, the federal government prevented private development, and in November 1885 a small parcel of land was reserved around the springs as Canada's first national park. An additional 270 square miles (700 sq km), featuring some of the world's most stunning mountain scenery, was annexed two years later to form Rocky Mountains Park (later known as Banff National Park), and Lake Louise was added in 1902. Banff and the three adjacent national parks—Yoho, Kootenay, and Jasper—together protect almost 8,000 square miles (20,700 sq km) of wilderness.

CANADA'S MOST POPULAR PARK

To many overseas visitors, Canada is epitomized by a red-coated Mountie (Royal Canadian Mounted Policeman) on horseback in front of the turquoise waters of Lake Louise, and with over 4 million tourists annually, Banff is certainly the country's most visited national park.

Lake Louise (above) is one of the highlights of Banff.
Bighorn sheep (right) roam the park's high country.

It is also the most heavily developed. Two major highways cut north and west through its center and the town of Banff has a permanent population of over 4,000. Easy access has put increasing pressure on fragile lowland ecosystems, and strict regulations have now been placed on backcountry camping.

Although visitors initially came for the hot springs, unparalleled mountain scenery is now Banff's main attraction. Even to the untrained eye, these mountains look varied. Near the town of Banff , the tilted summit of Mount Rundle and the serrated ridges of the Sawback, Sundance, and Palliser ranges were formed by a folding of the Earth's crust.

Canoes on Moraine Lake in Valley of the Ten Peaks (above).
Skaters take to the ice on Lake Louise (below).

TRAVELER'S NOTES

Information *The Superintendent, Banff National Park, Box 900, Banff, AB T0L-0C0; tel. (403) 762-1550, fax (403) 762-1551*

Hours *Always open*

Visitor centers *Banff: 224 Banff Ave, mid-May to early Sept, 8 am–6 pm. Early Sept to mid-May, 9 am–5 pm. Lake Louise: Samson Mall mid-May to early Sept, 8 am–6 pm. Early Sept to mid-May, 9 am–5 pm.*

Fees *Admission*

Permits *Camping, backcountry camping, fishing*

Camping *14 campgrounds (over 2,700 sites). No charge after Sept 27*

Lodging *Many hotels and motels in Banff and Lake Louise. Overflow in Canmore and Field*

Supplies *Banff, Lake Louise and along Icefields Parkway (summer only)*

Access for people with disabilities *Banff Visitor Center. Cave and Basin hot springs, nature and discovery tours wheelchair accessible. Wheelchair accessible camping at Tunnel Mountain II, Two Jack Lakeside, Johnston Canyon, Lake Louise, and Waterfowl Lake*

When to visit *June, Sept–Oct, excellent hiking and camping; few crowds. Nov–March, excellent skiing (downhill and cross-country). July–Aug, busy highways and campground congestion*

Backcountry maps *CMO Banff National Park*

Scaling the peaks of Banff.

THE ALPINE LARCH

The displays of fall coloring found in eastern hardwood forests are largely absent in the west because of extensive stands of evergreen conifers such as fir, spruce, hemlock, and pine. Out west, colorful deciduous trees are confined mainly to river banks and lakeshores.

Growing close to the treeline, however, the alpine larch is one conifer that does change color in fall. Found in thick stands where the soil is rocky and the growing season short, the larch is spindly and stunted, its sole redeeming feature being its long, delicate, pale green needles.

From early September to mid-October, frosty nights and shorter days limit the amount of chlorophyll the larch produces, and its needles turn bright yellow, then golden, then brown. The best place to see these trees is near Moraine Lake on the eastern edge of the park, where Larch Valley blazes with color each fall. Winter storms knock the needles off and the trees remain bare until spring, when new needles grow.

Unlike lowland conifers, the larches in western Canada do not grow to a size that makes them valuable for either pulp or building material.

In fall, larch trees are easy to distinguish from other conifers.

The area around Peyto Lake, near Bow Pass, offers superb climbing and hiking.

These peaks thrust skyward at extreme angles and you can see layers of limestone and shale that were once the beds of ancient inland seas. Farther north, summits such as Mount Temple and Castle Mountain are more square and upright, resulting from vast chunks of rock being pushed upward.

For the most part, these peaks are barren and rugged, but in alpine areas, such as Simpson Pass and Paradise Valley, you'll find delightful meadows where wildflowers bloom in the brief Rocky Mountain summer. Look, in particular, for alpine buttercup, Indian paintbrush, mountain fleabane, and white, yellow, and red heather. Lower slopes bear dense forests of conifers; mainly spruce, fir, hemlock, and pine.

In the valleys you will find extensive hardwood forests, stunning turquoise lakes, and, somewhat unexpectedly, wet-land areas such as Vermilion and Waterfowl lakes.

Castle Mountain (above). Cotton grass (left) grows in cool, damp areas, flowering in the late spring and summer.

LARGE ANIMALS

The most common and best-loved of Banff's wandering wildlife is the Bow Valley elk herd, which has become used to living with human visitors. The reluctance of the elk's natural predators, such as wolf, cougar, and grizzly, to come down to the valley, where human contact is likely, has resulted in a proliferation of elk, which has had dire consequences for the aspens. Elk browse on suckers sent up from the trees' roots, and continued grazing will eventually kill not only new saplings, but parent trees as well. Some aspen stands near the townsite are over 1,000 years old, and will die off if elk numbers continue to grow. Elk may have to be trapped and moved away to a natural environment where their numbers can be controlled through predation.

Bears—both black and grizzly—are fairly common in alpine meadows and can also be seen in the valleys, where they are drawn to settlements and campgrounds in search of carelessly discarded or inadequately stored food. Contact between bears and humans has not benefitted either; tourists have been mauled and the offending bears have been trapped and destroyed.

Visitors are unlikely to see reclusive animals such as the mountain lion and the gray wolf, unless they spend time hiking in the backcountry. ST

The mountain goat's hooves have a sharp rim, for edging, and rubbery soles for grip.

Gwaii Haanas National Park Reserve

British Columbia

Haida Gwaii (Islands of the People), otherwise known as the Queen Charlotte Islands, is a crescent-shaped series of islands lying 80 miles (130 km) off the coast of British Columbia. Separated from the mainland for millenia, the natural and cultural development of these islands has been unique.

Haida tribes, which trace their roots on these islands back 10,000 years, and European settlers, who arrived in the nineteenth century, coexisted relatively peacefully until the 1980s. At that time, proposed clear-cut logging pitted

Sea stars (right) are abundant along the rocky shores. Kayaking on a calm day, in among the islands (below).

local Haida people against timber companies and forestry unions. Subsequent negotiations produced a moratorium on logging on the southern part of Moresby Island and on Lyell Island, and created a national park covering 15 percent of the Queen Charlotte Islands.

This area, known as the Gwaii Haanas Archipelago, consists of 138 islands extending 54 miles (87 km) from north to south. There are no permanent settlements on the archipelago, but 500 Haida cultural sites have been identified. The most impressive is the remnants of a village at Ninstints on Anthony Island. Three of these sites are supervised by Haida Watchmen.

THE SAN CHRISTOVAL MOUNTAINS

The backbone of Gwaii Haanas is the rugged San Christoval mountain range, its flanks covered in dense old-growth temperate rain forest. Storms lash the islands in winter, but on land and within the sea, wildlife has proliferated.

Haida totem poles at Ninstints, on Anthony Island (above).
Old-growth rain forest on the San Christoval Mountains (right).

The most common animals are black bears, hairy woodpeckers, deer mice, and pine martens.

The eastern shore of the archipelago teems with marine life. The strong tides ensure a rich supply of nutrients which support a wide variety of fish and crustaceans. Steller's sea lions cling to the rocks, and sea otters, once hunted to near-extinction, are making a comeback. Around 750,000 seabirds nest along the archipelago. In all, over 100 bird species can be seen offshore and inland, among them ancient murrelets, Cassin's auklets, storm petrels, tufted puffins, horned puffins, and bald eagles. Each spring, a gray whale migration passes nearby, and there are resident orcas; minke, sperm, and humpback whales; plus porpoises and dolphins.

There are daily flights from Vancouver to Sandspit, and ferries run between Prince Rupert and the islands. The park has no roads, few trails, and no services. Most visitors tour by boat or sea-kayak, and many commercial operators offer expeditions of several days or more. Only the most experienced mariners should visit on their own. ST

TRAVELER'S NOTES

Information Superintendent, Gwaii Haanas National Park, Box 37, Queen Charlotte, BC V0T-1S0; tel. (250) 559-8818, fax (250) 559-8366

Hours Always open

Visitor centers Queen Charlotte: Sept 12–July 1, Mon–Fri, 8 am–4.30 pm. July 2–Sept 11, extended hours plus Sat–Sun. Sandspit: June, Mon–Fri, 9.30 am–6 pm. July 2–Sept 11, extended hours plus Sat–Sun

Fees None

Permits Fishing

Camping Backcountry only. Restricted in some bird rookeries and on islands with cultural sites

Lodging Queen Charlotte, Sandspit

Supplies Queen Charlotte, Sandspit

When to visit June–Sept offer best weather and safest marine conditions. Some fog on outer coast in summer

Backcountry maps Canadian Hydrographic Service nautical map no. 3853 (Cape St James and Tasu Sound). More detailed maps may be required for some areas

Black oystercatchers nest along the rocky shores.

Pacific Rim National Park

British Columbia

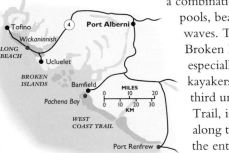

The ceaseless roar of the ocean is a constant companion for visitors to Pacific Rim National Park. Hundreds of thousands of them are drawn every year to this rugged park situated on the west coast of Vancouver Island.

The park is comprised of three units: Long Beach, Broken Islands, and the West Coast Trail. Long Beach is the most accessible and the most visited unit, providing a combination of rain forest, tide pools, beaches, and spectacular waves. To the south lies the Broken Islands Unit, which is especially popular with sea-kayakers and canoeists. The third unit, the West Coast Trail, is a thin strip of land along the coast. A track runs the entire length of the unit connecting dozens of beaches and coves. Although it's an arduous 44 mile (70 km) hike, taking six days or so to complete, it is Canada's most popular hiking trail and a quota system is enforced in order to preserve its unique wilderness values.

At Long Beach, nine short hiking trails have been cut through some of the last stands of old-growth forest still left unlogged on Vancouver Island. Sitka spruce, western red cedar, amabilis fir, and western hemlock grow here to astonishing heights. The coastal rain forest is a dynamic environment: trees thrust hundreds of feet skyward, are knocked down by violent winter storms, and then rapidly decay as they provide nutrients for ferns, mosses, lichens, fungi, and herbs. Huckleberry, blueberry, salal, skunk cabbage, and salmonberry all compete for soil and moisture on the forest floor.

The West Coast Trail is one of the most popular and challenging hiking tracks in North America.

Sunrise at Schooner Cove in the Long Beach Unit (above). Sea-kayaking near the Broken Islands demands caution and skill (right).

This rich environment is home to the ubiquitous yellow banana slug, whose gelatin-like mass can be found sticking to almost every leaf and branch. Black bears and mountain lions often forage in the forest, but they are reclusive and mostly nocturnal, so visitors seldom spot them.

THE LURE OF THE SEA

The spellbinding power of the sea eventually lures everyone to the beach, but people should watch out for rogue waves which can sneak up without warning and sweep them out to sea, even in benign weather. During winter storms, it is easy to see how this coastline became known as the graveyard of the Pacific. Indeed, the West Coast Trail was originally a lifesaving route hacked through the forest to provide safe passage for survivors of the region's many shipwrecks. ST

Steller's sea lion.

TRAVELER'S NOTES

Information Pacific Rim National Park, Box 280 Ucluelet, BC VOR-3A0; tel. (250) 726-7721, fax (250) 726-4720

Hours Always open

Visitor centers Wickaninnish (Long Beach Unit): daily mid-May to Labor Day, hours vary. Maps, displays, restaurant. West Coast Trailhead Information Centers; North, Pachena Bay 3 miles (5 km) from Bamfield; South, next to Port Renfrew Community Center. Mon–Fri, 9 am–5 pm

Fees Parking, camping

Permits Backcountry camping

Camping Greenpoint: (94 sites), flush toilets, fire pits, wood. Schooner: primitive, not recommended in winter

Lodging Tofino, Ucluelet, Port Renfrew

Supplies Tofino, Ucluelet, Port Renfrew, Bamfield

Access for people with disabilities Wickaninnish center. Shorepine Bog Trail in Long Beach Unit

When to visit May–June, Sept. Nov–Feb good for watching storms. July–Aug crowded. Mar–Apr for whale migration

Note Tide tables for Tofino are essential. Broken Islands Unit is marine-access only. cars are parked at Long Beach. Trail maps available at visitor centers. Registration for West Coast Trail can be done by phone. Track may be closed during periods of heavy rainfall

Fundy National Park

New Brunswick

The Bay of Fundy tides are the strongest in the world; the amount of water that ebbs and flows in this bay each day is roughly equal to the daily outflow of all the rivers in the world. At high tide, visitors to Fundy National Park see a typical shoreline of water, sand, and trees, but six and a half hours later the water will have receded several miles, leaving great stretches of mud.

Most of the bird species in Fundy are found in the forest. They include warblers, thrushes, and juncos, and species, such as the boreal chickadee and pine grosbeak, which are normally found much farther north but are attracted to Fundy's cool climate. It's on the mud flats, however, that you'll see the greatest number of birds. During the fall migration, over a million semipalmated sandpipers stop over to feed on the tiny mud shrimp that live just below the surface. The fat that the birds store from this feast enables them to fly nonstop over open ocean to their wintering grounds in South America.

Back from the shore, the Caledonia Highlands, which are part of the glacially eroded Appalachian chain, rise to a forested plateau where rapids and waterfalls tumble in deep valleys and visitors are likely to see white-tailed deer, raccoons, and snowshoe hares. The upland forests are mainly red spruce and balsam fir, interspersed with hardwoods such as sugar maple and yellow birch.

In places, ice-age glaciers gouged out the soil, creating wetlands known as bogs. The Caribou Plain Trail provides an easy walk through both forest and bog country, where the birdwatching is excellent. A boardwalk enables visitors to take a close look at beaver habitat.

Dickson Falls can be visited on a loop trail, via several boardwalks and stairs.

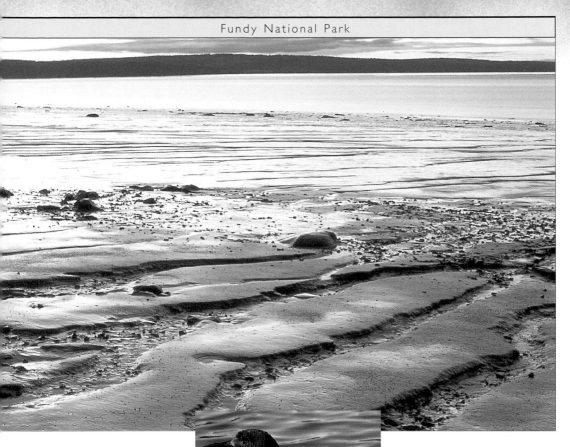

The Fundy mud flats, where 100 billion tons of water ebb and flow each day. The common loon (left) is one of the park's regular visitors. Atlantic salmon swimming upstream (below).

REINTRODUCTIONS

Pine martens, Atlantic salmon, and peregrine falcons have recently been reintroduced to Fundy. The American pine marten was widely trapped for its fur during the last century, and became extinct in this part of Canada around 1910. In 1984, wild breeding stock from northern New Brunswick was brought to the park and several animals have now been successfully bred within its boundaries.

Before the park was commissioned in 1948, dams were built on the Point Wolfe and Salmon rivers. They were constructed without fish ladders, which meant that migrating Atlantic salmon could not return to these, their native rivers, to spawn. A stocking program has reintroduced salmon to Fundy and the Point Wolfe river dam has now been removed, enabling them to swim upstream once more.

The most successful reintroduction has been that of the peregrine falcon, which nearly became extinct in the 1950s in eastern Canada through poisoning by agricultural pesticides. Peregrine falcons were released from various sites in 1985, and breeding pairs found in the vicinity of the park show the program is working.

Habitat enhancement for other endangered species, such as the common loon and two types of salamander, is currently underway, in the hope of increasing their numbers as well. ST

TRAVELER'S NOTES

Information Fundy National Park, P.O. Box 1001, Alma, New Brunswick, Canada, E4H 1B4; tel. (506) 887-6000, fax (506) 887-6008. TDD (506) 887-6015

Hours Always open

Visitor centers Alma: Mid-May to mid-June, early Sept to mid-Oct, Mon–Fri, 8.15 am–4.30 pm, Sat–Sun, 10 am–5 pm. Mid-June to early Sept, daily, 8 am–9 pm. Jan–Feb, Mon–Fri, 8.15 am–4.30 pm, Sat–Sun, 9 am–5 pm. Guided walks, evening programs. Wolfe Lake: summer only, 10 am–6 pm

Fees Admission, camping

Permits Backcountry camping, fishing

Camping 4 campgrounds (600 sites), backcountry sites

Lodging Fundy Park Chalets, Caledonia Highlands Inn, chalets within park; Alma

Supplies Alma

Access for people with disabilities Visitor center, picnic areas, Caribou Plain Trail, Chignecto and HQ campgrounds, boardwalks at Alma Beach, Point Wolfe

When to visit June, Sept best. July–Aug crowded. Winter, cross-country skiing

Backcountry maps CMO Fundy National Park

Gros Morne National Park

Newfoundland

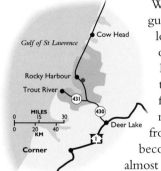

The rare harlequin duck.

Gros Morne National Park is a region of land-locked freshwater fjords, steep-walled headlands and a range of unique geological features. Gros Morne (meaning "big lone mountain") is the park's highest peak—a rounded summit providing spectacular views for miles around.

Despite the region's harsh conditions, humans have often made their home here. Evidence of Stone Age tribes from 3,000 years ago has been found. They were followed a thousand years later by the Dorset Culture, and finally by Europeans, who established fishing villages on the shores of the Gulf of St Lawrence.

White-sand beaches border the gulf, while farther inland, bog lowlands and coastal forest take over. Tuckamore is the Newfoundland term for the tangled, stunted spruce and balsam found here—their growing tips nipped back by wind, hail, and frozen saltwater spray. The trees become so entwined that they are almost impenetrable.

Above the heath, the Long Range Mountains thrust steeply overhead, gradually diminishing in elevation toward the east. Western Brook Pond is a particularly striking sight—a deep, narrow lake gouged by ice-age glaciers. The word "pond" seems an understatement, when you consider that it is 10 miles (16 km) long and sheer granite walls rise over 2,600 feet (800 m) above the shoreline.

Magnesium in the rocks prevents plant growth in the barren tablelands in the park's south-west. These rocks are exposed sections of the Earth's mantle (the rock layer covering its molten core) and the oceanic crust (the layer above the mantle), seen nowhere else in the world.

Because Gros Morne is situated on an island, the animals either flew here, traveled on pack ice, or swam from the mainland.

Ten Mile Pond viewed from Gros Morne Mountain (above).
Granite cliffs line Western Brook Pond (right). Arctic hare (below).

Some species that are common elsewhere in
Canada (such as skunks, porcupines, groundhogs,
raccoons, moles, and snakes) never made it across
the water or have never been introduced.

RETURN OF THE CARIBOU

The woodland caribou is the park's most striking
indigenous animal. At the turn of the century,
up to 250,000 lived on the island, but their
numbers were heavily reduced by hunting.
There is now no legal caribou hunting within
the park, and since 1972 their numbers have
been increasing. The caribou are now returning
to overwinter on the coastal plain, which used to
be their cold weather range before they were
driven into the highlands by hunters.

Another alpine inhabitant is the arctic hare, a
large cousin of the snowshoe hare. Gros Morne
is the most southerly range of its habitat. Moose
are also common, but they are not native, having
been introduced at the turn of the century.

Whales are occasionally seen
in offshore waters, but are more
often spotted on Newfoundland's
east coast. Harbor seals breed on
islands in St Pauls Inlet. Birds
such as arctic terns, bald eagles,
ospreys, and rock ptarmigan
are common, but there are no
major seabird colonies in Gros
Morne. Keen-eyed birders
who spot the brilliant plumage
of the harlequin duck are
asked to report sightings to
the visitor center. Fewer
than 1,000 survive in eastern
North America. ST

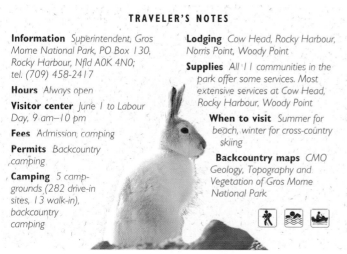

TRAVELER'S NOTES

Information Superintendent, Gros
Morne National Park, PO Box 130,
Rocky Harbour, Nfld A0K 4N0;
tel. (709) 458-2417

Hours Always open

Visitor center June 1 to Labour
Day, 9 am–10 pm

Fees Admission, camping

Permits Backcountry
camping

Camping 5 camp-
grounds (282 drive-in
sites, 13 walk-in),
backcountry
camping

Lodging Cow Head, Rocky Harbour,
Norris Point, Woody Point

Supplies All 11 communities in the
park offer some services. Most
extensive services at Cow Head,
Rocky Harbour, Woody Point

When to visit Summer for
beach, winter for cross-country
skiing

Backcountry maps CMO
Geology, Topography and
Vegetation of Gros Morne
National Park

263

Nahanni National Park Reserve

Northwest Territories

The South Nahanni River originates close to the Yukon Territory and flows southeast, cutting through the massive Mackenzie Mountains to form the deepest gorges and highest waterfalls in Canada. The Athapaskans used to refer to the tribes of the Mackenzie River valley and its tributaries as the Nahanni, meaning "people over there far away". In 1972, the heart of this remote, dramatic watershed was set aside for Parks Canada, as a response to a proposed hydroelectric dam at Virginia Falls.

After the Yukon gold rush, at the turn of the century, miners headed to the Nahanni amidst rumors of a motherlode. The bodies of three prospectors found dead by search parties led to tales of murders and ghosts, which live on in names such as the Funeral Range and Deadman Valley. In fact, very little gold was ever found in the Nahanni, but the region's worth as wilderness is incalculable.

There is no vehicle access to the region, and visitors must charter a float plane and fly into Rabbitkettle Lake or Virginia Falls. Canoes, rafts, or kayaks are the main mode of transport, and you can either organize your own trip or be guided by an approved outfitter.

Trumpeter swans are best identified by their loud, low-pitched trumpeting and their flat head and bill profile.

MASSIVE CANYONS

The upper Nahanni is serene for the first 75 miles (120 km) until it plummets 290 feet (90 m) over Virginia Falls—twice the height of Niagara—and then runs through four stunning canyons. At Third Canyon, which is 12 miles (19 km) long, the Nahanni narrows between sheer limestone cliffs that tower 3,000 feet (914 m) above, splitting through a narrow defile known as The Gate, or Pulpit Rock. As the river eases through First Canyon, it proceeds

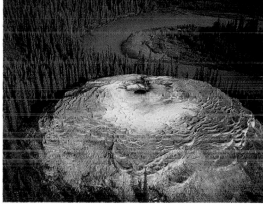

Virginia Falls (above) and the great mound of Rabbitkettle hot springs in Nahanni National Park (right).

through vertical walls untouched by ice-age glaciation and many water-eroded caves can be seen high in the limestone walls.

There are several examples of erosion of this sort (known as karst topography) within the park, such as caves, underground rivers, dry lakes, and bowl-shaped sinkholes (called dolines). Just below First Canyon, there are sulfur hot springs surrounded by lush vegetation, and there are also hot springs upriver at Rabbitkettle.

The South Nahanni spills out of the Mackenzie Mountains near the Yukon border. In the valleys, white spruce, balsam, and aspen thrive. Forest fires started by summer lightning often rage unchecked as part of nature's cycle, and within a year there is new growth for the large population of woodland caribou to browse on. The wet lowlands also provide excellent habitat for moose and beaver. Trumpeter swans and peregrine falcons, birds that are endangered elsewhere, are often seen in the park, particularly around Yohin Lake.

Because of the park's northerly location, trees stop growing at less than 4,000 feet (1,200 m) and alpine tundra takes over. Sedges, cotton grass, and wildflowers such as white mountain avens grow in this exposed world, which is home to black bear, mountain goat, and Dall sheep. Black bears frequent both the forest and the tundra, and travelers should take proper precautions when storing food. ST

Point Pelee National Park

Ontario

Point Pelee and offshore Pelee Island are the southernmost points in Canada. The sandy, triangular point extends for over 10 miles (16 km) into the waters of Lake Erie, shallowest of the Great Lakes. True deciduous forest reaches its northern boundary here, featuring flora and fauna found nowhere else in Canada.

Pelee lies at the intersection of the Mississippi and Atlantic flyways (see p. 239), and is at the northern limit of the ranges of a great number of birds.

Long recognized for its importance to wildlife, Point Pelee became a national park in 1918. The park is synonymous with birding, and any weekend during the spring or fall migration, thousands of spotting scopes will be trained on the hundreds of species that take refuge here.

In spring, nocturnal migrants traveling northward from the Gulf of Mexico sometimes find themselves over Lake Erie at dawn. Having already flown several hundred miles that night, they must continue or drown. On sighting Point Pelee they descend, exhausted, to the delight of birders. These groundings can occur over a period of a week or more, new arrivals landing in successive waves.

Three hundred and fifty species of bird have been identified in the park and some flocks reach into the thousands. Huge numbers of red-breasted mergansers, bank swallows, white-throated swallows, chimney swifts, and northern orioles have been seen here. Mid-May is the best time for spotting migrants and rarities such as

The Marsh Boardwalk (above). In fall, on their way to their winter home in the Sierra Madre Mountains in Central Mexico, monarch butterflies (left) pass through Point Pelee in their thousands.

266

piping plovers, Kentucky warblers, Bell's vireos, and summer tanagers.

A red-tailed hawk (left). Birders scan the shoreline (below).

One spectacular feature of the fall migration is the arrival of hawks traveling south. Unlike the spring migrants heading north, many raptors fly by day and do not like to cross water. Birds such as American kestrels and buteos follow the northern shore of Lake Erie to avoid crossing the lake.

MONARCH BUTTERFLIES

Many monarch butterflies spend summer in southwestern Ontario, and fly south to over-winter in the fir forests of Mexico's Sierra Madre Mountains. Both regions are home to the milkweed plant, the leaves of which are this butterfly's only food. The plants do not survive Ontario's harsh winters, and the monarch has not developed the ability to over-winter here. The monarchs therefore spend summer fattening themselves, and then fly south for a winter food source.

They begin their migration by following the shore of Lake Erie, which dips southward at Point Pelee. Here they can either fly across the lake or retreat northward and go around. Since flying back north goes against their migratory instinct, they stay at the southernmost tip, congregating on tree limbs while waiting for a combination of light winds and warm weather to cross the lake.

No individual butterfly makes the entire round trip. The monarchs breed on the way back north, and it is their offspring that return to the migration's starting point. ST

TRAVELER'S NOTES

Information Superintendent, Point Pelee National Park, RR #1 Leamington, Ontario N8H-3V4; tel./TDD (519) 322-2365, fax (519) 322-1277

Hours Always open

Visitor center Apr, 10 am–5 pm; May, 8 am–6 pm; June–Aug, 10 am–6 pm; Sept–Oct, 10 am–6 pm; Nov–Mar, Mon–Fri, 12 pm–4 pm, Sat–Sun, 10 am–5 pm

Fees Admission

Permits Fishing

Camping Group camping for registered non-profit groups only

Lodging Leamington

Supplies Leamington

Access for people with disabilities Visitor center, Marsh Boardwalk, transit buses to Tip all wheelchair accessible. Special wheelchairs for trail use available at visitor center and at trailhead for Marsh Boardwalk. Audio tapes at Marsh Boardwalk and visitor center

When to visit May for spring migration, Sept for monarch butterflies and fall migration. Crowded Apr–Sept

Kluane National Park

Yukon Territory

Each summer, thousands of travelers bound for Alaska drive along the eastern boundary of Kluane National Park in the southwest of Canada's Yukon Territory. The Alaska Highway, built during the Second World War to ensure a supply of oil to the United States in the event of a Japanese invasion, skirts the park and an adjacent game reserve for 150 miles (240 km). But few clues as to the park's wonders reveal themselves on this lonely stretch of highway. If the weather is clear, the rugged snow-capped summits of mounts Kennedy, Alverstone, and Hubbard can be seen just west of Whitehorse, towering thousands of feet above the foothills.

In fact, Kluane and the adjacent Wrangell–St Elias National Park in southern Alaska constitute the largest protected wilderness area in the world.

Skiers crossing a glacier in the heart of the massive St Elias Mountains.

GLACIER COUNTRY

The heart of Kluane National Park is a staggering network of glaciers fanning outward from the base of 19,341 foot (5,900 m) Mount Logan, Canada's highest peak. These vast glaciers make up the largest nonpolar icecap in the world, and climbers fly in from all corners of the globe to meet the challenge of the Icefields Ranges peaks.

For those who are not mountaineers, air tours offered by bush pilots based at Kluane Lake provide an inspiring, if somewhat expensive, way of seeing the glaciers. Most visitors restrict their visit to those attractions which are easily accessible from the highway, such as hiking and wildlife watching, or boating on the whitecapped waters of the lake which gives the park its name. Kluane is a Tutcheone Indian name meaning "lake of many fish".

The roiling Alsek River drains several of the huge

glaciers and flows through the heart of the park. Significant natural features such as the Alsek dunes (an extensive sand dune system on the eastern side of the upper valley) and the largest concentration of grizzly bears in Canada (bears regularly forage along the river's shrub-lined banks) have earned the Alsek the status of a Canadian Heritage River.

Farther downstream, near Goathead Mountain, the Alsek pools into a silty brown

Mount Logan viewed from Seward Glacier (above). A glacier, close up (left).

lake at the bottom of the Lowell Glacier. Turquoise icebergs break off from the glacier and crash into the water—a process known as calving—then float on the surface while they slowly melt. Adventure travel operators approved by Parks Canada run week-long guided rafting trips down the Alsek, introducing participants to an area of wilderness where there is virtually no sign of human intrusion.

Kluane boasts the largest concentration of grizzly bears in Canada. The population spends summer in the high meadows, returning to the valleys each winter.

TRAVELER'S NOTES

Information Superintendent, Kluane National Park Reserve, Box 5495, Haines Junction, Yukon Territory Y0B-1L0; tel. (867) 634-7250

Hours Always open

Visitor centers Haines Junction Visitor Reception Center: mid-May to mid-Sept, 9 am–9 pm; mid-Sept to mid-May, Mon–Fri, 9 am–4 pm, closed weekends. Publications, displays. Sheep Mountain Information Kiosk: mid-May to mid-Sept, 9 am–9 pm; closed mid-Sept to mid-May. Information, telescopes for wildlife viewing

Fees Camping

Permits Backcountry camping, mountaineering, river rafting, fishing, float plane landing

Camping 1 campground (43 sites) at Kathleen Lake. Primitive camping on Kluane Lake shores

Lodging Haines Junction

Supplies Food and gas in Haines Junction and at Bayshore Motel (km 1711, Alaska Hwy). Food, gas, and campsites at Destruction Bay. Food and gas at Kathleen Lake Lodge

Access for people with disabilities Haines Junction Visitor Center, boardwalk trail at Kathleen Lake

When to visit May–Sept. Summer visits peak early July to mid-Aug. Nov–Mar heavy drifting snow on highways

Backcountry maps CMO Dezadeash 115 A, Mount St Elias 115 B/C, Kluane Lake 115 G/F

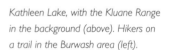

TAKING TO THE TRAILS

South of the Haines Visitor Center, the Alsek Pass Trail follows an old mining road for 14 miles (22 km) and can even be ridden on mountain bikes. Look for a distinct band of sandy soil, driftwood, and other debris high on the slopes above. This is the high-water mark that formed when the advancing Lowell Glacier blocked the Alsek River, forming a gigantic lake. When the glacier eventually melted and its ice-dam broke—in 1850—the lake drained out, with a flow comparable to that of the Amazon River.

Backpackers wishing to take a look at the huge icefields can hike up the Slims River Trail to the base of the Kaskawulsh Glacier, which is the source of the Alsek and the Slims rivers. (The Alsek flows into the Tatshenshini, which ends at Dry Bay, a wide coastal plain on the Gulf of Alaska, while the Slims flows north into the Yukon, which eventually empties into the Arctic Ocean.) A side-trip leads to the summit of Observation Mountain, providing expansive views of the country beyond.

Kluane provides sanctuary for golden eagles.

Kathleen Lake, with the Kluane Range in the background (above). Hikers on a trail in the Burwash area (left).

Kluane's low-elevation hikes provide excellent opportunities for viewing wildlife. Over 105 bird species, including arctic frequent-fliers such as the rock ptarmigan, peregrine falcon, and golden eagle, have been counted. Larger mammals such as mountain goats, moose, caribou, and grizzly bears roam through the mountain meadows and lowland river valleys for food during summer's short growing season.

SUBARCTIC FLORA

Kluane's proximity to the moderating influence of the Gulf of Alaska and the drier, often frigid interior, combined with its dramatic geological relief, provide an impressive diversity of flora. Despite its subarctic location, over 1,300 plant species have been able to adapt to harsh winters and extensive glaciation.

In some regions of Kluane, an impenetrable layer of permafrost (permanently frozen soil) prevents plant roots from growing more than a few feet deep. On south-facing hillsides which receive more sunshine, the soil does not freeze and normal growing patterns emerge.

*Mount Wallace in late summer (above).
Burwash Landing at Kluane Lake (below).*

In the valleys, wheat grass and sedges share rich alluvial soil with hardwoods such as balsam, white spruce, and quaking aspen. Higher up, mountain meadows come alive in summer in a blaze of color, with alpine forget-me-not, arctic poppy, purple saxifrage, and mountain avens growing in profusion. Even the rocky mountainside supports tiny flowers such as moss campion, which clings to the rocks like flowering barnacles, and yellow stonecrop, which pokes through rock crevices, growing in pockets of thin soil. ST

DALL SHEEP

High on precipitous rock faces above Kluane Lake, tiny specks of white can be seen sunning themselves in the brief Yukon summer. Viewed through a telescope or binoculars, they can be made out as chunky Dall sheep—snowy relatives of the Rocky Mountain bighorn—named for William Dall, an early Yukon surveyor. The rams, which weigh up to 200 pounds (90 kg), grow large curved horns, up to 3 feet (1 m) long. The ewes, distinguished by short, spiky horns, are roughly two-thirds as large.

Traveling in migrating herds of the same sex, males frequent higher areas and more northerly habitat, while ewes and lambs graze together at lower elevations.

The sheep feed on the lichens and wildflowers of the alpine tundra. At high elevations, they have few predators and their population is controlled mostly by mishap—either through tumbling off cliffs or by being caught in avalanches. Small lambs and old sheep may fall prey to golden eagles.

Kluane has the highest concentration of Dall sheep in North America—over 4,000 have been counted. High-powered telescopes are set up for sheep viewing at Sheep Mountain, and trails up Sheep and Bullion creeks often provide hikers with a closer look.

From nowhere we came; into nowhere we go. What is life? It is the flash of a firefly in the night. It is the breath of a buffalo in the winter time. It is as the little shadow that runs across the grass and loses itself in the sunset.

CROWFOOT,
Blackfoot tribe

Resources
Directory

FURTHER READING

History and Conservation

Cadillac Desert: The American West and its Disappearing Water, by Marc Reisner (Viking, 1988).

Call to Action: Handbook for Ecology, Peace, and Justice, edited by Brad Erickson (Sierra Club Books, 1990).

Clearcut: The Tragedy of Industrial Forestry, edited by Bill Devall (Sierra Club Books, 1995).

How Many Americans? Population, Immigration, and the Environment, by Leonard F. Bouvier and Lindsey Grant (Sierra Club Books, 1994).

Islands in a Far Sea: Nature and Man in Hawaii, by John Culliney (Sierra Club Books, 1988).

John Muir and His Legacy: The American Conservation Movement, by Stephen Fox (Little Brown, 1981).

National Parks: The American Experience, by Alfred Runte (University of Nebraska Press, 1979).

Olympic Battleground: The Power Politics of Timber Preservation, by Carsten Lien (Sierra Club Books, 1991).

Our Endangered Parks, by National Parks and Conservation Association (Foghorn Press, 1994).

Rediscovering America: John Muir in His Time and Ours, by Frederick Turner (Sierra Club Books, 1990).

Silent Spring, by Rachel Carson (Houghton Mifflin, 1962).

A Species of Eternity, by Joseph Kastner (Knopf, 1977). Travels of John and William Bartram.

Wildlife in America, by Peter Matthiessen (Penguin Nature Library, 1994).

Wolf Songs: The Classic Collection of Writing about Wolves, edited by Robert Busch (Sierra Club Books, 1994).

Nature Writing

American Nature Writing: 1994 (vol. 1) and *1995* (vol. 2), selected by John A. Murray (Sierra Club Books).

Autumn Across America, by Edwin Way Teale (Dodd Mead, 1956). First volume of tetralogy on experiencing the seasons in North America.

Beyond the One Hundredth Meridian: John Wesley Powell and the Second Opening of the American West, by Wallace Stegner (University of Nebraska Press, 1982).

The Dark Range: The Naturalist's Night Notebook, by David Rains Wallace, (Sierra Club Books, 1978).

The Desert, by John Van Dyke (Gibbs Smith Publishing, 1992).

Desert Solitaire: A Season in the Wilderness, by Edward Abbey (Simon & Schuster, 1968).

Downriver: A Yellowstone Journey, by Dean Krakel II (Sierra Club Books, 1988).

The Exploration of the Colorado River and its Canyons, by John Wesley Powell (Penguin Books, 1987).

The Immense Journey, by Loren Eiseley (Random House, 1957). Accounts of fossil hunting on the Great Plains and reflections on evolution.

The Intertidal Wilderness, by Anne Wertheim (Sierra Club Books, 1985). A photographic interpretation of the West Coast seashore.

John Muir: Eight Wilderness Discovery Books, (Diadem Books and The Mountaineers, 1992). A collection of Muir's nature writing in one volume.

Land of Little Rain, by Mary Austin (Penguin Nature Library, 1988). Classic account of the desert habitat.

A Natural History of Nature Writing, by Frank Stewart (Island Press, 1995).

North American Indians, by George Catlin (Penguin Nature Library, 1989).

Of Wolves and Men, by Barry Lopez (Macmillan, 1979).

One Day on Beetle Rock, by Sally Carrighar (Alfred A. Knopf, 1944). Closely observed account of Sierra Nevada wildlife.

The Oregon Trail, by Francis Parkman, Jr. (Penguin Classics, 1985).

Pilgrim at Tinker Creek, by Annie Dillard (Perennial Library, 1988). Fascinating record of author's relationship with the natural world in the Blue Ridge Mountains.

A Place on Earth, by Wendell Berry (North Point Press, 1983). Engaging novel about Kentucky farmlands and forests.

The Portable Thoreau, by Henry David Thoreau, edited by Carl Bode (Penguin, 1977).

The Practice of the Wild, by Gary Snyder (North Point Press, 1990). Essays on ecology and human culture.

Reflections from the North Country, by Sigurd F. Olson (Alfred A. Knopf, 1976). Observations on the environment of Minnesota.

Run River Run: A Naturalist's Journey Down One of the Great Rivers of the West, by Ann Zwinger (Harper & Row, 1975). Absorbing account of a trip down the Green River.

A Sand County Almanac, by Aldo Leopold (Oxford University Press, 1960).

The Sense of Wonder, by Rachel Carson (The Nature Company, 1991).

Spirit of Place: The Making of an American Literary Landscape, by Frederick Turner (Sierra Club Books, 1990).

Travels in Hawaii, by Robert Louis Stevenson (University of Hawaii Press, 1973).

Travels, by William Bartram (Penguin Nature Library, 1988).

Wanderer on My Native Shore: A Personal Guide and Tribute to the Ecology of the Atlantic Coast, by George Reiger (Simon & Schuster, 1983).

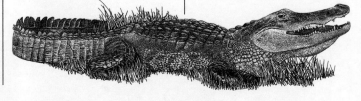

Preparation and Equipment

AMC Guide to Winter Camping, by Stephen Gorman (AMC Books, 1991).

Backcountry Skiing: The Sierra Club Guide to Skiing Off the Beaten Track, by Lito Tejada-Flores (Sierra Club Books, 1981).

Basic Essentials of Cross Country Skiing, by John Moynier (ICS Books, 1990).

Camper's Companion, by Hal Kahn and Rick Greenspan (Foghorn Press, 1994).

The Complete Walker III, by Colin Fletcher (Alfred A. Knopf, 1993).

The Cordes/LaFontaine Pocket Guide to Outdoor Photography, by Mary Mather (Greycliff Publishing, 1994).

The Essential Guide to Hiking in the United States, by Charles Cook (Michael Kesend Publishing, 1992).

Exploring Underwater: The Sierra Club Guide to Scuba Diving and Snorkeling, by John L. Culliney and Edward S. Crockett (Sierra Club Books, 1980).

Land Navigation Handbook: The Sierra Club Guide to Map and Compass, by W. S. Kals (Sierra Club Books, 1983).

Learning to Rock Climb, by Michael Loughman (Sierra Club Books, 1981).

Photography of Natural Things, by Freeman Patterson (Sierra Club Books, 1990).

Sharing Nature With Children, by Joseph Bharat Cornell (Ananda Publications, 1976).

The Sierra Club Family Outdoors Guide, by Marlyn Doan (Sierra Club Books, 1995).

The Sierra Club Guide to Sketching in Nature, by Cathy Johnson (Sierra Club Books, 1991).

The Sierra Club Guide to 35 mm Landscape Photography, by Tim Fitzharris (Sierra Club Books, 1994).

Simple Foods For the Pack: The Sierra Club Guide to Delicious Natural Foods for the Trail, by Claudia Axcell, Diana Cooke, and Vikki Kinmont (Sierra Club Books, 1986).

Walking Softly in the Wilderness: The Sierra Club Guide to Backpacking, by John Hart (Sierra Club Books, 1984).

Weathering in the Wilderness: The Sierra Club Guide to Practical Meteorology, by William Reifsnyder (Sierra Club Books, 1980).

The Weather Sourcebook, by Ronald Wagner and Bill Adler, Jr. (Globe Pequot, 1994).

Wilderness Basics: The Complete Handbook for Hikers and Backpackers, edited by Jerry Schad and David S. Moser (The Mountaineers, 1993).

Wildwater: The Sierra Club Guide to Kayaking and Whitewater Boating, by Lito Tejada-Flores (Sierra Club Books, 1978).

Books for Travelers with Disabilities

Access America Guide to the Southwestern National Parks: An Atlas and Guide for Visitors with Disabilities (Northern Cartographic, Inc., 1989).

Easy Access to National Parks, by Wendy Roth and Michael Tompane (Sierra Club Books, 1992).

Scuba Diving with Disabilities, by Jill Robinson and A. Dale Fox (Leisure Press, 1992).

Books for Younger Travelers

Ancient Ones: The World of the Old-Growth Douglas Fir, by Barbara Bash (Sierra Club Books, 1994).

And Then There Was One: The Mysteries of Extinction, by Margery Facklam (Sierra Club Books, 1993).

Bees Dance and Whales Sing: The Mysteries of Animal Communication, by Margery Facklam (Sierra Club Books, 1992).

The Big Bug Book, by Margery and Paul Facklam (Little, Brown, 1994).

Desert Giant: The World of the Saguaro Cactus, by Barbara Bash (Sierra Club Books, 1990).

Ecology for All Ages, by Jorie Hunken (Globe Pequot, 1994).

A Field Guide to Birds Coloring Book, by Roger Tory Peterson (Houghton Mifflin, 1982).

Frogs and Toads, by Steve Parker (Sierra Club Books, 1994).

Lost in the Woods: Child Survival for Parents and Teachers, by Colleen Politano (ICS Books, 1993).

Peterson First Guide: Birds, by Roger Tory Peterson (Houghton Mifflin, 1986).

Safari Beneath the Sea, by Diane Swanson (Sierra Club Books, 1994).

The Sierra Club Book of Our National Parks, by Donald Young (Sierra Club Books, 1990).

The Sierra Club Wayfinding Book, by Vicki McVey (Sierra Club Books, 1991).

The Sierra Club Wildlife Library: including *Snakes, Seals, Wolves, Bears, Eagles.* Various authors (Sierra Club Books).

Take a Hike!: The Sierra Club Kid's Guide to Hiking and Backpacking, by Lynne Foster (Sierra Club Books, 1991).

Whales and Dolphins, by Steve Parker (Sierra Club Books, 1994).

What is an Amphibian?, What is a Mammal?, What is a Fish?, all by Robert Snedden (Sierra Club Books).

Field Guides

The Amateur Naturalist, by Gerald Durrell (Alfred A. Knopf, 1982).

Between Pacific Tides, by Edward F. Ricketts, Jack Calvin, and Joel W. Hedgpeth (Stanford University Press, 1994).

Birding, by Joseph Forshaw, Steve Howell, Terry Lindsey, Rich Stallcup (The Nature Company, 1994).

Falcon Press Watchable Wildlife. State-by-state guides. 22 states. Various authors (Falcon Press).

Field Guide to the Birds of North America (National Geographic Society, 1983).

The Field Guide to Wildlife Habitats of the Eastern United States, by Janine M. Benyus (Simon & Schuster, 1989).

The Field Guide to Wildlife Habitats of the Western United States, by Janine M. Benyus (Simon & Schuster, 1989).

Fire on The Mountain: The Nature of Volcanoes, by Dorian Weisel and Carl Johnson (Chronicle Books, 1994).

Golden Guides to Field Identification: including Birds; Mammals; Trees; Reptiles; Amphibians; Rocks and Minerals; Skyguide. Various authors (Golden Press).

Habitats, by Tony Hare (Macmillan, 1994).

Audubon Society Field Guides: including Mushrooms; North American Butterflies; North American Birds; North American Seashells; Fishes, Whales, Dolphins; Fossils; Insects and Spiders; Mammals; Mushrooms; The Night Sky; Reptiles and Amphibians; Rocks and Minerals; Seashore Creatures; Eastern Trees; Western Trees; Weather. Various authors (Alfred A. Knopf).

Peterson Field Guides: including Advanced Birding; Eastern Birds; Western Birds; Mammals; Reptiles and Amphibians of Eastern and Central North America; Western Reptiles and Amphibians; Pacific Coast Fishes; Wildflowers; Venomous Animals and Poisonous Plants; Freshwater Fishes; Atmosphere. Various authors (Houghton Mifflin).

The Sierra Club Handbook of Seals and Sirenians, by Randall R. Reeves, Brent Stewart, and Stephen Leatherwood (Sierra Club Books, 1992).

The Sierra Club Handbook of Whales and Dolphins, by Stephen Leatherwood and Randall R. Reeves (Sierra Club Books, 1983).

Skywatching, by David H. Levy (The Nature Company, 1994).

Tracking and the Art of Seeing, by Paul Rezendes (Camden House Publishing, 1992).

Guides to Nature Areas

Alaska's Parklands: The Complete Guide, by Nancy Simmerman (The Mountaineers, 1991).

America's Secret Recreation Areas: Your Guide to the Forgotten Wild Lands of the Bureau of Land Management, by Michael Hodgson (Foghorn Press, 1995).

The Audubon Society Nature Guides: including Atlantic and Gulf Coasts; Deserts; Eastern Forests; Grasslands; Pacific Coast; Western Forests;

Wetlands. Various authors (Alfred A. Knopf).

Falcon Press Hiker's Guides: including Wyoming, Colorado, Utah, Alaska, Arizona, California, Florida, Georgia, Idaho, Montana, Nevada, New Mexico, Oregon, Texas, Utah, Virginia, Washington. Various authors (Falcon Press).

Fodor's National Parks and Seashores of the East (Fodor's, 1994).

Fodor's National Parks of the West (Fodor's, 1994).

Guide to the National Wildlife Refuges, by Laura and William Riley (Collier Books, 1992).

National Park Guide, by Michael Frome (Prentice Hall, 1994).

The National Parks of Canada, by Kevin McNamee (Key Porter Books, 1994).

1994–95 America's National Parks, by the National Parks Association (Fodor's, 1994).

The Sierra Club Adventure Travel Guides: including Gulf of Mexico; Alaska; British Columbia; Arizona; California Desert; Chesapeake Bay Area; Florida; Rockies; Southeast Coast. Various authors (Sierra Club Books).

The Sierra Club Guides to Natural Areas of the United States: including California; Colorado and Utah; Idaho, Montana, and Wyoming; Florida; New England; New Mexico, Arizona, and Nevada; Oregon and Washington. Various authors (Sierra Club Books).

The Sierra Club Guides to the National Parks: including Desert Southwest; East and Middle West; Pacific Northwest and Alaska; Pacific Southwest and Hawaii; Rocky Mountains and the Great Plains. Various authors (Stewart, Tabori & Chang).

The Sierra Club Naturalist Guides: including Deserts of the Southwest; Middle Atlantic Coast; North Woods of Michigan, Wisconsin, Minnesota, and Southern Ontario; Pacific Northwest; Sierra Nevada; Southern New England,

Southern Rockies. Various authors (Sierra Club Books).

The Sierra Club Totebooks: including Hiking Southwest Montana; Climber's Guide to High Sierra; Climber's Guide to Yosemite Valley; Exploring Yellowstone Backcountry; Hiking the Grand Canyon; Hiking the Great Basin; Hiking the Southwest; Hiking the Teton Backcountry. Various authors (Sierra Club Books).

Visitor's Guide to the Birds of the National Parks: Eastern; Central; Rocky Mountains, by Roland Wauer (John Muir Publisher).

Magazines

Adventure West, PO Box 3210, Incline Village, Nevada 89450

Audubon, 700 Broadway, New York, NY 10003

Backpacker, Rodale Press, 33 E Minor St, Emmaus, PA 18098

Birding, American Birding Association, PO Box 6599, Colorado Springs, CO 80934

Canoe and Kayak, PO Box 3146, Kirkland, WA 98083

EcoTraveler, P.O. Box 469003, Escondido, CA 92046-9850

Explore, 301 14th St NW, Suite 420, Calgary, Alberta, T2N 2A1

Natural History Magazine, Central Park W at 79th, New York, NY 10024

National Parks, 1701 18th St NW, Washington, DC 20009

National Wildlife, 8925 Leesburg Pike, Vienna, VA 22184

Outdoor Photographer, 12121 Wilshire Blvd, Suite 1220, Los Angeles, CA 90025-1175

Outside, 430 Montezuma Ave, Santa Fe, NM 87501

Sierra, 85 Second St., San Francisco, CA 94105-3441

Summit, 1221 May St, Hood River, OR 97031

Wildlife Conservation, Wildlife Conservation Society, Bronx River Parkway and Fordham, Bronx, NY 10451

FURTHER INFORMATION

Nature Areas
UNITED STATES
Bureau of Land Management
Department of the Interior,
1849 C St NW,
Washington DC 20240;
tel. (202) 452-0330
National Park Service,
Office of Public Inquiries,
Box 37127,
Washington DC 20013;
tel. (202) 208-4747
United States Forest Service,
3165 10th St,
Halfway
OR 97834;
tel. (541) 742-7511
United States Fish and Wildlife
Service,
PO Box 25486,
Denver Federal Center,
Denver, CO 80225;
tel. (303) 236-8152

THE FAR WEST
National Park Service,
Fort Mason,
Building 201,
San Francisco, CA 94123;
tel. (415) 556-0560.
National Park Service,
83 S King St, Suite 212,
Seattle, WA 98104

THE MOUNTAIN WEST
National Park Service,
Box 25287,
12795 West Alameda Pkwy,
Denver, CO 80225-0287;
tel. (303) 969-2000

THE SOUTHWEST
National Park Service,
Box 728,
1100 Old Santa Fe Trail,
Santa Fe, NM 87504-0728

THE MIDWEST AND GREAT PLAINS
National Park Service,
1709 Jackson St
Omaha, NE 68102-2571;
tel. (402) 221-3471

CANADA
Department of Canadian
Heritage, Publications Section,
Room 10H2,
25 Eddy St,
Hull, Quebec
Canada K1A 0M8;
tel. (819) 997-0055

Backcountry Maps
United States Geological Survey
(USGS), 807 National Center,
Reston, VA 20192;
tel. 1 (888) 275-8747
Trails Illustrated,
PO Box 4357,
Evergreeen, CO 80437;
tel. (303) 670-3457
Canadian Mapping Office,
Surveys and Mapping Section,
1615 Booth St, Ottawa,
Ontario Canada K1A 0E9;
tel. (800) 465-6277

Nature Organizations
American Birding Association,
PO Box 6599, Colorado
Springs, CO 80934;
tel. (800) 835-2473
American Hiking Society,
PO Box 20160,
Washington DC 20041-2160;
tel. (301) 565-6704
Appalachian Mountain Club,
PO Box 298, Route 16,
Gorham, NH 03581;
tel. (603) 466-2727
Canadian Nature Federation,
1 Nicholas Street, Suite 520,
Ottawa, Ontario,
Canada K1N 7B7;
tel. (613) 562-3447
Canadian Parks and Wilderness
Society, CPAWS National
Office, 880 Wellington St,
Suite 506, Ottowa, Ontario
Canada K1R 6K7;
tel. 1 (800) 333-WILD (9453)
Earth Island Institute,
300 Broadway, Suite 28,
San Francisco, CA 94133;
tel. (415) 788-3666
Ecotourism Society,
PO Box 755,
North Bennington,
VT 05257;
tel. (802) 447-2121
Friends of the Earth,
Global Building, Suite 300,
1025 Vermont Avenue NW,
Washington DC 20005;
tel. (202) 783-7400
Greenpeace,
1436 U St NW,
Washington DC 20009;
tel. (202) 232-1590
National Audubon Society,
700 Broadway,
New York, NY 10003;
tel. (212) 979-3000

The Nature Conservancy,
1815 North Lynn St
STE 400,
Arlington,
VA 22209;
tel. (703) 841-5300
National Parks and
Conservation Association,
1776 Massachusetts Ave NW,
Washington DC 20036;
tel. (202) 223-6722
National Wildlife Federation,
8925 Leesburg Pike,
Vienna, VA 22184;
tel. (703) 790-4000
Rainforest Action Network,
221 Pine St,
San Francisco,
CA 94104;
tel. (415) 398-4404
The Rainforest Alliance,
65 Bleecker St,
New York, NY 10012;
tel. (212) 677-1900
Sierra Club,
85 Second St, Second Floor,
San Francisco,
CA 94105-3441;
tel. (415) 977-5500
The Student Conservation
Association, Inc.,
PO Box 550,
Charleston, NH 03603;
tel. (603) 543-1700
The Trust For Public Land,
116 New Montgomery St,
4th Floor,
San Francisco, CA 94105;
tel. (415) 495-4014
Wilderness Society,
900 17th St NW,
Washington DC 20006;
tel. (202) 833-2300
Wildlife Conservation Society,
Bronx River Parkway and
Fordham, Bronx,
NY 10451;
tel. (718) 220-5100
World Wildlife Fund,
1250 24th St NW,
Washington DC 20037;
tel. (202) 293-4800

Educational and Volunteer Vacations
American Birding Association,
Volunteer Opportunities for
Birders Directory,
PO Box 6599, Colorado
Springs, CO 80934;
tel. (800) 835-2473

Appalachian Mountain Club,
  PO Box 298, Route 16,
  Gorham, NH 03581;
  tel. (603) 466-2727
Canyonlands Field Institute,
  PO Box 68,
  Moab, UT 84532;
  tel. (435) 259-7750
Earthwatch,
  680 Mount Auburn St,
  Watertown, MA 02472;
  tel. (781) 926-8200
Hawk Mountain Sanctuary,
  1700 Hawk Mountain Road,
  Kempton,
  Pennsylvania, 19529-9449;
  tel. (610) 756-6961
National Audubon Society,
  Audubon Ecology Camps
  and Workshops,
  613 Riversville Rd,
  Greenwich, CT 06831;
  tel. (203) 869-5272
National Wildlife Federation,
  8925 Leesburg Pike,
  Vienna, VA 22184;
  tel. (703) 790-4000
National Wildlife Research
  Center,
  4101 LaPorte Ave,
  Fort Collins,
  CO 80521-2154;
  tel. (970) 266-6000
Oceanic Society Expeditions,
  Fort Mason Center,
  Building E,
  San Francisco,
  CA 94123;
  tel. (800) 326-7491 or
  (415) 441-1106
Pacific Whale Foundation,
  101 N Kihei Rd,
  Kihei, HI 96753;
  tel. (808) 879-8860
Sierra Club,
  85 Second St, Second Floor,
  San Francisco,
  CA 94105-3441
  tel. (415) 977-5500
University Research Expeditions
  Program (UREP),
  University of California,
  2223 Fulton St,
  Berkeley, CA 94720;
  tel. (510) 642-6586
Yellowstone Institute,
  PO Box 117,
  Yellowstone National Park,
  WY 82190;
  tel. (307) 344-7749
Yosemite Association,
  5020 El Portal Rd,
  El Portal, CA 95318;
  tel. (209) 379-2646
Wildlife Studies,
  3 Mosswood Circle,
  Cazadero,

CA 95421;
  tel. (707) 632-5665
  Summer staff tel.
  (406) 763 5467

Nature Travel Tour Operators
NORTH AMERICA
Backroads,
  801 Cedar St,
  Berkeley, CA 94710;
  tel. (800) 462-2848,
  (510) 527-1555
  Biking, walking, and
  cross-country skiing tours
Mountain Travel-Sobek,
  6420 Fairmont Ave,
  El Cerrito, CA 94530;
  tel. (800) 227-2384,
  (510) 527-8100
  River running,
  backpacking tours

Sierra Club, Outing
  Department,
  85 Second St, Second Floor,
  San Francisco,
  CA 94105-3441;
  24-hour voicemail tel.
  (415) 977-5630

THE FAR WEST
Alaska Wildland Adventures,
  PO Box 389,
  Girdwood, AK 99587;
  tel. (800) 334-8730,
  (907) 783-2928
Camp Denali,
  PO Box 67, Denali
  National Park, AK 99755;
  tel. (907) 683-2290 (summer)
Hawaiian Walkways,
  PO Box 1307,
  Honokaa, HI 96727;
  tel. (808) 775-0372
Northern Lights Expeditions,
  PO Box 4289,
  Bellingham, WA 98227;
  tel. (800) 754-7402, or
  (360) 734-6334
Osprey Expeditions, Box 209,
  Denali National Park,
  Healy, AK 99743;
  tel. (907) 683-2734
Sea Trek, PO Box 561
  Woodacre, CA 94973;
  tel. (415) 488-1000

Sea kayaking trips in California
Southern Yosemite Mountain
  Guides, PO Box 301,
  Bass Lake, CA 93604;
  tel. (559) 658-8735
Wilderness Alaska,
  P.O. Box 113063,
  Anchorage, AK 99511;
  tel. (907) 345-3567
Wilderness Birding Adventures,
  PO Box 103747,
  Anchorage, AK 99510;
  tel. (907) 694-7442

THE MOUNTAIN WEST
Adventure Bound River
  Expeditions,
  2392 H Road, Grand
  Junction, CO 81505;
  tel. (970) 241-5633
Western River Expeditions,
  7258 Racquet Club Drive,
  Salt Lake City,
  UT 84121
Glacier Guides,
  PO Box 535,
  West Glacier, MT 59936;
  tel. (800) 521-RAFT
  Backpacking, river running
Kaibab Mountain Bike Tours,
  391 South Main Street,
  Moab, UT 84532;
  tel. (800) 451-1133
Timberline Bicycle Tours,
  7975 E Harvard,
  Denver, CO 80231;
  tel. (303) 368-4418
Yellowstone Expeditions,
  PO Box 865,
  West Yellowstone,
  MT 59758;
  tel. (406) 646-9333
  Cross-country skiing tours
Yellowstone Mountain Guides,
  PO Box 30067130,
  Bozeman, MT 59772;
  tel. (406) 388-0148
  Horseback, hiking tours
Wild Horizons Expeditions,
  P.O. Box 7627,
  Jackson Hole,
  Wyoming 83002;
  Toll free tel. (888) 734-4453
  Backpacking tours

THE SOUTHWEST
Crow Canyon
  Archaeological Center,
  23390 Country Rd K,
  Cortez, CO 81321;
  tel. (970) 565-8975
Dvorak's Kayak & Rafting
  Expeditions,
  17921 US Highway 285,
  Nathrop, CO 81236;
  tel. (800) 824-3795,
  (719) 539-6851

James Henry River Journeys,
 PO Box 807,
 Bolinas, CA 94924;
 tel. (800) 786-1830,
 (415) 868-1836
OARS, PO Box 67,
 PO Box 67,
 2687 S. Hwy. 49;
 Angels Camp, CA 95222;
 tel. (800) 346-6277 or
 (209) 736-4677,
 fax. (209) 736-2902.
 River running,
 kayaking tours
Sheri Griffith Expeditions,
 PO Box 1324,
 Moab, UT 84532;
 tel. (435) 259-8229
 River running.

THE MIDWEST AND GREAT PLAINS

Clearwater Canoe Outfitters,
 355 Gunflint Trail,
 Grand Marais, MN 55604;
 tel. (800) 527-0554,
 (218) 388-2254
Gunflint Northwoods Outfitter,
 143 South Gunflint Lake,
 Grand Marais,
 MN 55604-9706;
 tel. (800) 362-5251,
 (218) 388-2296
 Canoeing.
Seagull Outfitters,
 12208 Gunflint Trail,
 Grand Marais, MN 55604;
 tel. (800) 346-2205,
 (218) 388-2216.
 Canoeing
Wilderness Canoe Trips,
 PO Box 30, Ely, MN 55731;
 tel. (218) 365-4046 or
 (800) 752-2306

THE NORTHEAST

Allagash Canoe Trips,
 Box 713-W,
 Greenville,
 Maine 04441;
 tel. (207) 695-3668.
Battenkill Canoe Ltd,
 Historic Rte 7a,
 Arlington,
 Vermont 05250-2445;
 tel. (800) 421-5268.
Coastal Kayaking
 Tours,
 PO Box 405,
 Bar Harbor,
 ME 04609;
 tel. (800) 526-8615 or
 (207) 288-9605
Highlander Hiking,
 416 Ferris Lane,
 New Britain, PA 18901;
 tel. (800) 429-8268 or
 (215) 345-7725

THE SOUTHEAST

Appalachian Wildwaters,
 PO Box 100,
 Rowlesburg, WV 26425;
 tel. (800) 624-8060 or
 (304) 454-2475
Wilderness Southeast,
 711 Sandtown Road,
 Savannah, GA 31410;
 tel. (912) 897-5108
 Hiking.

CANADA

Canadian River Expeditions,
 PO Box 1023,
 Whistler, BC,
 Canada V0N 1B0;
 tel. 1 (604) 938-6651
Canadian Outback Adventure
 Company,
 100–657 Marine Drive,
 West Vancouver, BC,
 Canada V7T 1A4;
 tel. (604) 921-7250
Ecosummer Expeditions,
 PO Box 1765, Clearwater,
 BC, Canada V0E 1N0;
 US Sales office: 936 Peace
 Portal Drive,
 #240 Blaine, WA 98231
 tel. (250) 674-0102 (US),
 (800) 465-8884 (Canada).
 Kayaking and trekking trips.
Natural Outings,
 Box 100, Mansfield,
 ON, Canada L0N 1MO;
 tel. (705) 434-0848
 Backpacking.
Tofino Expeditions,
 P.O. Box 15280,
 Seattle, WA 98115-0280,
 tel. (206) 517-5244

Tours for Travelers with Disabilities

All Outdoors,
 20436 Clay Pidgeon CT,
 Bend, OR 97702;
 tel. (541) 388-8103
Cooperative Wilderness
 Handicapped Outdoor Group,
 PO Box 8128,
 Pocatello, ID 83209;
 tel. (208) 282-3812
 Environmental
 Traveling
 Companions (ETC),
 Fort Mason
 Center,

Building C,
 San Francisco, CA 94123;
 tel. (415) 474-7662
Wilderness Inquiry,
 1313 5th St SE,
 Minneapolis,
 MN 55414;
 tel. (612) 379-3858

Travel Services

The following companies
serve as information centers
and booking agents for a wide
variety of nature and adventure
tour operators.
Adventure Center,
 1311 63rd St,
 Suite 200,
 Emeryville,
 CA 94608;
 tel. (800) 227-8747,
 (510) 654-1879
REI Adventures,
 PO Box 1938,
 Sumner, WA 98390-0800;
 tel. (253) 437-1100

Equipment Suppliers

The following suppliers offer
mail order services.
Black Diamond Equipment, Ltd,
 2084 East 3900 South,
 Salt Lake City,
 UT 84124-1723;
 tel. (801) 278-5533
Campmor,
 PO Box 700,
 Saddle River,
 NJ 07458-0700;
 tel. 1 (800) 525-4784
The Nature Company,
 750 Hearst Avenue,
 Berkeley, CA 94710;
 tel. (800) 227-1114
North Face,
 999 Harrison St,
 Berkeley, CA 94710;
 tel. (800) 362-4963
Patagonia,
 8550 White Fir St,
 PO Box 32050,
 Reno,
 Nevada 89533-2050;
 tel. (800) 638 6464 or
 (212) 343-1776
REI (Recreational Equipment,
 Inc.),
 1700 45th St E,
 Sumner, WA 98352;
 tel. (800) 426-4840 or
 (206) 891-2500;
 TDD (800) 443-1988 or
 (253) 891-2500
 Sierra Trading Post,
 5025 Camp Stool Road,
 Cheyenne, WY 82007;
 tel. (307) 775-8050

INDEX and GLOSSARY

In this combined index and glossary, bold page numbers indicate the main reference, and italics indicate illustrations and photographs.

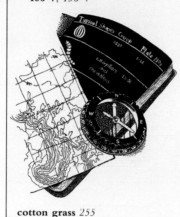

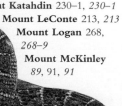

CAPTIONS

Page 1: Snowshoes will allow you to get off the beaten track in winter.

Page 2: Mule deer tracks and maple leaves.

Page 3: Claretcup cactus in bloom.

Pages 4–5: The Half Dome in Yosemite National Park, California, at sunset.

Pages 6–7: The extraordinary colors of the Prismatic Springs in Yellowstone National Park, Wyoming.

Pages 8–9: A bull caribou pauses on its way across a mountain stream in the Rockies.

Pages 10–11: A lone skier on the John Muir Trail in Kings Canyon National Park, California.

Pages 12–13: The Chasm of the Colorado River (1873–74), by Thomas Moran.

Pages 30–1: A camper prepares for another day of discovery in Banff National Park, Alberta, Canada.

Pages 62–3: A visitor is dwarfed by old-growth forest in Olympic National Park, Washington.

Pages 76–7: Sea-kayaking at the foot of a calving glacier in southeast Alaska.

Page 86–7: Snow clings to Sentinel Rock in Yosemite National Park, California.

Page 122–3: Mammoth Hot Springs in Yellowstone National Park, Wyoming.

Page 154–5: Grand Canyon National Park, Arizona.

Page 174–5: Park rangers rounding up feral horses in Theodore Roosevelt National Park, North Dakota.

Page 198–9: A great egret foraging in the swamps of the Everglades in Florida.

Page 222–3: Waves pounding the rocky shore at Bass Harbor Head in Acadia National Park, Maine.

Page 250–1: Moraine Lake in the Valley of the Ten Peaks in Banff National Park, Alberta, Canada.

Page 272–3: Bison stampeding across the prairies.

CONTRIBUTORS

Edward L. Bowen (EB) is a veteran author and editor on the subject of thoroughbred racing. He recently co-authored *The Smithsonian Guide to Natural America: Appalachia*.

Ben Davidson (BD) is a San Francisco-based writer and photographer specializing in outdoor recreation and adventure travel. He has been a travel editor at *Sunset Magazine* and currently contributes to numerous magazines and newspapers.

Dwight Holing (DH) writes on natural history and conservation issues for a wide range of national and international magazines. He has authored a number of nature travel books including *California Wild Lands: A Guide to The Nature Conservancy Preserves*, *Earthtrips: A Guide to Nature Travel on a Fragile Planet*, and *The Smithsonian Guide to Natural America: The Far West*.

Susanne Methvin (SM) is General Manager of Inca Floats, a nature travel tour operator specializing in tours to the Galápagos Islands and mainland Ecuador. A former Safari Director at the Nature Company, she has been active in organizing and leading nature tours throughout the world since 1979.

Edward R. Ricciuti (ER) has written over 50 books on nature, outdoor recreation, and science for a range of international publishers and has contributed articles to magazines such as *Audubon*, *National Wildlife*, and *Wildlife Conservation*. He is a former Curator of Publications and Public Relations for the New York Zoological Society.

Michele Strutin (MS) has worked as a writer and editor for various national magazines including *National Parks*, *Outside*, and *Rolling Stone*. From a beginning with outdoor adventure and travel subjects, her interests have focused on natural and cultural history. She is the author of *Chaco: A Cultural Legacy* and *The Smithsonian Guide to Natural America: The Great Lakes*.

Steven Threndyle (ST) is a Vancouver-based freelance writer and photographer specializing in outdoor activities. He has published articles in over 30 magazines and newspapers throughout North America and is the editor of *COAST*, British Columbia's outdoor recreation magazine.

David Rains Wallace is the author of numerous books on natural history and conservation, including *Life in the Balance, Idle Weeds*, and *The Klamath Knot*, for which he won the John Burroughs Medal for Nature Writing in 1984. He is a regular contributor to such magazines as *Sierra, Wilderness, The New York Times Book Review*, and *The Los Angeles Times*.

Eugene J. Walter Jr (EW) is a New Jersey-based freelance writer specializing in natural history and environmental conservation. From 1974 to 1991 he was Director of Publications at the New York Zoological Society and Editor-in-Chief of the Society's *Wildlife Conservation* magazine. He is the author of *Why Animals Behave the Way They Do* and *The Smithsonian Guide to Natural America: The Mid-Atlantic States*.

Suzanne Winckler (SW) has been writing on nature and environmental issues for over ten years in publications such as *Atlantic Monthly, Texas Monthly, Audubon*, and *The New York Times*. Among her books are *The Plains States* and *The Great Lakes* volumes in the series *The Smithsonian Guide to Historic America*.

Bettman Archive/APL **59**tl, cr and bl Colin McRae Photography; tr UPI/The Bettman Archive/APL; cl Kevin T Karlson; br David Young-Wolff/PhotoEdit **60**t Sam C Pierson/PR; bl Galen Rowell/ML; br Gary Braasch **61**tl Jeff Foott/TS; tr Renee Lynn/PR; bl and br Oliver Strewe **62–63** Jean-Paul Ferrero/A **64**tl, tc and b Gerry Ellis; r Mickey Gibson/AA/ES **65**l Gerry Ellis; r Ken Cole/AA/ES; b Breck P Kent/AA/ES **66**tl Thomas Kitchin/TS; tr Jeff Gnass; br Gerry Ellis **67**tl Galen Rowell/ML; tc Daniel J Cox/DJC; tr Stephen J Krasemann/DRK; bl Pat O'Hara; br Ralph A Reinhold/AA/ES **68** tl and tr Harvey Payne; c Jeff Foott; cr John and Karen Hollingsworth **69** tl Thomas Kitchin/TS; tr Wayne Lynch/DRK; cl Jeff Foott; cr Jeff Gnass; b John Shaw/TS **70**tl C Allan Morgan/DRK; tr John Gerlach/TS; bl Ted Levin/AA/ES; bc John Gerlach/AA/ES **71**tl Wayne Lynch/DRK; r Francois Gohier/A; cl John Shaw; bl Tom McHugh/PR **72**tl Brian Parker/TS; tr Grant Black/FL; c Gerry Ellis; b Don Enger/AA/ES **73** tl Alan D Briere; tc Ken Cole/AA/ES; bl S Nielsen/DRK; br Thomas Kitchin/TS **74**tl Randy Morse/TS; tr Matt Bradley; cr Alan D Briere; l Frans Lanting/MP; bc Tim Fitzharris/M/SP **75**t Daniel J Cox/DJC; tr Gil Lopez-Espina/NS; cr Kevin T Karlson; l Ed Robinson/TS; br Gerry Ellis **76–77** Jeff Foott/A **78**tl Larry Lipsky/TS; tr Culver Pictures; b John Eastcott/Yva Momatiuk/AA/ES; bl Galen Rowell/ML **79**t Ken Cole/AA/ES; r Jeff Gnass; bl Robert Winslow/TS; b Harvey Payne **80**tl courtesy Paddy Pallin; tr Galen Rowell/ML; bl Gunner Conrad/PR; bc Jeff Gnass; br Appalachian Trail Conference **81**t Chromosohn/PR; bl Maresa Pryor/AA/ES; bc Gerry Ellis **82**t Randy Olson/NGS; b Daniel J Cox/DJC; **83**tl The Granger Collection; tc Melissa Farlow/NGS; bl The Wilderness Society; br Galen Rowell/ML **84** Ben Davidson **86–87** Roy C Bishop/SB **88**b Johnny Johnson/DRK **88–89** Jeff Gnass **89**c Johnny Johnson/AA/ES; bl Kim Heacox/DRK; br Jeff Gnass **90**t Jeff Gnass; b Johnny Johnson/DRK **91**t Kim Heacox/DRK; c and bl Pat O'Hara; br Galen Rowell/ML **92–93** Tom Bean/DRK **93**c Jeff Gnass; b Gerry Ellis **94**l Jeff Gnass; r Wolfgang Kaehler **94–95** Jeff Gnass **95** Daniel J Cox/DJC **96**cl Francois Gohier/A; bl Zig Leszczynski/AA/ES **96–97** Susan G Drinker/Drinker/Durrance Graphics **97** c John Elk III/BCI; b Pat O'Hara **98**b John Gerlach/DRK **98–99** Galen Rowell/ML **99**c Wayne Lankinen/DRK; b The Bettman Archive/APL **100–101** Randy Morse/TS **101**l Larry Ulrich; r Bruce Watkins/AA/ES **102** John C Parker/PI **102–103** Larry Ulrich/DRK **103**c Randy Morse/TS; b Joe McDonald/AA/ES **104–105** Robert Rowan/Tony Stone Images/PLS **105**c Zig Leszczynski/AA/ES; b Galen Rowell/ML **106**l ER Degginger/BCI; c Larry Ulrich/DRK **106–107** Matthias Breiter/OSF **107**c Larry Ulrich/DRK; bl Jeff Foott/BCL **108**t Ed Cooper; c and br Galen Rowell/ML; bl Jeff Foott; bc Jack Wilburn/AA/ES **109**c Jeff Gnass; b Underwood Collection, The Bettman Archive/APL **110–111** Jeff Gnass **111**c David Muench; b Jack Wilburn/AA/ES **112**bl Larry Ulrich/DRK; br Stephen Trimble/DRK **112–113** G Brad Lewis/Tony Stone Worldwide/PLS **113**c John C Parker/PI; b Philip Rosenberg/A **114**t Philip Rosenberg/A; bl Jeff Gnass; br Gerry Ellis **115**t Larry Ulrich/DRK; c Jim Brandenberg/MP; b Ben Davidson **116** Frans Lanting/MP; c John and Karen Hollingsworth **116–117** Douglas Peebles **117** Keith Gillett/AA/ES **118**bl Sharon Gerig/TS; br Gerry Ellis **118–119** Dennis Frates/PI **119** Pat O'Hara **120** Gerry Ellis **120–121** Joanne Lotter/TS **121**c Jean-Paul Ferrero/A; b Pat O'Hara **122–123** Dorothy Kerper Monnelly **124** Stan Osolinski/OSF **124–125** Barbara von Hoffman/TS **125**c Tom and Pat Leeson/DRK; b Daniel J Cox/DJC **126**c Michael Fogden/OSF; l Spencer Swanger/TS; br Joe McDonald/BCI **127**t Jeff Gnass; l John and Ann Mahan; b John C Parker **128** John Shaw/TS; **128–129** Jon Gnass **129**b William Smithey Jr/Planet Earth Pictures **130–131** John and Karen Hollingsworth **131**c and br John and Karen Hollingsworth; bl Keith Gunner/BCI **132** l John C Parker/PI; r Jeff Gnass **132–133** Daniel J Cox/DJC **133**c Steve Kaufman/DRK; b Gerry Ellis **134** Paul Rezendez/PI **134–135** John and Karen Hollingsworth **136**bl Victoria Hurst/TS; br David L Brown/TS **136–137** Jim Brandenburg/MP **137**r Jeff Gnass; l John Shaw **138–139** Robert Bornemann/PR **139**c Jeff Gnass; b Gerry Ellis **140**bl Daniel Heuclin/NHPA; br Tom Bean/DRK **140–141** Larry Ulrich/DRK **141**c Pat O'Hara **142**b Tom Till/A; c Pat O'Hara **142–143** Pat O'Hara **143**c Joanne Lotter/TS; b Michael Fogden/AA/ES **144** Jeff Gnass **144–145** Ben Davidson/Backroads **145**c Ben Davidson/Backroads; b John Shaw **146**t John Shaw/A; b Hardie Truesdale **147**t John Shaw/A; c Patti Murray/AA/ES; bl Jeff Foott; br Gerald and Buff Corsi/TS **148** Pat O'Hara **148–149** Pat O'Hara **149**c Galen Rowell/ML; b Daniel J Cox/DJC **150** Jim Brandenburg/MP **150–151** Dick Durrance/Durrance Graphics **151**c Tom Till/A; b Jeff Gnass; b Erwin and Peggy Bauer/BCL **152**t Jeff Foott/DRK; c Dennis Frates/PI; b Culver Pictures **153**t Jeff Gnass; bl Patti Murray/AA/ES; br Spencer Swanger/TS **154–155** Jean-Claude Lejeune/SB **156**bl Mark Gibson; bc G Kelly/TS **156–157** Michael Fogden/AA/ES **157** Don and Esther Phillips/TS **158**bl Kim Heacox/DRK; bc Harald Lange/BCL **158–159** Ron Sanford/Trannys Lab and Paintbox **159** c Pat O'Hara; b Tom Bean/DRK**160** t Hardie Truesdale; bl The Bettman Archive/APL; br Pat O'Hara **161**t Dick Canby/PI; c Mary Clay/Planet Earth Pictures; b CC Lockwood/DRK **162** Daniel J Cox/DJC **162–163** Ron Sanford **163**c GC Kelly/TS; b Wayne Lankinen/DRK **164–165** John and Karen Hollingsworth **165** John and Karen Hollingsworth **166** John Shaw/NHPA **166–167** David Hiser/Aspen **167**c Phil Degginger/Color-Pic

Inc; b National Park Service **168**b David Muench; c Anthony Mercieca/PR **168–169** Jeff Foott/TS **169** David Muench **170**l John Shaw; r Steve Bentsen **170–171** Matt Bradley **171**c Jeff Foott; b Jeff Simon/BCI **172–173** Jeff Foott/BCI **173**l Calvin Larsen/PR; r Joe McDonald/BCI **174–175** Thomas Sennett/Magnum Photos **176**bl Les Campbell/PI; c ER Degginger/BCI **176–177** Richard Day/Daybreak Imagery **177**c DP Burnside/PR; l Robert C Simpson/TS **178**b JH Robinson/AA/ES; br Ted Levin/AA/ES **178–179** John Lemker/AA/ES **179** Joe McDonald/AA/ES **180** John and Ann Mahan **180–181** John and Ann Mahan **181**c Ron Sauter/NS; b Stephen J Krasemann/DRK **182**b Jeff Gnass **182–183** Daniel J Cox/DJC **183**c Stephen J Krasemann/DRK; b John and Ann Mahan **184** John and Ann Mahan **184–185** Daniel J Cox/DJC **185**c Chuck Wyrostok/AppaLight; b Daniel J Cox/DJC **186** Jeff Gnass **187**t John and Ann Mahan; c Stephen J Krasemann/DRK; b Wayne Lankinen/BCL **188–189** Dorothy Kerper Monnelly **189**c Gene Ahrens/BCI; b Stephen J Krasemann/PR **190** Jeff Gnass **190–191** Tom Algire/TS **191**c Wendy Shattil and Bob Rozinski/TS; b Jim Brandenburg/MP **192** Harvey Payne **193** Harvey Payne **194**bl Ken Cole/AA/ES; br Richard Thom/TS **194–195** Harvey Payne **195**c Jeff Gnass; b Jeff Foott **196**t Jack Dermid/OSF; c Bates Littlehales/AA/ES **197**t Wendell Metzei/BCI; c Larry Brock/TS; b Wildlife Conservation Society **198–199** Peter Menzel/SB **200**bl Mike Bacon/PI; l Gerry Ellis **200–201** John Hall/AA/ES **201**c Gerry Ellis; cr Jim Brandenburg/MP; b Marty Cordano/DRK **202**t Brian Parker/TS; l Jim Brandenburg/MP; r Schneidermeyer/OSF; b Jeff Foott **203**t Larry Lipsky/DRK; bl Ken Cole/AA/ES; bc Kathy Willens/AP/Wide World Photos **204** Mike Bacon/TS **204–205** Larry Lipsky/TS **205** Larry Lipsky/TS **206** Fred Whitehead/AA/ES **206–207** Fred Whitehead/AA/ES **207** Doug Wechsler/Vireo **208**l Dr ER Degginger/Color-Pic Inc; r National Parks Service **208–209** Dr ER Degginger/Color-Pic Inc **209**c Jeff Gnass; b Chet Dowell/AppaLight **210**l Tim Davis/PR; r Jeff Gnass **210–211** Jeff Gnass **211**c Phil A Dotson/PR; b Nancy Adams/TS **212**t John Netherton/OSF; b Daniel J Cox/DJC **213**t Gerry Ellis; c Jeff Gnass; bl Kenneth Murray/PR; br Andre Jenny/Stock South, Atlanta **214**b Breck P Kent/AA/ES **214–215** David Muench **216**b The Library of Virginia **216–217** Jeff Gnass **217**l John C Shaw/A; b Joe McDonald/NS **218** Jeff Gnass **219**t NW; l Jeff Gnass; r Kennan Ward/DRK **220** Jeff Gnass **220–221** Ric MacDowell/AppaLight **221**c Hardie Truesdale; b Ric MacDowell/AppaLight **222–223** Joseph Schuyler/SB **224–225** Gil Lopez-Espina/NS **225** Henry Ausloos/AA/ES **226** Jeff Gnass **226–227** Jeff Gnass **227**c Paul Rezendez/PI; b Tom Tietz/Tony Stone Images/PLS **228** Alan D Briere; r AH Rider/PR; b NW **229**t Farley Lewis/PR; c Daniel J Cox/DJC **230** Alan D Briere **230–231** Paul Rezendez/PI **231** Jeremy Woodhouse/DRK **232** Jerry Howard/PI **232–233** William E Ferguson **233** MP Kahl/DRK **234** Tom Till/DRK **234–235** Jim Brandenburg/MP **235**c Tom Till/A; b Dale Wilson/M/SP **236** Phil Degginger/Color-Pic Inc **236–237** Shawneen Finnegan **237**c Johnny Johnson/AA/ES **237**b Kevin T Karlson **238**t and r ER Degginger/Color-Pic Inc; l ER Degginger/AA/ES; b Phil Degginger/Color-Pic Inc **239** Frans Lanting/MP **240** ER Degginger/BCI **240–241** Gil Lopez-Espina/NS **241**c Gary Meslaros/BCI; b Frank W Mantlik/PR **242**l Gerry Ellis; r Hardie Truesdale **242–243** Hardie Truesdale **243**c Hardie Truesdale; b Jeff Gnass **244**l CC Lockwood/AA/ES; r Harry Engels/AA/ES **244–245** John and Karen Hollingsworth **245** Bill Byrne/NS **246** Daniel J Cox/DJC **246–247** Daniel J Cox/DJC **247** Johnny Johnson/DRK **248** Gordon Langsbury/BCI **248–249** John and Karen Hollingsworth **249**l John Hicks/DRK; r Steve Maslowski/PR **250–251** Roy Bishop/SB **252**bl Darwin R Wiggett/FL; br John C Parker/PI **252–253** Tom and Pat Leeson/DRK **253**c Wolfgang Kaehler; b Galen Rowell/ML **254**t Dennis Frates/PI; b Pat O'Hara/DRK **255**t John C Parker/PI; c George F Godfrey/AA/ES; b Jim Brandenburg/MP **256**b Jerry Kobalenko/FL; r Randy Morse/TS **256–257** Jerry Kobalenko/FL **257**c JA Kraulis/M/SP; b Thomas Kitchin/TS **258** David Nunuk/TS **258–259** Alec Pytlowany/M/SP **259**c Ionas Kaltenbach; b Thomas Kitchin/TS **260** Mike Dobel/M/SP **260–261** Peter Griffith/M/SP **261** Stephen J Krasemann/BCL **262–263** Wayne Lynch/M/SP **263**c Barrett and Mackay/M/SP; b Sherman Hines/M/SP **264** Barbara Gerlach/DRK **264–265**John Foster/M/SP **265** Janet Foster/M/SP **266–267** Bill Brooks/M/SP **267**c Tom Bledsoe/DRK; b Wayne Wegner/FL **268** Patrick Morrow/FL **268–269** Richard Hartmier/FL **269**c Stephen J Krasemann/DRK; b Thomas Kitchin/FL **270**t Jeff Gnass; c AE Sirulnikoff/FL; b Tim Fitzharris/M/SP **271**t Jeff Gnass; l Richard Hartmier/FL; b James Kevin Jackson/AA/ES **272–273** Jim Brandenburg/MP **ILLUSTRATIONS: David Wood** 16-17, 18, 34, 81; **Ngaire Sales** 64-65, 66, 68-69, 70-71, 72-73, 74-75; **Rob Mancini** 92, 100, 104, 110, 130, 135, 138, 146, 157, 164, 172, 179, 188, 196, 207, 215, 218, 224, 229, 233, 236, 247, 261, 262, 266; **Genevieve Wallace** Resources Directory **MAPS: Stan Lamond** 85, 86, 122, 154, 174, 198, 222, 250; **Anne Bowman** 239; **Mark Watson, Pictogram** all other maps **JACKET: Front** Francois Gohier/PR; John C. Parker/PI; John and Karen Hollingsworth; Ben Davidson/Backroads; Jeff Gnass; Tom Till/A; Steve Kaufman/DRK; Oliver Strewe; The Nature Company; Larry Lipsky; Randy Morse/TS; David Fleetham/OSF; Hardie Truesdale; Ron Sauter/NS; Bob Winsett/TS; Larry Ulrich/DRK **Back** Steven J. Krasemann/DRK; Joanne Lotter/TS; Colin McRae Photography; Galen Rowell/ML; Daniel J. Cox/DJC **Front flap** Tom Bean/DRK; Galen Rowell/ML; Keith Gillett/AA/ES **Back flap** The Bettman Archive/APL

ACKNOWLEDGEMENTS The publishers wish to thank the following people for their assistance in the production of this book: Julia Burke, Melanie Corfield, Edan Corkill, Simon Darby, Monique Filo, Stephen Foster, Diane Harriman, Ionas Kaltenbach, Margaret McPhee, Paddy Pallin Ltd, Gail Page, Patagonia, REI (Recreational Equipment Inc.), Oliver Strewe.